Interrupting Auschwitz

Interrupting Auschwitz

Art, Religion, Philosophy

JOSH COHEN

continuum
NEW YORK • LONDON

Continuum

The Tower Building, 11 York Road, London SE1 7NX

370 Lexington Avenue, New York, NY 10017-6503

First published 2003

British Library Cataloguing-in-Publication Data
A catalogue record for this book is available from the British Library.

ISBN 0–8264–5551–4 (hardback)
     0–8264–5552–2 (paperback)

Typeset by Aarontype Limited, Easton, Bristol
Printed and bound in Great Britain by Bookcraft (Bath) Ltd, Midsomer Norton, Somerset

For Ethan

Wer
sagt, daß uns alles erstarb,
da uns das Aug brach?
Alles erwachte, alles hob an.

Who
says that everything died for us
when the eye broke for us?
Everything awakened, everything rose.

Paul Celan, 'With All My Thoughts'

Contents

Acknowledgements

Thanks to the following institutions for their invaluable help in granting me time and financial support to complete the book's research and writing: the Arts and Humanities Research Board for a Research Leave Award in 2001 and the Goldsmiths College Research Committee for both a generous research grant and a Hoggart Fellowship for study leave.

Thanks also to those readers of and interlocutors with the work in progress for so enriching the experience of writing this book: Howard Caygill, Rick Crownshaw, Garin Dowd, Bob Gibbs, Dennis Keenan, Julian Levinson, Nigel Tubbs and especially Andrew Benjamin, without whose unfailingly attentive reading and unstinting support this book would be much the poorer. To the many friends and colleagues who have thought with and – much worse – listened to me, especially: Bob Eaglestone, Vic Seidler, Andrew Renton, Alex Gordon, Tamra Wright, Philip McGowan, Helen Carr, Peter Nicholls, Andrew Gibson, Forrest Gander. And of course to my graduate students past and present, especially Zac Baker, Liz Crossley, Barbara Mella, Evin O'Riordan and Angie Simon.

Thanks as always and for more than I could list here to my parents. And above all, to my wife Abigail; only she and I know how much this book's completion owes to her unconditional love, interest and humour. During the course of its writing, she gave birth to our son Ethan, the most glorious of interruptions. It's to him, the ungraspable future, that this book is dedicated.

Abbreviations

A	G. W. F. Hegel, *Aesthetics* (2 volumes, trans. T. M. Knox, Oxford: Clarendon Press, 1975).
AA	Richard Rubinstein, *After Auschwitz: History, Theology and Contemporary Judaism*, second edition (Baltimore, MD: Johns Hopkins University Press, 1992).
AE	Emmanuel Levinas, *Autrement qu'être ou au delà de l'essence* (The Hague: Martinus Nijhoff, 1981).
AEL	Jacques Derrida, *Adieu to Emmanuel Levinas* (trans. P.-A. Brault and M. Naas, Stanford, CA: Stanford University Press, 1999); *Adieu à Emmanuel Levinas* (Paris: Galilée, 1997).
AFC	Edmond Jabès, *A Foreigner Carrying in the Crook of His Arm a Tiny Book* (trans. R. Waldrop, Hanover, NH: Wesleyan University Press, 1993).
ALH	Emmanuel Levinas, *A L'heure des Nations* (Paris: Editions Minuit, 1988).
AT	Theodor W. Adorno, *Aesthetic Theory* (trans. R. Hullot-Kentor, Minneapolis, MN: Minnesota University Press, 1997).
AV	Emmanuel Levinas, *L'Au-Delà du Verset: Lectures et Discours Talmudiques* (Paris: Editions Minuit, 1982).
BM	Edmond Jabès, *The Book of Margins* (trans. R. Waldrop, Chicago, IL: University of Chicago Press, 1993).
BQ1	Edmond Jabès, *The Book of Questions*, Volume I: *The Book of Questions, The Book of Yukel, Return to the Book* (trans. R. Waldrop, Hanover, NH: Wesleyan University Press, 1991).
BQ2	Edmond Jabès, *The Book of Questions*, Volume 2: *Yaël, Elya, Aely, • El, or The Last Book* (trans. R. Waldrop, Hanover, NH: Wesleyan University Press, 1991).

BR1   Edmond Jabès, *The Book of Resemblances* (trans. R. Waldrop, Hanover, NH: Wesleyan University Press, 1990).

BR2   Edmond Jabès, *The Book of Resemblances 2: Intimations The Desert* (trans. R. Waldrop, Hanover, NH: Wesleyan University Press, 1991).

BR3   Edmond Jabès, *The Book of Resemblances 3: The Ineffaceable The Unperceived* (trans. R. Waldrop, Hanover, NH: Wesleyan University Press, 1992).

BS   Edmond Jabès, *The Book of Shares* (trans. R. Waldrop, Chicago, IL: Chicago University Press, 1989).

BV   Emmanuel Levinas, *Beyond the Verse: Talmudic Readings and Lectures* (trans. G. B. Mole, London: Athlone Press, 1994).

CM   Theodor W. Adorno, *Critical Models* (trans. H. W. Pickford, New York: Columbia University Press, 1998).

CPR   Immanuel Kant, *Critique of Pure Reason* (trans. N. Kemp Smith, Basingstoke: Macmillan, 1929).

DDQ   Emmanuel Levinas, *De Dieu qui vient à l'idée* (Paris: Vrin, 1982).

DE   Theodor W. Adorno, *Dialectic of Enlightenment* (trans. J. Cumming, London: Verso, 1979).

DEE   Emmanuel Levinas, *De L'existence à L'existant* (Paris: Vrin, 1969).

DF   Emmanuel Levinas, *Difficult Freedom: Essays on Judaism* (trans. S. Hand, Baltimore, MD: Johns Hopkins University Press, 1997).

DL   Emmanuel Levinas, *Difficile Liberté: Essais sur le judaïsme* (Paris: Albin Michel, 1976).

DSS   Emmanuel Levinas, *Du Sacré au Saint* (Paris: Editions Minuit, 1947).

EAS   Edmond Jabès, *Un Étranger avec, sous le bras, un livre de petit format* (Paris: Gallimard, 1989).

ED   Maurice Blanchot, *L'écriture du desastre* (Paris: Gallimard, 1980).

EE   Emmanuel Levinas, *Existence and Existents* (trans. A. Lingis, Dordrecht: Kluwer Academic, 1978).

EH   Robert Antelme, *L'espèce humaine* (Paris: Gallimard, 1978).

EI   Maurice Blanchot, *L'entretien infini* (Paris: Gallimard, 1969).

EN   Emmanuel Levinas, *Entre Nous: On Thinking of the Other* (trans. M. B. Smith, London: Athlone, 1998); *Entre-Nous: Essais sur le penser-à-l'autre* (Paris: Editions Bernard Grasset et Fasquelle, 1991).

FAH   Eliezer Berkowitz, *Faith After the Holocaust* (New York: Ktav, 1973).

FEL   *Face to Face with Emmanuel Levinas* (ed. R. A. Cohen, Albany, NY: SUNY
         Press, 1986).

GS   Theodor W. Adorno, *Gessamelte Schriften* (20 volumes, ed. R. Tiedemann,
         Frankfurt am Main: Suhrkamp Verlag, 1986).

H   Theodor W. Adorno, *Hegel: Three Studies* (trans. S. W. Nicholsen, Cam-
         bridge, MA: MIT Press, 1993).

HR   Robert Antelme, *The Human Race* (trans. J. Haight and A. Mahler, Evan-
         ston, IL: Northwestern University Press, 1998).

HS   Giorgio Agamben, *Homo Sacer: Sovereign Power and Bare Life* (trans.
         D. Heller-Roazen, Stanford, CA: Stanford University Press, 1995).

IC   Maurice Blanchot, *The Infinite Conversation* (trans. S. Hanson, Minneapolis,
         MN: Minnesota University Press, 1993).

ITN   Emmanuel Levinas, *In the Time of the Nations* (trans. M. B. Smith, London:
         Athlone Press, 1994).

KRV   Immanuel Kant, *Kritik der reinen Vernunft* (Riga: J. F. Hartnoch, 1787).

LBUS   Edmond Jabès, *The Little Book of Unsuspected Subversion* (trans. R. Waldrop,
         Stanford CA: Stanford, CA: University Press, 1996).

LDP   Edmond Jabès, *Le Livre du Partage* (Paris: Gallimard, 1987).

LM   Edmond Jabès, *Le Livre des Marges* (Paris: Fata Morgana, 1984).

LP   Edmond Jabès, *Le Parcours* (Paris: Gallimard, 1985).

LQ1   Edmond Jabès, *Le Livre des Questions, 1: Le Livres des Questions, Le Livre de
         Yukel, Le Retour au Livre* (Paris: Gallimard, 1988).

LQ2   Edmond Jabès, *Le Livre des Questions, 2: Yaël, Elya, Aely, • El, ou le dernier
         livre* (Paris: Gallimard, 1989)

LR   Edmond Jabès, *Le Livre des Ressemblances: Le Livre des Ressemblances, Le
         Soupçon Le Désert, L'ineffeçable L'inaperçu* (Paris: Gallimard, 1991).

MDM   Edmond Jabès, *Le Memoire des Mots: Comment je lis Paul Celan* (Paris: Four-
         bis, 1990).

MM   Theodor W. Adorno, *Minima Moralia: Reflections from Damaged Life* (trans.
         E. Jephcott, London: Verso, 1974).

MW   Emil Fackenheim, *To Mend the World: Foundations of Post-Holocaust
         Jewish Thought*, second edition (Bloomington, IN: Indiana University
         Press, 1994).

ND   Theodor W. Adorno, *Negative Dialectics* (trans. E. B. Ashton, London: Routledge, 1973).

NL1   Theodor W. Adorno, *Notes to Literature*, Volume 1 (trans. S. W. Nicholsen, New York: Columbia University Press, 1991).

NL2   Theodor W. Adorno, *Notes to Literature*, Volume 2 (trans. S. W. Nicholsen, New York: Columbia University Press, 1992).

NP   Emmanuel Levinas, *Noms propres* (Montpellier: Fata Morgana, 1976).

NTR   Emmanuel Levinas, *Nine Talmudic Readings* (trans. A. Aronowicz, Bloomington, IN: Indiana University Press, 1990).

OB   Emmanuel Levinas, *Otherwise Than Being, or Beyond Essence* (trans. A. Lingis, Pittsburgh, PA: Duquesne University Press, 1998).

OGW   Emmanuel Levinas, *Of God Who Comes to Mind* (trans. B. Bergo, Stanford, CA: Stanford University Press, 1998).

P   Theodor W. Adorno, *Prisms* (trans. S. Weber, Cambridge MA: MIT Press, 1983).

PG   G. W. F. Hegel, *Phänomenologie des Geistes* (Volume 3 of *Werke*, Frankfurt am Main: Suhrkamp Verlag, 1970).

PH   Andrew Benjamin, *Present Hope: Philosophy, Achitecture, Judaism* (London: Routledge, 1997).

PLS   Edmond Jabès, *Le petit livre de la subversion hors de soupçon* (Paris: Gallimard, 1982).

PN   Emmanuel Levinas, *Proper Names* (trans. M. B. Smith, Stanford, CA: Stanford University Press, 1996).

PS   G. W. F. Hegel, *Phenomenology of the Spirit* (trans. A. V. Miller, Oxford: Clarendon Press, 1979).

QLT   Emmanuel Levinas, *Quatres Lectures Talmudiques* (Paris: Editions Minuit, 1968).

RA   Giorgio Agamben, *Remnants of Auschwitz: The Witness and the Archive* (trans. D. Heller-Roazen, New York: Zone Books, 1999).

'RO'   Emmanuel Levinas, 'La réalité et son ombre', *Les Temps Modernes* 38 (1948).

'RPH'   Emmanuel Levinas, 'Reflections on the Philosophy of Hitlerism' (trans. S. Hand), *Critical Inquiry*, 17 (1990).

'RS'   Emmanuel Levinas, 'Reality and Its Shadow' in *The Levinas Reader* (trans. S. Hand, Oxford: Blackwell, 1989).

SE   Franz Rosenzweig, *Der Stern Der Erlösung* (Frankfurt am Main: Suhrkamp Verlag, 1988).

SMB   Emmanuel Levinas, *Sur Maurice Blanchot* (Montpellier: Fata Morgana, 1975).

SP   Paul Celan, *Selected Poems* (trans. M. Hamburger, London: Penguin, 1990).

SR   Franz Rosenzweig, *The Star of Redemption* (trans. W. Hallo, Notre Dame, IN: Notre Dame University Press, 1971).

TaI   Emmanuel Levinas, *Totality and Infinity* (trans. A. Lingis, Pittsgurgh, PA: Duquesne University Press, 1969).

TeI   Emmanuel Levinas, *Totalité et Infini* (The Hague: Martinus Nijhoff, 1971).

TLR   *The Levinas Reader* (ed. S. Hand, Oxford: Blackwell, 1992).

VA   G. W. F. Hegel, *Vorlesungen über die Ästhetik* (Volumes 1–3, 12, 13 and 14 of *Werke*, Frankfurt am Main: Suhrkamp Verlag, 1970).

WD   Maurice Blanchot, *The Writing of the Disaster* (trans. A. Smock, Lincoln, NE: Bison Books, 1995).

Preface

It was in personal rather than professional interest that this book began life. Some years ago I began, alongside the reading in modern literature and Continental philosophy which had long informed my research and teaching, to read deeply in Jewish thought since the Nazi genocide. The question that impelled this reading was simple, and no different from the one asked by modern Jews of all shades of religious commitment: how is Judaism possible in the wake of the camps?

As the first chapter of this book should indicate, I found myself increasingly frustrated by the responses on offer. Whether the intention was to discredit or to reassert the continued relevance of Judaic tradition, an implicit, and sometimes explicit, theodicy consistently set the terms of inquiry. For some, the extermination camps provided an empirical disconfirmation of a providential and benign God; for others, while incomprehensible in themselves, the camps could not be understood in isolation from a broader sacred–historical and ultimately redemptive narrative. Either way, the premise governing each argument was that God – the Absolute – can be thought of only in terms of what one leading Holocaust theologian calls His 'presence in History'.[1] If history is judged empty of this presence, then Judaism itself, at least in its traditional forms, is invalidated; if history appears on the other hand to confirm this presence, Judaism's integrity and truth remain intact.

The philosophical inadequacies of these positions soon revealed the artificiality of the boundary I had interposed between 'private' and 'professional' inquiry. For all their very real differences, the key figures about whom I had long been thinking, writing and teaching – Benjamin, Adorno, Heidegger, Levinas, Blanchot, Derrida and Jabès, among others – shared an essential commitment to think the Absolute outside the economy of presence and absence bequeathed by philosophical and theological tradition. Each of them in their own singular register had put in question irrevocably the conception of God as transcendent guarantor of the meaning of History to which the various Holocaust theologians remained stubbornly attached, whether by way of negation or affirmation.

Nowhere was this critique of theodicy more explicit than in the writings of Emmanuel Levinas, both in his formal phenomenological works and his confessional essays on Judaism. Religion for Levinas, far from drawing God into a determinate relation with human history, is that which maintains a relation to God '*despite* the impossibility of the whole' (*TaI*, 80; *TeI*, 53, my emphasis). The Levinasian God is not an Absolute that redeems itself in history, but that ' "absolves" itself from the relation in which it presents itself' (*TaI*, 50; *TeI*, 21). As that which discloses itself by withdrawing or 'absolving' itself, God can no longer be thought of within a teleological or redemptive horizon.

The affinity of this religious perspective to the discourse on 'writing' in the thought of Levinas' contemporaries could hardly go unnoticed. Indeed, the on-going commentaries on Levinas by Blanchot and Derrida, as well as the explicit dialogues between them, have made this affinity – with all its attendant tension and complexity – explicit.[2] For both Blanchot and Derrida, writing names precisely that movement of language which discloses truth only by perpetually withdrawing or deferring its presence. Moreover, Blanchot's 1980 book *The Writing of the Disaster*, ties this movement explicitly to the ethical demand of thinking after Auschwitz.

Via Blanchot, the Levinasian path out of theodicy became inextricably associated with the paradoxical logic of writing. In spite of their complex and significant differences, both thinkers posited the task of thinking the meaning (and resistance to meaning) of Auschwitz as indissociable from a radical rethinking of the Absolute. It was at the point of this convergence of religion with art, and of Judaism with writing, that the idea for *Interrupting Auschwitz* emerged. To renew thought after Auschwitz would involve stepping out of the confines of a 'religious' philosophy in which the Absolute is thought in terms of its self-completion, and exploring traditions – philosophical and poetic as well as religious – for which the presence of the Absolute is one with its own *interruption*. As Chapter 3 will attempt to show, Levinas' writings on Judaism and Zionism elaborate the concrete ethico-political implications of such a conception of the Absolute for the task of thinking after Auschwitz.

If Levinas provided the most significant religious elaboration of this interruptive Absolute, its twin aesthetic elaboration was found in the thought of T. W. Adorno, and especially in its development (to use his own phrase) 'after Auschwitz'. Many commentators have observed that Adorno's ethico-political project is borne increasingly by art in his late work; what made this conjunction of the ethical and the aesthetic especially significant in the context of this project was its traumatic intrication with the fact of Auschwitz. As I argue throughout the book, Auschwitz imposes not simply a new demand on thinking, but a transformation in the very mode of thinking. This transformation is intimated in Adorno's well-known and apparently straightforward declaration of a 'new categorical imperative', namely 'to arrange ... thoughts and actions so that Auschwitz will not repeat itself, so that nothing similar will happen' (*ND*, 465; *GS6*, 358).

The structure of this imperative came to reveal itself as the very structure of thinking that would be elaborated here. The imperative allows for the judgement of its violation, but not of its achievement, which belongs of necessity to an unachieved and unachievable future. Thus, the redemptive horizon at which 'nothing similar will happen' cannot be thought of apart from the impossibility of its actualization. This impossibility founds the task of thinking undertaken by each of the thinkers constellated by this book; in each of their authorships, to think is also and always to refuse to bring thought to completion.

In Adorno's late work, this ethical demand is carried above all by the aesthetic. Art is characterized by a doubled gesture whereby to approach the Absolute is simultaneously to be withheld from it; indeed, for Adorno, redemption itself is nothing other than this simultaneity of approach and withdrawal. Chapter 2 will unfold the philosophical implications of this simultaneity by way of readings in the Adornian aesthetic, and especially in his essays on poetry.

Moreover, just as Levinas' religious thought reveals an implicitly 'writerly' logic when cast in Blanchot's light, so Adorno's aesthetic will be seen to be implicitly informed by a certain construal of Judaism. The source for this 'unspeakable' Judaic itinerary will be located in Franz Rosenzweig's 'messianic politics', though divested by Adorno's post-Auschwitz 'negative dialectic' of its positive theological content. Adorno's 'atheism', it will be argued, is the symptom not of a disavowal of transcendence, but of a distinctly Judaic prohibition of its positive expression.

The philosophical force of the Adornian aesthetic and of Levinasian religion derives in part, however, from their preservation of the distinctness of these two terms by privileging the true transcendence of the one over the suspect transcendence of the other. Religion in Adorno and art in Levinas are never admitted to the elevated status of their counterparts. Nor would such a reconciliation be desirable, if by this is meant some homogenizing synthesis of the two terms. A different relation between these terms was to be found in the unclassifiable texts of the poet-thinker Edmond Jabès. This relation is encapsulated in his famous pronouncement that 'Judaism and writing are but the same waiting, the same hope, the same wearing out (*usure*)' (*BQ*1, 122; *LQ*1, 136).

As Chapter 4 will argue, the sameness of Judaism and writing to which Jabès points here is not the cancellation of their differences. It intimates rather the logic of 'incompletion' – 'waiting', 'hope', 'wearing out' – that each of these irreducibly different languages and traditions articulates. The chapter will explore Jabès' relationship to, and interlacing of, poetic and Judaic traditions. What binds these traditions as read and rewritten by Jabès is a thinking of the Absloute as that which is maintained in its promise rather than its realization, a thinking concentrated in the figure of the *question* – that form which subsists only in its irresolution – which organizes all of his texts.

Jabès, then, provided me with the most explicit and sustained confirmation of the two thoughts that gave birth to this book: that to think Judaism after Auschwitz is radically to rethink the Absolute, and that such a rethinking finds its exemplary enactment through the modality of writing.

While Adorno, Levinas and Jabès are the central figures through which this rethinking of the Absolute is staged, other thinkers have been indispensable to its development across the book as a whole. Chief among these are, as already indicated, Blanchot and Rosenzweig, as well as Giorgio Agamben. Others invoked both explicitly and implicitly in elaborating the idea of the incompletion of the Absolute include Benjamin, Derrida, Philippe Lacoue-Labarthe, Jean-Luc Nancy, Marc-Alain Ouaknin and Paul Celan. This network of thinkers has helped in different ways to delineate the urgent and always incomplete task of thinking after Auschwitz.

I have given this task the name of 'interrupting'. Within the book's title, it signifies in two distinct but inextricable ways. Read as participial adjective it suggests the effect of the inassimilable trauma of Auschwitz on thinking (' "Auschwitz" interrupts'); read as present participle, 'interrupting' suggests the imperative of thinking and acting against the recurrence of Auschwitz (' "Auschwitz" must be interrupted'). Needless to say, readers of this book should have both these meanings in mind: if Auschwitz is what destroys thought, it is equally what conditions its urgent renewal.

CHAPTER I

The Interrupted Absolute: Art, Religion and the 'New Categorical Imperative'

In confronting the Nazi genocide, contemporary thought has attested repeatedly to an experience of its own limit. By their own accounts, historical, sociological, psychological, philosophical and theological reason encounter here less a contained object of inquiry than an uncontainable rupture and exhaustion of their explanatory resources. The death camps, it seems, harbour an excess to knowledge which neither empirical analysis nor speculative metaphysics succeed in appeasing.

The hybrid sub-disciplinary formation known as Holocaust Studies can be understood as both symptom of and response to this crisis of rational cognition; indeed, perhaps its most persistent motif is the inadequacy of resources within existing disciplines for comprehending its object. To be sure, this inadequacy has not prevented the ongoing achievement of its most immediate and urgent task, namely the exhaustive documentation and reconstruction of the ideological, political, legal, bureaucratic and technical processes which culminated in the *Endlösung* of European Jewry (not to mention the murderous persecution of many other peoples and groups). These indispensable gains in positive knowledge do little, however, to abate the conceptual crisis that the events themselves engender. On the contrary, they seem to exacerbate it – the more facts accumulate, the more stubbornly they resist accommodation to any rule of reason.[1]

The question which this resistance immediately raises, and to which this book addresses itself, is both starkly simple and implacably difficult: exposed by history to its own limit, how is thought to continue? More particularly, if Auschwitz[2] has ruined the philosophical ideal of transparent and total knowledge, is thought consigned to the impotent mourning of its own failure? How might this fate be avoided without recourse to an easy disavowal of recent history and its corrosive implications?

These questions are posed in full awareness of their having been posed before. Indeed, if anything can be said to distinguish the major texts of theoretical reflection on Auschwitz, it is an insistently critical self-consciousness towards their own conceptual premises. Reflection on the Nazi genocide demands simultaneously reflection on reflection itself, and especially on the ethico-political entailments of the means by which thought approaches its object.

REDEEMING KNOWLEDGE: ZYGMUNT BAUMAN'S MODERNITY AND THE HOLOCAUST

Nowhere is this critical self-consciousness exemplified more overtly than in Zygmunt Bauman's influential sociology of Nazi anti-Semitism, *Modernity and the Holocaust*.[3] The guiding thesis of Bauman's book is that no such sociology is possible without an attendant critique of sociological morality itself. Auschwitz confronts the discipline with the moral and political inadequacy of its implicit founding premise, namely that social phenomena should be read in terms of their conformity to the narrative of the West's ongoing 'civilizing process'. This premise dictates that any violation of that process is at best explained as an aberration and at worst elided altogether; because sociology assumes a continuity between social reason and historical progress, it cannot account for any break in that continuity.

Such a break, however, is irrefutably evident in the genocidal methods of the Nazis, which placed the most advanced technical rationality 'in the service of a goal incomprehensible in its irrationality' (Bauman, 136). In exposing the chasm that the darkest historical forces can interpose between technical and ethical rationality, Auschwitz simultaneously shows up the ethical blindness of sociology itself. In its theoretical impotence before this chasm, sociology unwittingly discloses its complicity with the amorality of technical rationality.

The struggle to undo this complicity requires first of all an attentiveness to those phenomena which escape normative sociological categories, the most exemplary of which is the ambiguous place of the Jew in the modern West. This ambiguity is a function above all of the Jew's inassimilability to a determinate national identity: '*The world tightly packed with nation-states abhorred the non-national void. Jews were in such a void: they were such a void*' (Bauman, 53, Bauman's emphasis). As 'non-national void', '*the opacity of the world fighting for clarity*' (Bauman, 56), the Jews presented an insuperable obstacle and challenge to the classifying logic of the modern nation and its claims for 'the ascribed character of nationhood, heredity and naturalness of national entities' (Bauman, 55). From this perspective, racism is a kind of protective ideological wall placed around these claims to naturalness and the cognitive clarity they guarantee.

Sociology's dependence on the same classifying logic – its assumption of society's conformity to 'causal laws and statistical probabilities' (Bauman, 3) – renders it powerless to interpret phenomena other than in terms of this logic. It is for this reason that orthodox sociological analysis of Auschwitz has been unable to recognize its intrication with the processes and institutions of modernity. Its assumption of the essential benignity of modern rationality prevents it from understanding modern genocide as anything other than 'a temporary suspension of the civilizational grip in which human behaviour is normally held' (Bauman, 4).

As a response to the demand imposed on thought by the horror of Auschwitz, the intense critical reflexivity of Bauman's book is indissociable from his attempt to point a way out of the moral indifference of sociological method. Sociology's paucity of resources for thinking the mutual implication of modernity and barbarism raises a demand for the transformation of its (and indeed every) conception of knowledge.

Bauman seeks to effect this transformation by recasting sociology in the light of a Levinasian ethics. Given the pivotal place of Levinas' thought in the present work, it is important to distinguish Bauman's uses of his key terms from my own; the distance between these construals of 'ethics as first philosophy' should hint at the perspective to be developed in the chapters that follow.

Bauman's theory of morality turns on the sociological adaptation of Levinas' idea of the face. In order to prevent possible dissent against the extermination of the Jews, Bauman argues, the Nazis had to ensure the removal of the victims from public visibility. The process of displacing Jews from the visible centre to the invisible margins of civic life brought with it a concomitant decrease in moral inhibition towards them. This pattern illuminates an intimate connection between human proximity and social morality: '*Responsibility is silenced once proximity is eroded; it may eventually be replaced with resentment once the fellow human subject is transformed into an Other*' (Bauman, 184, Bauman's emphasis).

Readers of Levinas will recognize the provenance of Bauman's terminology here. 'Proximity' is Levinas' term for the simultaneity of 'contact' and 'separation' by which the human other discloses himself to me, while 'responsibility' is the infinite and unchosen obligation to which I am commanded by this disclosure. The problem with Bauman's invocation of this vocabulary stems from its use as a means to describe a determinate social content. Sociologically recoded, 'proximity' is divested of the paradoxical identity it connotes between the absolute immediacy and infinite distance of the Other, and is reduced to its ordinary connotation of spatial nearness. Similarly, once responsibility is made contingent on the visible presence of the Other, it becomes a derivative effect of a particular social relation rather than – as in Levinas – the very condition of possibility for relationality as such.

Thus, where Levinas' ethics reads as an explicit challenge to the thinking of the Other as a mere datum of phenomenal experience, Bauman's post-Auschwitz ethics rests on just this phenomenalization of alterity. According to Bauman, 'Moral behaviour ... Emmanuel Levinas tells us, is triggered off by the mere presence of the Other as a *face*, that is, as an authority without force' (Bauman, 214).[4] This understanding of the face as a 'trigger' to moral behaviour assimilates it to the very economy of the visible and invisible which Levinas everywhere seeks to interrupt. Bauman's insistence on thinking the Other in terms of her social visibility – in the name of a correction and expansion of sociological reason – is tacitly complicit with the very coercive logic it seeks to criticize.

The point of this brief critical excursus into Bauman's post-Auschwitz ethics is not simply to take issue with his use of Levinas. Nor is it to deny the undoubted power of his critique of sociological reason's ethical blindness. It is rather to suggest the difficulty of responding to the demand imposed on thought by Auschwitz without falling back into the very gestures thought seeks to escape. Bauman's path to an ethical transformation of sociology leads equally to a sociological transformation of ethics – an account of the social conditions that enable ethical behaviour rather than of the ethical itself. As such, it is an essentially *expansive* move, an assimilation to sociology of an ethics it previously lacked. *Modernity and the Holocaust* remains within a comprehensive model of knowledge. To be sure, Auschwitz raises the demand for a new attentiveness to alterity; but where in Levinas this alterity refuses any instrumental logic, in Bauman it is put to the work of redeeming sociology.

THE 'NEW CATEGORICAL IMPERATIVE'

The argument staged across this book is that responding to the task of thinking after Auschwitz demands above all a vigilant resistance to alterity's assimilation to knowledge. This demand is famously intimated by Adorno, in a passage from *Negative Dialectic*:

> A new categorical imperative has been imposed by Hitler on unfree mankind: to arrange their thoughts and actions so that Auschwitz will not repeat itself, so that nothing similar will happen. (*ND*, 465; *GS*6, 358)

This imperative haunts each member in the constellation of thinkers which structures this book. Each of these thinkers, in very different conceptual and terminological registers, responds to its demand by way of a refusal to bring thought or action to completion or consummation. Indeed, this refusal is intrinsic to the structure of the imperative itself; history can judge the imperative violated (and the landscape of history after Auschwitz is shamefully littered with such violations), but the judgement of its fulfilment belongs of necessity to an unachieved and unachievable future. Thus, if Adorno points to a redemptive horizon at the point of which 'nothing similar will happen', this horizon is always already intricated with the impossibility of its actualization. The redemptive is, paradoxically, indissociable from this impossibility.

If art as thought by Adorno, religion as thought by Levinas, and their troubled sameness as 'writing' and 'Judaism' in Jabès, are carriers of the ethico-political task of thinking after Auschwitz, it is because they are each bound to an irreducible alterity in excess of conceptual comprehension. As long as thought is governed by the horizon of a completed future, it will fall short of the demand of the new categorical imperative. The possibility opened up by the inter-articulation of art and religion in this constellation of thinkers is nothing less than a radical rethinking of the redemptive – and so of the Absolute – as conceived by both metaphysical and materialist philosophies of history.

The Absolute to be thought of here is not the completion of history and experience in Hegelian Absolute Knowledge, nor even the Kantian regulative Ideal of the realization of the highest good in the Kingdom of God. It is rather that which, according to Levinas ' "absolves" itself from the relation in which it presents itself' (*TaI*, 50; *TeI*, 21). The Absolute's self-absolution from presence is what always prevents its coming to completion. The 'end' signified by this Absolute is neither telos nor Ideal but rather to invoke Maurice Blanchot's term 'a *measureless* end'[5] which dissolves the will to realize it.

NAZISM, THE WEST AND THE ABSOLUTE: LEVINAS AND AGAMBEN

The chasm between this thinking of the Absolute and its determination by Nazism as the fulfilment of a biological metaphysics hardly needs remarking upon. And yet Adorno's imperative bids us recognize the bleak fact that Western philosophical and theological tradition offered no resources for understanding, much less preventing, Nazism's Absolute and its demonic consequences. Auschwitz confronts us, in other words, with two urgent questions: what is Nazism?; and what is its relation to Western rationality? Levinas had recognized the urgency of these questions as early as 1934, and his essay of that year, 'Reflections on the Philosophy of Hitlerism', constitutes the embryo of a response.

According to Levinas' 1990 'Prefatory note' to the translation of this essay, its central thesis is that,

> the bloody barbarism of National Socialism lies not in some contingent anomaly within human reasoning, nor in some accidental ideological misunderstanding. This article expresses the conviction that this source stems from the essential possibility of *elemental Evil* into which we can be led by logic and against which Western philosophy had not sufficiently insured itself. ('RPH', 63, Levinas' emphasis)

According to the essay itself, this vulnerability of Western philosophy to evil[6] is concentrated in the 'Judeo-Christian leitmotif of freedom' ('RPH', 66), as expressed in the Christian doctrine of the soul. The Christian soul's 'noumenal nature' sets it above the entanglements of finite history 'in which concrete man nonetheless is placed'. This power to detach itself from material conditions is no 'abstract state', but on the contrary a 'concrete and positive power ... to free itself from *what has been*, from everything that linked it to something or engaged it with something [*engageé*], so it can regain its first virginity' ('RPH', 66).

The Christian hierarchy of soul over body, whose legacy is so clearly visible in the French Enlightenment's proclamation of the sovereignty of reason, interposes a permanent distance between spirit and 'physical, psychological and social matter' ('RPH', 66). The cardinal virtue of such a doctrine is that it liberates the human from the suffocating grasp of mythic nature,[7] such that his possibilities are no longer legislated in advance by 'a series of restless powers that seethe within him and already push him down a determined path' ('RPH', 66).[8]

If the first break with this tradition of liberal autonomy comes with Marx's assertion of the priority of being over consciousness, this break remains partial, inasmuch as '[t]o become conscious of one's social situation is, even for Marx, to free oneself of the fatalism entailed by that situation' ('RPH', 67). In Marx, consciousness continues to enjoy a relative autonomy from the being that conditions it. The decisive break with the Western conception of the human can occur only when 'the situation to which he was bound was not added to him but formed the very foundation of his being' ('RPH', 67). In this inversion of liberal Christendom's governing logic, being's truth is now identified not in the noumenal intelligibility of the soul, but in the material experience of the body.

Levinas goes on to show how the phenomenological analysis of physical pain appears to confirm the truth of this inversion; in its expression of opposition to this pain, the spirit betrays precisely the impossibility of escaping it. Indeed, pain is in its essence this ineluctable rivetedness[9] of the spirit to the body: 'The body is not only a happy or unhappy accident that relates us to the implacable world of matter. *Its adherence to the Self is of value in itself*. It is an adherence that *one does not escape*' ('RPH', 68, Levinas' emphases).

The West's vulnerability to the ideological and political onslaught of Nazism lies in its unwillingness to confront this fact of inescapability. This evasiveness on the part of Western tradition clears a space for a 'new conception of man' which puts the biological at the heart of spiritual life:

The mysterious urgings of the blood, the appeals of heredity and the past for which the body serves as an enigmatic vehicle, lose the character of being problems that are subject to a solution put forward by a sovereignly free Self ... Man's essence no longer lies in freedom, but in a kind of bondage [*enchaînement*]. To be truly oneself does not mean taking flight once more above contingent events that always remain foreign to the Self's freedom; on the contrary, it means becoming aware of the ineluctable chain that is unique to our bodies, and above all accepting this chaining. ('RPH', 69)

Once biology determines human essence, there is no escaping the destiny it imposes. The body to which I am chained becomes the bearer of a spiritual value which no act of thought or speech[10] can alter, and which places me irrevocably inside or outside of an 'authentic' community of 'consanguinity'.

Some seven years before Nazism's genocidal ambitions would take ultimate form, Levinas had here exposed the already exterminist logic of its metaphysics. More importantly still, he illuminates the troubling relation of this metaphysics to the governing philosophical categories of Western tradition. Nazism's corporealization of spirit constitutes less a demonic aberration from, than a strictly symmetrical *inversion* of, this tradition. The symmetry between these radically opposed metaphysics points to their shared structure of truth; the elevated Absolute of Western soul is reflected in the degraded Absolute of the Nazi body. This inversion, moreover, as a permanent possibility within Western rationality itself, is inseparable from its history.

If we have thus tarried at length with Levinas' reflections on Hitlerism, it is because they intimate the conceptual and ethico-political difficulties raised by the imperative to 'arrange thoughts and actions so that Auschwitz will not repeat itself'. More particularly, they point up the inadequacy to the imperative of an appeal simply to restore the violated rule of reason. To insist on this inadequacy is to posit not the logical continuity of Auschwitz with reason, but reason's vulnerability to its murderous inversion. For Levinas, as for many of the contemporary theorists of Nazism his essay anticipates, this vulnerability is disclosed in the thinking of the Absolute. To locate truth in the uncontaminated noumenality of the soul is to confer a transcendent substantiality on the human; a substantiality which in biological racism passes without remainder into the immanence of the body. The term common to both accounts of the human essence, however, is substance; whether figured as noumenal soul or spiritual body, the Absolute is comprehended as ultimate foundation, final guarantor of the meaning of experience. It is against the background of this construal of the Absolute that this book will attempt to configure a different arrangement of thought after Auschwitz.

The significance of Levinas' contribution to the understanding of Nazism's logic and of its relation to the political and philosophical history of the West has been recognized by one of its most significant contemporary theorists, Giorgio Agamben. In an excursus towards the end of *Homo Sacer*, his influential study of the logic of political sovereignty, he credits Levinas' essay as being even today 'the most valuable contribution to an understanding of National Socialism' (*HS*, 151). The force of Levinas' insight, according to Agamben, lies in its identification of the 'indissoluble cohesion of body and spirit' (*HS*, 151) as the philosophical condition of possibility for Nazism's politics.[11] Moreover, the 1990 prefatory note to the essay hints unambiguously at the complicity of Heideggerean ontology with this politics; Heidegger's 'ontology of a being concerned with being' ('RPH', 63) similarly collapses transcendence into finitude such that the terms cannot be held apart.

This statement of Nazism's rootedness 'in the same experience of facticity from which Heidegger departs' (*HS*, 152) is instructive in illuminating not only the proximity but equally the radical divergence between Heideggerian and Nazi ontologies. For Agamben, the ethico-political stakes of this divergence are high; if Western tradition conditions Nazism's metaphysics, then Auschwitz imposes the demand for a thinking of truth which escapes the economy of body and spirit into which both Christendom and its demonic other are locked. If Heidegger provides the point of entry for such a thinking, it is because his account of the 'indissoluble cohesion' of transcendence and finitude (or of Being and time) rigorously refuses the temptation of biologism.

This refusal is cast into relief by Agamben's theory of 'bare life'. This theory begins from the Aristotelian distinction between *zoe*, the naked *fact* of life common to all beings, and *bios*, the mode of life proper to individuals or groups. The structure of political sovereignty is premised on the incorporation of *zoe* into *bios* in the form of an 'inclusive exclusion'; *zoe* is that which enters community only in the form of a ban or non-belonging. Every political community, Agamben argues, founds itself on the paradox of inclusive exclusion, defining itself through that which it casts out. In modern sovereignty, this paradox is manifested in the form of the nation-state. In contrast to the strict separation of *zoe* and *bios* in the classical world, the nation-state, by tying rights to territoriality, makes bare life 'the earthly foundation of the state's legitimacy and sovereignty' (*HS*, 127). As the exponentially growing numbers of refugees today dramatically attests, this territorial definition of the human has engendered an insoluble crisis for modern sovereignty. The history of the last century can be read in terms of this crisis, of the challenge posed to power by a bare life discontinuous with and unassimilable to nationality. If, as Agamben audaciously goes on to claim, the concentration camp is 'the biopolitical paradigm of the modern', it is because it constitutes the most radical attempt to manage this crisis. Nazism finds in biology the basis for the determination, isolation and eventual annihilation of bare life.

This biologism is precisely the point at which Nazism and Heidegger part company. According to Agamben,

Nazism determines the bare life of *homo sacer* in a biological and eugenic key, making it into the site of an incessant decision on value and nonvalue in which biopolitics continually turns into thanato-politics and in which the camp, consequently, becomes the absolute political space. In Heidegger, on the other hand, *homo sacer* – whose very own life is always at issue in its every act – instead becomes Dasein, the inseparable unity of Being and ways of being, of subject and qualities, life and world, 'whose own Being is at issue in its very Being.' (HS, 153).

The irrevocable difference between Hitler and Heidegger, in other words, lies in their respective thinking of the Absolute. The biological determination of bare life in the former confers a corporeal substantiality on Being, which authorizes a legal and physical separation of the Aryan body (now the embodiment of Being) from its contaminating Jewish other (embodiment of non-Being). In Heidegger, however, it is just this isolation of bare life which is impossible.[12] As Dasein, Being is always already consigned to its 'ways of being' or 'qualities', such that it can never be determined *as such*. Being is that which is destined in advance to its own conceal-ment in finite being, and which can never be thought apart from this concealment. This refusal of the segregation of life from its forms, of the reduction of life to the brute facticity of survival, points to nothing less than the ethico-political task of thought after Auschwitz.[13]

It is this task which the present study will seek to unfold by way of its readings in Adorno, Levinas and Jabès. Central to each of the these readings will be an unre-lenting – Levinas would say 'insomniac' – resistance to the determination of the Absolute as fixed and ultimate substance, whether that substance is defined in terms of its immanence or its transcendence. As Levinas and Agamben's analyses have shown, the possibility of Auschwitz and its repetition cannot be thought apart from this substantialization of Spirit.

THE TEMPTATION OF THEODICY: AMERICAN-JEWISH THOUGHT AFTER AUSCHWITZ

This intrication suggests why the majority of religious, and specifically Jewish reli-gious philosophical responses to Auschwitz have repeatedly fallen short of its demand. This limitation is especially evident, as will presently be argued, in the field of North American-Jewish philosophical theology which has dominated post-Auschwitz religious discourse in recent years. As a number of commentators have shown, this is a large and internally variegated field;[14] undoubtedly, however, its most prominent and influential figures are the 'triumvirate' of Richard Rubin-stein, Eliezer Berkowits and Emil Fackenheim, representatives respectively of death-of-God theology,[15] neo-Orthodoxy and the space between these poles. My intention here is to show that in spite of their real and substantial religious differences, these positions are structured by the same premise, a premise which cannot but be inadequate to the Adornian imperative, namely that God (or the Absolute) can be understood only as guarantor of the meaning of historical experi-ence.[16] This premise, to be sure, manifests itself in very different guises across this body of work; but none of the thinkers in question are able to avoid the theodicical trap into which this premise leads.

IMMANENT THEODICY: RICHARD RUBINSTEIN

The ascription of a theodicy to Richard Rubinstein will surprise readers of his major theological work, *After Auschwitz*.[17] Rubinstein's book is, after all, a concerted refutation of traditional covenantal theology, asserting the absolute irreconcilability of the Jewish doctrine of election with the historical fact of the Nazi genocide: 'To see any purpose in the death camps, the traditional believer is forced to regard the most demonic, antihuman explosion of all history as a meaningful expression of God's purposes' (*AA*, 171).[18] The necessary condition for the renewal of Jewish theology, if it is to avoid such a morally and metaphysically objectionable conclusion, is the eschewal of the God of the Bible – 'the ultimate, omnipotent actor in the historical drama' (*AA*, 171).

This portrayal of the God of the Hebrew Bible rests on two unquestioned presuppositions. The first is that Jewish tradition cannot think God other than as the transcendent Author of a sacred History; as Zachary Braiterman points out, to make such a claim is to bypass the many rabbinic texts which trouble the relationship between divine authority and human experience.[19] The second and related presupposition is that the text of Jewish tradition can be reduced to a determinate communicative content whose meaning is transparent; but this premise depends on a blindness to one of that tradition's essential principles, namely that holy texts can be read only via a continuing and incessant process of interpretation and counter-interpretation.[20] Indeed, Rubinstein implicitly acknowledges the anomalousness to Jewish tradition of his interpretative literalism when he ascribes it to the deep and persistent influence of 'conservative American Protestantism' (*AA*, 178).

Both Rubinstein's account of normative Judaic theology and his attempt at its radical revision are thought within the dichotomy between spirit and matter, transcendence and immanence which, Levinas teaches, structures both Western tradition and its demonic other. If the theology of the Covenant is predicated on the transcendent Creator God, Rubinstein's post-Auschwitz alternative 'gives priority to the indwelling immanence of the Divine' (*AA*, 295). In this scheme, religion is to express a displacement of the Divine presence from heaven to earth.

What authorizes such a displacement? In Rubinstein as in Berkowits and Fackenheim, the sign and site of theological renewal is the State of Israel. In *After Auschwitz*, the creation of the State portends a recovery of pre-Biblical paganism: '*Increasingly, Israel's return to the earth elicits a return to the archaic earth religion of ancient Palestine*'. This return, moreover, far from being counter-historical, is 'fully in keeping with the twentieth century's return to primal origins and primal circularities' (*AA*, 205). The restoration of the Land to the People of Israel is a restoration of immanence to the Divine, and 'of humanity ... to its only true hearth – the bosom of Mother Earth' (*AA*, 209). As such, it is symptomatic of a more general world-cultural movement against the estrangement wrought by technological modernity.

If this neo-pagan God dwells in phenomenal nature rather than a noumenal super-nature, Rubinstein is nonetheless careful, particularly in his more recent essays, not to represent Him as a determinate and incarnate form. Indeed, it is in his attempt to reimagine the Divine that he identifies some valuable motifs in Jewish tradition, notably the Kabbalistic '*En-Sof*, that which is without limit or end' (*AA*, 298). As infinite Source or Ground of Being that conditions all, but cannot be identified with any finite being, God is '*no-thing* ... the dark unnameable Abyss' (*AA*, 298).

The explicit echo of Heidegger here is unmistakable. As that which is simultaneously radically distinct *and* indissociable from finite being, Heideggerian Being perhaps lends itself to this rewriting as immanent God of nature. Yet an ambiguity attaches itself to Rubinstein's use of Heidegger; if Being is the infinite Ground that refuses identification with any entity, it is also the primordial origin or *omphalos* from which humanity finds itself estranged. As the primary agent through which the people of Israel overcome this estrangement, the State of Israel is the condition for the recovery of this lost origin. Rubinstein himself makes the link between Zionism and Heidegger unambiguously:

> One of the most important but least noticed aspects of Zionism is the extent to which it represents a Jewish expression of the twentieth century's urge to return to primal origins. This is evident in many of the cultural endeavours of our times. In philosophy, Martin Heidegger has characterized his thought as an attempt to get behind more than two thousand years of European philosophy's estrangement from 'Being'. (*AA*, 201)

In this passage, the force of Levinas' warning against the ethico-political dangers into which Heidegger's philosophy can lead is unwittingly confirmed. The diagnosis of estrangement from Being authorizes Zionism not in ethical or political but in *sacral* terms; the Land of Israel is the authentic repository of Being to which the State grants the people access. Where for Agamben, Heidegger's philosophy is directed against '*facticity* ... presenting itself as a *fact*' (*HS*, 152), that is, against the condition of any fact's possibility being itself reduced to a fact, for Rubinstein it enables precisely this reduction: the facticity of the Divine is presented in the fact of the Land. The Land of Israel, in short, enables a turning from inauthentic to authentic existence;[22] such a turning, however, involves determining the 'Holy Nothingness' as the earth. In spite of Rubinstein's insistence on the incommensurablity of

God with any category of relation, it is clear that spatial nearness to and distance from the Land are precisely forms of, respectively, authentic and inauthentic relation to the Divine. Such a distinction would not be possible without a determination of the Absolute as earthly substance.

Nor does this dramatic shift in theological orientation enable Rubinstein to escape the temptations of theodicy. As holy Abyss, God remains source, if not providential Author, of all good and evil. Rubinstein does not shy from the logical entailments of this conception of divinity; if his account of the divine foregrounds its destructive elements, it is, he remarks, 'because *this aspect of divinity has hardly received the attention in recent Jewish thought which recent Jewish experience suggests it deserves*' (*AA*, 245, Rubinstein's emphasis). It is to the destructive force of the divine, in other words, that Auschwitz can be ascribed: 'No people has known as deeply as have we how truly God in His holiness slays those to whom he gives life' (*AA*, 246). It is difficult to interpret this statement as anything other than violently theodicical, or to state what makes the anonymity and fatality of divine destruction either morally or metaphysically preferable to destruction in the name of providential history. Such a shift involves little more than an arbitrary transfer of force from transcendence to immanence.

The motivation for this transfer seems to be less ethical or religious than epistemological. A theology of immanence appears to Rubinstein to provide a means of overcoming the incomprehension into which Auschwitz casts traditional covenantal theology. This motivation is made evident in the last essay of *After Auschwitz* ('God after the Death of God'), which formulates the transition from a theology of transcendence to one of immanence in terms of a preference for Hegelian *Vernunft* (Reason) over Kantian *Verstand* (Understanding), or for a 'system of continuity' over a 'system of gaps'. The Hegelian critique of *Verstand* states that the partial and finite perspective of empirical experience is 'actually the self-manifestation of the single universal, infinite Ground and Source' (*AA*, 297). If covenantal theology is rendered incoherent by Auschwitz, it is thus because it leaves an insuperable gap in comprehension between God and history. From this perspective, a neo-pagan theology of nature is preferable because it fills this gap, rendering all historical experience continuous with the anonymous creative–destructive capacity of God. If Auschwitz calls rational cognition into question, Rubinstein's response appears to be to transform cognition's structure such that it would be invulnerable to questioning. On this model, the Hegelian task of theology after Auschwitz, and of its actualization in the State of Israel, is to heal the wounds that history has wrought against spirit, 'so that they reveal no scar' (*AA*, 206). The very theodicy that Rubinstein begins by refuting returns here with all the more violence for being unacknowledged. The anonymous Creator–Destroyer of his neo-pagan theology provides an explanatory source for Auschwitz more stubbornly impregnable than the Biblical God he refuses.

TRANSCENDENT THEODICY: ELIEZER BERKOWITS

In contrast to Rubinstein, Eliezer Berkowits' neo-Orthodox[23] theology appears to resist the temptation to close the gap insinuated by Auschwitz into religious comprehension. Certainly, he shows persuasively that the very premises of the test to which Rubinstein subjects the God of Hebrew tradition are based on a profound misreading of that tradition. In response to the portrayal of this God as the absolute Subject of a providential History, Berkowits excavates from tradition a God whose concealment is not a refutation of His presence but a mode of its *manifestation*. This is the God of whom, for example, Isaiah says, 'Verily Thou art a God that hidest Thyself,/O God of Israel, the Saviour' (Isaiah 45: 15, cited in *FAH*, 101). Glossing this passage, Berkowits finds that in it, 'God's self-hiding is not a reaction to human behavior, when the Hiding of the Face represents God's turning away from man as a punishment. For Isaiah, God's self-hiding is an attribute of divine nature' (*FAH*, 101).

Berkowits' nuanced reading appears to take the Jewish God out of the economy of visible and invisible, immanent and transcendent. Instead of opposing revelation to concealment, which would make of history a permanent empirical testing-ground for the presence or absence of God (a ground from which atheism is bound always to emerge vindicated), he insists on the indissociability of the two terms. Admittedly, this conception of God is placed in the service of a more traditional theological argument which sees evil as the necessary price paid for His divinely generous withdrawal from the world to create space for free human action. But Berkowits refuses to allow this argument to alleviate the agonizing paradox 'that God's direct concern for the wrongdoer should be directly responsible for so much pain and sorrow on earth' (*FAH*, 106). Instead, this experience of radical abandonment becomes the only means of attesting to Him: 'The God of History must be absent and present concurrently. He hides his presence. He is present without being indubitably manifest; he is absent without being hopelessly inaccessible' (*FAH*, 107).

By distinguishing God's presence from His active intervention in history, Berkowits appears to have taken Auschwitz definitively beyond the reach of theodicy. Yet precisely the tradition which enables this refusal of theodicy is employed to reinforce it in his subsequent reflections on Auschwitz's relation to the broader sweep of Jewish history. Berkowits portrays this history as the site of conflict between two radically incompatible modes of historical existence: the 'power history' of the nations and the 'faith history' of Israel. Where the nations represent 'naturalistic history, explainable in terms of power and economics', Israel 'testifies to a supra-natural dimension jutting into history' (*FAH*, 111). Had these histories developed separately, each might have been left to unfold itself according to its own internal logic; but the presence of Israel within the nations meant their inevitable interpenetration.

This interpenetration has led, on the one hand, to the occasional glimpse within 'the naturalistic realm' of the divine Voice. On the other, it has led far more frequently to the violent incursion into the 'supra-natural' realm of the nations' rage and resentment. What Berkowits calls the political history of the 'is' finds its very foundations put in question when confronted by the ethical history of the 'ought'. Auschwitz is the logic of this confrontation taken to its demonic limit. The genocide was based not, as suggested by Nazism's hysterical rhetoric, in fear of the economic and political forces the Jews had secretly ranged against the Aryan, but in 'a metaphysical fear of the true mystery of God's "powerless" presence in history as "revealed" in the continued survival of Israel' (FAH, 117). The death camps are from this perspective the concrete expression of the will to silence the witness to this presence.

Notwithstanding the power of his analysis of the metaphysics of Nazi violence, Berkowits' account of Jewish history rests on a fundamentally ahistorical mystification. Like Rubinstein, his religious and ethical perspective is caught within a hierarchy of transcendence and immanence which governs his every historical judgement. Once Israel and the nations are assigned to such radically opposed metaphysical destinies in world history, the meaning of any and every event in that history must be determined in advance.

The consequences of this metaphysically determined reading of history are made evident in Berkowits' interpretation of the State of Israel and its theological meaning. Collapsing the people into the State of Israel, he renders the latter the world's sole carrier of 'faith history', a nation witnessing to the transcendent in the midst of nations tethered to the earthly. This manifestation of transcendence on the stage of world history is, moreover, the hither side of God's absent presence in Auschwitz:

> Jewish survival through the ages and the ingathering of the exiles into the land
> of their fathers after the holocaust proclaim God's holy presence at the very
> heart of his inscrutable hiddenness. We recognized in it the hand of divine
> providence because it was exactly what, after the holocaust, the Jewish people
> needed in order to survive. (FAH, 134)

What is disclosed above all by this passage is a thoroughgoing dialectical symmetry between God's manifest absence at Auschwitz and his manifest presence in the State. The Nazi attempt to annihilate all vestiges of faith history is overturned by that history's triumphal resurrection in the Land of Israel. This insertion of Auschwitz into the broader narrative of Jewish history casts Berkowits' earlier reading of Isaiah into a new light. Where previously the 'hester panim' ('hiding face') of God appeared to place him beyond the economy of presence and absence, visible and invisible, the interpretation of the State as evidence of 'the divine hand

of providence' pulls Him forcibly back into it. God's silence at Auschwitz is
redeemed by His voice in Israel; the opacity of the first is merely the necessary
corollary of the transparency of the second.

The State, then, has once again proved the means by which an apparently discred-
ited theodicy insinuates itself back into religious thought. The State phenomena-
lizes the transcendence which appeared to confound phenomenality. Furthermore,
the a priori character of the opposition between Israel and the nations, and the
unquestioned conflation of the State with the former, means that Berkowits at
the outset rules out of court any possibility of their contamination. In insisting on
Israel's absolute distance from power, he effectively sacralizes the history of the
State (as well as providing a metaphysical endorsement for its every act) and in
turn redeems the apparently irredeemable fact of Auschwitz. As the culmination
of faith history, the State confers a new sense on what, seen in isolation, appeared
senseless: 'Seen in this light, Jewish history does make sense: it is part of the cosmic
drama of redemption. In it the massive martyrdom of Israel finds its significance:
nothing of the sorrow and the suffering was in vain, for all the time the path was
being paved for the Messiah' (FAH, 152).

As extermination, Auschwitz refused redemption; as martyrdom, it becomes an
indispensable part of its narrative. Nor can such a narrative be dismissed as supple-
mentary to Berkowits' theological treatment of Auschwitz; on the contrary, it
emerges seamlessly from the metaphysical division of history into the forces of
transcendent faith and immanent power. Such a division cannot but end in the
reassertion of the very theodicy it sought to refuse.

WEAK SPECULATIVE THEODICY: EMIL FACKENHEIM

A similar metaphysics of history ultimately prevents Fackenheim's 'foundations of
post-Holocaust Jewish thought'[24] from breaking out of theodicy. Fackenheim's
major work, To Mend the World, self-consciously positions itself between the
extremes of fideism and materialism, the twin temptations of religious thinking
after Auschwitz. It is this precarious space which thought is forced to inhabit
when history ruptures the narratives of divine providence and rational progress
alike: 'this catastrophe, though in history – the history of the humanly possible –
is not quite of it' (MW, xiv, Fackenheim's emphasis).[25] Faced with the exhaustion
of its own (and indeed all other) explanatory resources, Judaism is thrown into a
crisis of self-understanding which it can overcome only by confronting head-on.

Neither the authority of the Sinaitic witnesses of Biblical tradition nor its
modern transformation by Rosenzweig into the authority of personal revelation
is tenable in the face of the radical violation of the Covenantal relation signified
by Auschwitz. While Rosenzweig's phenomenology of revelation provides a basis

for faith other than blind fideism, its insistence on the eternality of revelation inoculates it against all historical disconfirmation. The lesson of Auschwitz, to the contrary, is that 'historicity, whether a curse, a blessing, or something of both, has become inescapable for Jewish thought' (*MW*, 94).

Fackenheim's claim to have confronted thought's historicity in contradistinction to Rosenzweig's avoidance of it rests on a common misreading of the latter. Moreover, this misreading obscures Fackenheim's own vulnerability to the very charge he levels against his predecessor, namely the sacralization of Jewish history.

For Fackenheim, 'Jewish eternity' in Rosenzweig's great work of philosophical theology, *The Star of Redemption* (*Der Stern der Erlösung*) signifies unambiguously an 'ahistorical' conception of Jewish existence. Certainly, there are moments in the *Star*'s remarkable descriptive phenomenology of Judaism and Christianity (Part 3) which appear to confirm such a claim. In the chapter on Christianity (Part 3, Book 2), for example, Rosenzweig graphically removes the Jew from the time of the nations: 'God withdrew the Jew from this life by arching the bridge of his law high above the current of time, which henceforth and to all eternity rushes powerlessly along under its arches' (*SR*, 339; *SE*, 376).

If initially this sentence appears a ready confirmation of Fackenheim's charge against Rosenzweig, close reading discloses in it an instructive ambiguity: it is crucially the bridge of Jewish *law*, carrier of revelation, rather than the Jew himself, that the text envisions arched over time. Rosenzweig's earlier account of the pitfalls and possibilities of Jewish community and prayer accentuates this distinction between Jew and Judaism. For the Jew to walk across the bridge of eternity would be to conflate God's time and earthly time, a conflation against which Rosenzweig expressly warns in his Introduction to Part 3:

> For the future is not, for God, anticipation. He is eternal, he alone is eternal, he is the Eternal per se. In his mouth, 'I am' is like 'I shall be' and finds explanation in it.
>
> For man and the world, however, life is not eternal by nature. They live in the mere moment or in the broad present. (*SR*, 272; *SE*, 303)

For the Jew, as for all of humanity, there is no *experience* of eternity – Jewish existence is no anticipation of the Hegelian reconciliation of finite and infinite. Far from seeking to effect such a reconciliation, Judaism is directed firmly towards preserving the *finitude* of experience. Judaism consists precisely for Rosenzweig in sustaining rather than closing the gap between finite and infinite.[26]

In contrast, Fackenheim, like Berkowits before him, is far less cautious in maintaining the distance between finite and sacred history. To be sure, Auschwitz is pronounced an irreparable rupture in history, beyond recuperation even by a Hegelian speculative metaphysics: '*where the Holocaust is there is no overcoming; and where there is an overcoming the Holocaust is not'* (*MW*, 135, Fackenheim's emphasis). Yet from the outset, this failure of *aufhebung* is construed in explicitly Hegelian terms. Thus Fackenheim charges that in rejecting Hegel, Rosenzweig 'did not consider sufficiently the possibility that the failure of Hegel's enterprise might be a "process" with dialectical "results"' (*MW*, 106). Fackenheim appears oblivious here to the irony of any 'result' issuing from such a failure; as a result attained through the labour of the negative, failure can only pass into – be succeeded by – success.[27] The impossibility of overcoming is tethered dialectically to the overcoming of impossibility.

This dialectical relation is disclosed by an ambiguity in the signficance Fackenheim gives to 'impossibility'. If impossibility is at one level of the text insuperable, at another it becomes the necessary condition for what he calls 'the Jewish return into history'.[28] This return – what Jewish tradition names *Teshuva* – signifies a bridging of the chasm opened by Auschwitz between God and his people. Such a return is present in the inexplicable and different forms of resistance attested to during the course of the Nazi genocide: survivor Pelagia Lewinska's attestation to the experience of an imperative, in the midst of the horrors of Auschwitz, to live through them; the exchange by a group of Hasidim in Buchenwald of four rations of bread for a set of *tefillin*; and of course the scattered instances of armed Jewish resistance.

Fackenheim insists that these instances of resistance exceed the reach of historical or psychological explanation. They attest rather to a positive epistemological and ontological limit: 'our ecstatic thought must point to their resistance – the resistance in thought and the resistance in life – as *ontologically ultimate. Resistance in that extremity was a way of being. For our thought now, it is an ontological category*' (*MW*, 248, Fackenheim's emphasis).

Fackenheim's agenda for post-Auschwitz Jewish thought turns on just this ontologization of resistance; indeed, it is the carrying of this ontology into the future that constitutes its authentic task. But what form might such a task take? Quite simply, all forms of Jewish self-affirmation (or at least all those adjudged to be such by Fackenheim himself) in and after Auschwitz are conferred with ontological status,[29] and so placed outside questioning or contestation. As with Berkowits and Rubinstein, it is Zionism that serves as the privileged expression of this ontology. As such, it is an imperative rather than a choice for the Jew after Auschwitz: 'Anti- or non-Zionism remains a possibility for Jews today. But it is a possibility without self-respect' (*MW*, 97).

As the sole available means of forging such self-respect, Zionism is heir to the resistance of the Jewish victims, and has the same metaphysical status. It represents less a 'Jewish return into history' (from what, one might ask, are Jews returning?) than history's return to the Jews and to their sacred destiny. If the task of Jewish thought today is *Tikkun* – a term borrowed from Lurianic *kabbalah*, signifying the

mending of the shattered vessels of divinity – then this task is identical with the
State of Israel itself:

> What then is the *Tikkun*? It is Israel itself. It is a state founded, maintained,
> defended by a people who – so it was once thought – had lost the arts of state-
> craft and self-defense forever. It is the replanting and reforestation of a land
> that – so it once seemed – was unredeemable swamps and desert. ... It is a
> City rebuilt that – so once the consensus of mankind once had it – was destined
> to remain holy ruins. (*MW*, 312–13)

As *Tikkun* itself – rather than as a potential means for *Tikkun* (which would
maintain it as an object of ethical and political judgement) – the State has ultimate
ontological status; as in Berkowits, it is made impervious to any critical questioning
by being removed from the sphere of finite history. There is an absence in both
thinkers of the *tension* which structures the people–State relation in Rosenzweig.[30]
Far from being a mere oversight, this absence is a necessary consequence of con-
flating the presence of God with His *appearance in history*.

The ontological significance conferred by Fackenheim on Auschwitz, the State
of Israel and their relation[31] discloses the danger into which any attempt to think of
Auschwitz must avoid falling: as long as the Absolute is thought in terms of its
determinate realization in the historical present, philosophy will be powerless to
escape Hegel, not least where it claims to distance itself from him. Fackenheim contrasts his 'fragmentary *Tikkun*' which leaves visible the historical scars of spirit, with
the teleological realization of History in the Hegelian State. Yet the Hegelian State is
never ontologized to the point of separation from finite history and invulnerability
to its judgement. Retaining Hegel's horizon of redemption while refusing its strong
metaphysical determination does not render Fackenheim's State less of an imposed
resolution; it merely conveys more reticence about directly naming its ontological
source, and as such might be termed a 'weak' speculative theodicy.

That the 'fragmentary *Tikkun*' of the State has already been construed by Hegel
as a mere phenomenological misrecognition of its own wholeness is made unwittingly evident in Fackenheim's expression of 'open-ended wonder before the
Six-Day-War' (*MW*, 146). This wonder, to which he contrasts the absoluteness of
the Hegelian telos, swiftly loses its open-endedness when read through his narrative of Jewish resistance. As the culmination of an ontologically ultimate History
inaugurated by the resisters, the meaning of the State of Israel is precisely *not* open-
ended or contestable, a point tacitly acknowledged at the book's conclusion, when
Fackenheim once again remarks his astonishment 'that in this of all ages the Jewish
people have returned – *have been* returned? – to Jerusalem' (*MW*, 313). The question mark appended to 'have been returned' is scarcely necessary, for the sacralized
narrative of Jewish history to which the question belongs has given its answer in
advance. The Absolute realized in history is invulnerable to the question.

THE ABSOLUTE IN QUESTION

The thought to be developed here, in contrast, is of an Absolute *structured* by the question, by an intrinsic resistance to its own fulfilment. But how is such a thinking otherwise of the Absolute to be staged? What resources does tradition in its various guises provide for such a thinking? A valuable response to these questions is intimated by Andrew Benjamin in his 1997 book *Present Hope*. Benjamin's rethinking of philosophical and aesthetic tradition in the ineliminable shadow of Auschwitz points to the new itinerary of thought to be traced presently and across the chapters that follow. He begins by asking in what sense philosophy can continue once 'its projects of completion and finality have been rendered redundant', (*PH*, 2) and responds by pointing to two possible futures for philosophy in the wake of this exhaustion:

> The first laments the impossibility of philosophy's project, and thus condemns itself to a ceaseless preoccupation with impossibility, the aporetic and a thoughtful melancholia. The second involves a complex re-reading of philosophy's history in which what comes to be affirmed is the identification of the productive presence of the incomplete as always having formed part of the philosophical project. (*PH*, 2)

The thinkers constellated in this study are each in different ways staked in recovering this 'productive presence of the incomplete' from tradition. Each of them draws what Benjamin terms the 'hope' of philosophy away from a horizon of futural redemption and towards the 'inherently incomplete nature' (A. Benjamin, 10) of the present. The philosophical, aesthetic and religious practice of 'incompletion' carries the ethico-political imperative to which thinking after Auschwitz is perpetually subject.

Undoubtedly, the figure most indissociable from philosophy's dream of completion is Hegel. It is perhaps unsurprising, then, that it is precisely in Hegel himself that the resources for awakening from this dream can be identified; his critique of the speculative failings of romanticism in the realm of art, and of Judaism in the realm of religion, delineate with uncanny precision the features of the thinking to be mapped here.

The literary Absolute: Romanticism

In his critique of the 'romantic form of art' in its late guise, Hegel questions 'whether such productions [i.e late romantic artworks] in general are still to be called works of art'. This question is provoked by romantic art's increasingly brazen failure to conform to 'the essential nature of works of art proper (i.e. of the Ideal), where the important thing is both a subject-matter not inherently arbitrary and transient, and also a mode of portrayal fully in correspondence with such a subject-matter' (*A*1, 596; *VA*2, 224). Rather than recognizing its own arbitrariness as symptom of the ever-widening divide between the inner life and the external world, romantic art exacerbates this divide, divesting each side – and the relation between them – of all but the most frivolous of meanings.

The butt of Hegel's most vituperative criticism in this regard is Jena Romanticism – the poets and thinkers who orbited around the Schlegel brothers and Novalis at the turn of the nineteenth century. Jena Romanticism's invocation of the fragmentary and transient illuminations of *Witz* and irony as means to the attainment of truth abandons the labour of the Concept and with it the universality and wholeness of knowledge. This always already lost universality renders its thinkers little more than 'worthless yearning natures' (*A*1, 68; *VA*1, 98), condemned to fall short of the redemption towards which it perpetually and impotently gestures.

This construal of Romanticism, however, makes no distinction between its and Hegel's own Absolute; as such, it can only be read by Hegel as a tragically unattainable telos. Philippe Lacoue-Labarthe and Jean-Luc Nancy's influential re-reading of Schlegel and the Jena Romantics is significant for drawing from their texts an altogether different thinking of the Absolute.[33] The *literary* Absolute, they argue, is constituted by, indeed *is*, the impossibility of its own fulfilment. It has as its structure the question rather than its resolution:

> literature, as its own infinite questioning and as the perpetual positing of its own question, dates from romanticism and as romanticism . . . the romantic question, the question of romanticism, does not and cannot have an answer. Or, at least . . . its answer can only be terminally deferred, continually deceiving, endlessly recalling the question.[33]

The text which most famously and explicitly stages this poetics of truth is the 116th of Schlegel's *Athenaeum Fragments*. Elaborating the 'progressive, universal' essence of Romantic poetry, the fragment discloses a structure of infinite reflection which enables the poem's perpetual self-production: 'And it can also – more than any other form – hover . . . on the wings of poetic reflection, and can raise that reflection again and again to a higher power, can multiply it in an endless succession of mirrors'.[34] The poem's yielding of itself to this mirroring effect places it outside any horizon of finality, such that completion becomes one with its interruption:

> Other kinds of poetry are finished and are now capable of being fully analyzed. The romantic kind of poetry is still in the state of becoming; that, in fact, is its real essence: that it should forever be becoming and never be perfected. It can be exhausted by no theory and only a divinatory criticism would dare to try to characterize its ideal. (Schlegel, 32/29–30)

Romantic poetry's state of becoming, in other words, is not a transient condition to be overcome with the moment of romanticism itself, but its paradoxical *essence*. The romantic poem is the very site of the Absolute as incompletion, one that realizes itself only in not realizing itself. Thought this way, the incomplete can no longer be opposed to the complete, for the incomplete as Absolute – or as Lacoue-Labarthe and Nancy put it, the 'incompletion of completion' (*l'inachèvement de l'achèvement*) – decisively undoes any such economy of opposition.

It is in this paradoxical logic of the incomplete that the poetic to be traced across the chapters that follow finds its point of departure. After Auschwitz, art is impelled not by the fulfilment but by the 'ab-solution' of the Absolute; '[a]rt', in Adorno's words, 'must turn against itself, in opposition to its own concept, and thus become uncertain of itself right into its innermost fiber' (*AT*, 2; *GS*7, 10). In order to keep faith with itself – *to be art* – art must negate its own essence or *not be art* – that is, refuse its historical ideal. Art is caught in a homonymous logic whereby it signifies both itself and something other than, even opposed to itself. The truth of the poem consists in renouncing its own ideal, exacerbating rather than healing the non-reconciliation of its inner life and external object. For Hegel, 'the keynote of romantic art is ... *lyrical*' (*A*1, 528; *VA*2, 225) and this lyricism – the shaping of art by inner life or '*depth of feeling*' (*A*1, 527; *VA*2, 224, Hegel's emphasis) – is what leads art inexorably to the fatal divorce of finite and infinite. For Adorno (as Chapter 2 will show), it is just this inner tendency towards self-division that constitutes the truth of the lyric after Auschwitz. And as Chapter 4 will show, for Jabès, poetry – or 'writing', or 'the book' – will be born of the same irreconcilability, by which it is consigned to a condition of perpetual self-prolongation: 'the book is always the beginning of an incomplete book defined by its very incompleteness, the beginning of an interrupted rebeginning ...' (*BR*2, 76; *LR*, 236).

THE INCOMPLETE MESSIAH: JUDAISM

If religion constitutes art's twin path in this itinerary of incompletion, it is once again Hegelian critique which provides the means of its unfolding. The terms of Hegel's critique of romantic art are echoed resoundingly in his critique of the Jewish religion. The *Lectures on the Philosophy of Religion* (like the penultimate chapter of the *Phenomenology*) trace across the development of the religious spirit a progressive enriching of the knowledge of God, which reaches its culmination in the Incarnation and its redemption in the speculative Good Friday. As a religion of the sublimity of God, placing an insuperable gap between Him and his creation, Judaism blocks in advance this reconciliation of finite and infinite. The text of Hebrew tradition is confirmation of this gap, as Hegel's gloss on Psalm 29 suggests. The 'lyrical sublimity' through which the Psalmist expresses God's infinity engenders a perpetual restlessness of spirit, whereby 'imagination seizes on external phenomena and juxtaposes them fragmentarily and in disorder' (*A* 2, 1140; *VA* 3, 453). Like romantic art, Judaism is condemned to unhappiness by its inability to recognize its transient place in the history of Spirit's self-completion.

The resistance to this history of Spirit unearthed in Lacoue-Labarthe and Nancy's (as well as Adorno's) excavation of a discontinuous romantic poetics finds its religious analogue in a number of contemporary texts and thinkers tying the Judaic motif of redemption to the impossibility of its fulfilment. Exemplary in this context is Marc-Alain Ouaknin's influential work on Talmudic hermeneutics, *The Burnt Book*.[36] Like Lacoue-Labarthe and Nancy's readings in Schlegel, Ouaknin's readings in Talmud undo the Hegelian Absolute by thinking the Absolute otherwise, by refusing its definition as a realized universal. The holiness of the Talmudic text is tied intimately to the process of questioning that structures it, and that prevents its resolution:

> To really enter Talmudic thought, each time a certainty is asserted one should seek the opposite assertion that it is related to. In this way, Talmudic thought never stops opposing itself, yet without ever contenting itself with satisfying this opposition. (Ouaknin, 86; 128)

This 'questioning word' consigns rabbinic discussion to a state of constitutive incompletion, one which cannot be opposed to completion, but whose completion consists in its prolongation. In a motif that will become familiar through both Levinas and Jabès, the Book as construed by the Talmud projects the culmination of knowledge into an unachievable future, a future (*avenir*), always yet to come (*à-venir*): 'The Book, by its impossibility of settling down in the "now", helps us to attain discontinuity and time-as-discontinuity' (Ouaknin, 169; 234).

From this perspective, the messianic horizon of Jewish hope is not a determinate state to be attained in a known or even unknown future. Drawing on the kabbalistic writings of Rabbi Nachman of Bratslav, Ouaknin develops a different understanding of the messianic:

> For Rabbi Nachman, the messianic era is not the *Tikkun*, a repairing that effaces the fissure [*Shevirah*]. The messianic era is not the time when the Messiah is here. On the contrary: it is the time during which the Messiah is awaited. To exaggerate a little: the Messiah is made for not coming . . . and yet, he is awaited. The Messiah allows time to be continually deferred [*se différer continuellement*], to generate time. (Ouaknin, 302; 395–6)

The chapters which follow will elaborate this (non)experience of the messianic as thought through the interplay of art and religion pervading three very distinct authorships. The *Bilderverbot* (prohibition of images) which governs Adorno's negative utopian aesthetic; the vigilant wresting by Levinas of the Judaic Messiah from every association with eschatological finality; and the designation by Jabès of the Messiah as 'the ultimate [*extrême*] opening of the book', will each be read as intricate responses to the urgent question issuing from the new categorical imperative: what would it mean 'to arrange thoughts and actions so that nothing similar will happen'?

CHAPTER 2

'The Ever-Broken Promise of Happiness':
Interrupting Art, or Adorno

Adorno's new categorical imperative, it has been shown, is structured by the insuperable paradox that its urgent moral necessity is indissociable from its impossibility. Precisely because the fulfilment of the imperative – the non-occurrence of anything similar – belongs to a future unachieved and unachievable, its claim on thought is all the more binding.[1] The impossibility of actualizing the imperative prevents thinking from coming to rest, from seeking a future in which it would be redeemed from its demand.

It will be argued in this chapter that this conjunction of necessity and impossibility structures Adorno's complex and internally variegated authorship. It is articulated above all in the paradoxical thinking of redemption that crosses his writings on metaphysics, politics, ethics and above all art after Auschwitz: that redemption must take the form of its unceasing refusal. To respect the thought of a reconciled future is to refuse its coercion into the present, that is, to recognize its impossibility. This impossibility is not, moreover, the temporary condition of late capitalist society patiently awaiting its dialectical supersession, but a constitutive condition of any future politics. Any politics which comes to rest, which seeks to free itself from the entanglements of finitude, ceases to be a politics. The authentically redemptive gesture must always be a turning away from redemption. This doubled thought is famously and beautifully elaborated in the 'Zum Ende' ('Finale' in Jephcott's translation)[2] of *Minima Moralia*. The centrality of this text for our argument demands its quotation in full:

The only philosophy which can be responsibly practiced in face of despair is the attempt to contemplate all things as they would present themselves from the standpoint of redemption (*Standpunkt der Erlösung*). Knowledge has no light but that shed on the world by redemption: all else is reconstruction, mere technique. Perspectives must be fashioned that displace and estrange the world, reveal it to be, with its rifts and crevices, as indigent and distorted as it will appear one day in the messianic light. To gain such perspectives without velleity (*Willkür*) or violence, entirely from felt contact with objects – this alone is the task of thought. It is the simplest of all things, because the situation calls imperatively for such knowledge, indeed because consummate negativity, once squarely faced, delineates the mirror image of its opposite. But it is also the utterly impossible thing, because it presupposes a standpoint removed, even though by a hair's breath (*wäre es auch nur um ein Winziges*), from the scope of existence, whereas we well know that any possible knowledge must not only be wrested from what is, if it shall hold good, but is also marked, for this very reason, by the same distortion and indigence which it seeks to escape. The more passionately thought denies its conditionality for the sake of the unconditional, the more unconsciously, and so calamitously (*verhängnisvoller*), it is delivered up to the world. Even its own impossibility it must at last comprehend for the sake of the possible. But beside the demand thus placed on thought, the question of the reality or the unreality of redemption itself hardly matters. (*MM*, 247; *GS* 4, 283).

Let us try to draw out the pivotal dilemma of the task delineated here. It is 'the simplest of all things' (*das Allereinfachtse*), because animated by the imperative which 'consummate negativity' (*vollendete Negativität*) – the irreparably 'damaged life'[3] of the West after Auschwitz – calls into being. It is simultaneously 'utterly impossible' because the standpoint of redemption is radically inaccessible to us, locked as we are within 'the scope of existence'. If it is thus solely via 'felt contact with objects' (*der Fühlung mit den Gegenständen*) – what Adorno elsewhere terms a *micrology* – that this demand on thought can be maintained in all its difficulty, it is because such contact begins from our ineluctable finitude, our entanglement in things. The refusal to acknowledge this conditionality of experience 'for the sake of the unconditional' is what delivers thought 'calamitously . . . to the world'. Conditionality and redemption, then, are bound together in being held apart, for only recognition of the finitude that suspends redemption keeps intact its possibility.

What is the terrain proper to the standpoint of redemption? That is, where might it be possible to hold to the conditionality of experience *and* the promise of redemption without hypostatizing either? Adorno's post-war corpus offers a number of possible answers, including philosophy, education or ethics. Undoubtedly, however, the privileged carrier of the sole 'task of thought' after Auschwitz is art. The 'nonconceptual language' of art, he writes in *Aesthetic Theory*, the second of his major late texts, 'is the only figure, at the contemporary stage of rationality, in which something like the language of divine creation is reflected, qualified by the paradox that what is reflected is blocked' (*AT*, 78; *GS* 7, 121). Art, as Adorno conceives it, is alone sufficiently self-reflective to recognize that the divine language towards which it gestures is blocked, that to move towards redemption is to be forced to step back from it. The ways in which this doubled gesture is worked out in particular artworks – and especially poetic artworks[4] – will be discussed later. In order to understand the thorny logic of Adorno's aesthetic, however, we must turn to art's great companion and antagonist in the thought of transcendence: religion.

KEEPING RELIGION OUT OF SIGHT

What of religion? Can it no longer have a place in the thinking of redemption? The evident answer to this question, at least as far as Adorno is concerned, would seem to be indeed not. For evidence of this view, we can turn to his 1957 essay 'Reason and Revelation' ('*Vernunft und Offenbarung*'), in which he argues that revealed religion is no longer in a position to articulate the truth of the Absolute. Modern religious institutions are only the degraded social–psychological symptoms of the insistent anxieties of modernity itself. Religion today is driven not by 'the truth and authenticity of the revelation . . . but rather the need for guidance, the confirmation of what is already firmly established, and also the hope that by means of a resolute decision alone one could breathe back that meaning into the disenchanted world under whose absence we have been suffering so long, as though we were spectators staring at something meaningless' (*CM*, 137; *GS* 10.2, 610). The impulse towards positive religion is thus a mere epiphenomenon of the social despair endemic to capitalist modernity, 'a screen-image (*Deckbild*) for immanent, social hopelessness' (*CM*, 139; *GS* 10.2, 612).

Modern positive religion, then, has a coercive relationship to redemption; it seeks to disavow worldly experience by leaping unreflectively and despairingly into (sham) transcendence. The consequence of such denial of conditionality for the sake of the unconditioned is, to adapt the closing lines of *Minima Moralia*, religion's calamitous (because unacknowledged) deliverance to the world. Sociology shows up positive religion as despair, philosophy exposes its unreflected metaphysics; either way, religion appears to have little to say to the 'task of thought' confronting us after Auschwitz.

This being the case, what are we to make of the religious, and especially Judaic vocabulary that pervades Adorno's authorship (especially the late work)? In particular, of those twin motifs of messianic yearning and the 'prohibition of images' (*Bilderverbot*) in which he invests so much? One response would be simply to dismiss such motifs as precisely that: mere rhetorical figures which give symbolic shape to a thoroughly materialist (if negative) utopianism.[5] But such a gesture conceives of Adorno's writing in terms of a Kantian form–content opposition which he is concerned everywhere to resist. To be sure, Adorno's aesthetic is not to be reduced to coded religion; nor, however, can his religious language be explained away as a heuristic device.

The third of Adorno's 'Theses on Art and Religion Today', a short but significant English-language piece of 1945, begins to clarify the difficult meaning of religion in his authorship. The thesis is largely, and in line with the critique of positive
religion already outlined, an attack on the 'aspect of the "ornamental" assumed
by religion when treated in modern poetry', as evinced in 'the pseudomysticism of
Rainer Maria Rilke'; in such poetry, '[r]eligious symbolism deteriorates into an
unctuous expression of a substance which is actually of this world' (*NL2*, 293–4;
GS 11, 648). Adorno concludes the thesis, however, by pointing to the possibility
of a different relationship between art and religion:

> Against this sort of thing, art can keep faith to its true affinity with religion, the
> relationship with truth, only by an almost ascetic abstinence from any religious
> claim or any touching upon religious subject matter. Religious art today is noth-
> ing but blasphemy. (*NL2*, 294; *GS* 11, 649)

What is immediately striking about this passage is the simultaneity of its critique
of religious content and the *preservation* of religion's 'relationship with truth'. Art,
that is, neither usurps nor supersedes religion;[6] rather, it is the place into which the
truth of religion migrates once it can no longer be positively expressed. The content of religion must be sacrificed if it is not to be delivered up to the world. Far
from being untrue, religion is in a sense *too* true, insofar as its inner content cannot
be articulated without being traduced. Only in the conjunction of art and philosophy (both, of course, understood in radically transformed ways) can this truth
content be preserved, because they alone – and unlike modern positive religion –
refuse to lay unreflective claim to the unconditioned. 'A changed philosophy',
Adorno writes in *Negative Dialectic*, 'would have to cease persuading others and
itself that it has the infinite at its disposal [*sie verfüge übers Unendliche*]' (*ND*, 13;
GS 6, 25). In preserving the infinite from the grasp of the concept, the authentic
work of art (we will return to this problematic term) keeps faith with the truth of
religion more steadfastly than positive religion.

How is this refusal of religion for the sake of its truth to be understood? Any
response to this question must depart from Adorno's relationship to Judaism, and
more particularly to his Jewish philosophical and literary contemporaries.

In an interview given to *Der Spiegel* towards the end of his life, Max Horkheimer,
co-author of *Dialectic of Enlightenment* and Adorno's closest and most consistent
intellectual collaborator, attempts to recode the entire project of Critical Theory in
terms of a Judaic negative theology, claiming that a '*Sehnsucht nach dem ganz Anderen*'
('longing for the wholly other') lies at the heart of his and Adorno's writings.[7] Asked
early on by his interviewer, Helmut Gumnior, what it is that gives rise in human
beings to their consciousness of their abandonment by God, he replies:

To that I would say that we can't even say anything about God. This is not only, as you may have guessed, a claim going back to my Judaism, but a decisive principle of Critical Theory. (57)

Horkheimer continues to elaborate the idea of an unspeakable God as the hidden heart of Critical Theory's ethics and politics. For Adorno and himself, 'theology stands behind all authentic human deeds' (60).[8] It is important, however, to distinguish this Judaic theology from Christian positive religion; where the latter seeks reconciliation with the Absolute in time, the Jew knows and respects his untraversible *distance* from it. Thus, where the Christian martyr was prepared to sacrifice his being as a 'shorter pathway (*Durchgang*) to his eternal happiness', the Jewish martyr could enjoy no such guarantees; he 'sacrifices his life not for his own holiness, but for that of his people (*nicht für eigenes Heil, sondern für das Heil des Volkes*)' (62). From this perspective, Jewish faith is not an unreflected leap into the unconditioned, but a tenacious holding to the ethical demands of finite experience; the Jew's thought of the absolute always throws him back onto his irreducible finitude.

Certainly, Horkheimer's retrospective Judaicizing of Critical Theory seems to be borne out by a number of passages both in *Dialectic of Enlightenment* and Adorno's own corpus. In the former, they argue that 'Jewish religion allows no word that would alleviate the despair of all that is mortal. It associates hope only with the prohibition against calling on what is false as God, against invoking the finite as the infinite, lies as truth' (*DE*, 23; *GS* 4, 40). To hope is thus to refuse to disavow despair, to resist the allure of a sham infinite; finitude can be neither escaped nor overcome. They later go on to contrast this sobriety towards the absolute with Christianity's absolutization of the finite, which they term 'idolatry ... in a spiritualized form'; '[m]an's self-reflection in the absolute, the humanization of God by Christ' (*DE*, 77; *GS* 3, 201–2) lies at the heart of Christendom's governing logic. Insofar as it annihilates the distance between man and Other, Christian religion is of a piece with the domination of nature. Adorno, writing in his major philosophical work twenty years later, takes this defence of Jewish sobriety yet further: 'one who believes in God cannot believe in God ... the possibility represented by the divine name is maintained (*festgehalten*), rather, by him who does not believe' (*ND*, 401–2; *GS* 6, 394).

Taken together, these citations attest to the complex and ambiguous entailments of Adorno's engagement with Judaism, and above all to a radical fidelity to the interdiction on pronouncing the divine Name, a fidelity which preserves the truth content of religion more resolutely than positive religion. This, as we shall see, will be the governing theme of Adorno's aesthetic: transcendence approached by way of an unrelenting abstemiousness.

If it has been established that Adorno is concerned above all to preserve the truth content of religion, it remains to specify fully the nature of this content. Indeed, the difficulty is that any such explicitness on his part would fall foul of his refusal to give any positive expression to religion. Acknowledging this difficulty, it will be suggested that the religious truth which for Adorno can be preserved only by being 'kept out of sight'[9] is systematized in much more direct form in Franz Rosenzweig's great work of theological philosophy, *The Star of Redemption* (*Der Stern der Erlösung*). While a number of commentators have speculated on the impact of Rosenzweig on Adorno,[10] there is little indication of his impression of the book either in his published writings or his correspondence. Scattered allusions, however, leave us in no doubt that Adorno had read Rosenzweig. As we shall see, the Jewish thinkers to whom he appears readiest to acknowledge his proximity are those – most notably Bloch, Kafka and of course Benjamin – whose religious or theological content is worked out in secular form. From this perspective, his near silence on the subject of Rosenzweig can be read in terms of his unwillingness to affirm any positively expressed religious content. Indeed this, rather than any particular claim, may be the problem with Horkheimer's *Spiegel* interview – that it directly identifies a filiation whose significance lies precisely in its concealment. Adorno's project is not theology in another guise, but an ongoing struggle to think the absolute in the wake of theology's impossibility.

MESSIANIC POLITICS: ADORNO AND ROSENZWEIG

Turning now to Rosenzweig, the nature of this thinking comes to light in the form of three key and related affinities between *The Star of Redemption* and Adorno's thought, namely: the primacy of particulars, constellational form and, most importantly, a negative 'messianic politics'.

1   First, then, the primacy of particulars: from the outset of the *Star*, Rosenzweig is concerned to give philosophical voice to that which the Western tradition has variously evaded, denied and voided, namely the experience of finitude. Thus Rosenzweig's opening sentence: 'All cognition of the All originates in death, in the fear of death' (*Vom Tode, von der Furcht des Todes, hebt alles Erkennen des All an*) (*SR*, 3; *SE*, 3). As that which is irreducibly singular ('[o]nly the singular can die and everything mortal is solitary' (*SR*, 4; *SE*, 4)), death is what places philosophy's supreme ambition in peril. The All tolerates no mortality and hence no singularity ('idealism, with its denial (*Verleugnung*) of everything that distinguishes the singular from the All, is the tool of the philosopher's trade' (*SR*, 4; *SE*, 4)). A 'new thinking' must thus begin by liberating phenomena from 'the omnipotence of the logos' which characterizes 'philosophy as a whole from Parmenides to Hegel' (*SR*, 47; *SE*, 50). The phenomenon is to be thought anew, transformed from the 'dead given' of idealism to the ever-renewed gift,

'the miracle in the world of spirit' (*SR*, 47; *SE*, 50). This rescue of particulars will find its echo, of course, in Adorno's 'micrological' thinking.[11]

Where Rosenzweig's thinking of the phenomenon displays its most exact affinity to Adorno, however, is in its refusal to collapse into an unreflected immediacy. For, in becoming aware of itself *as* particular, it is awakened to its own essence, that is, 'conscious of its attracted movement [*gezogenen Bewegung*] toward the universal' (*SR*, 48; *SE*, 51). Both thinkers seek to rescue the particular from its idealist subsumption without thereby denying its ineluctable conceptuality. As we shall see, this complex simultaneity of universal and particular, in which the latter neither escapes nor is sublated by the former, finds its exemplary expression, for Adorno, in the work of art, as these lines from *Aesthetic Theory* indicate:

> That universal elements are irrevocably part of art at the same time that art opposes them, is to be understood in terms of art's likeness to language [*Sprachähnlichkeit*]. For language is hostile to the particular and nevertheless seeks its rescue. (*AT*, 204; *GS*7, 304)

2   Rosenzweig's challenge to the 'omnipotence of the logos' is continued in his critique of the *form* of the idealist system. The relationship between Rosenzweig's 'star' and Adorno's 'constellation' is more than a mere happy coincidence of terms.[12] Both terms signal a new, non-hierarchical relationship between the elements of a system. Rosenzweig describes this reconstituted relationship as a 'new unity', opposed to 'the kind of unity which philosophy had previously sought and consequently presupposed ... the unity of the sphere which everywhere returns unto itself' (*SR*, 254; *SE*, 283). In the new unity, the elements God – World – Man form a triangle which is intersected by a second, inverted triangle of the elements Creation – Revelation – Redemption, to form a star.[13] This star is 'no "figure" at all but – a configuration [*Gestalt*]' (*SR*, 256; *SE*, 285), that is, a geometrical form which doesn't subsume its separate elements under an overarching unity. This new unity corresponds very precisely to the 'configurational form' – a kind of 'totality' of the 'non-total' (*NL*1, 17; *GS*11, 26) – which Adorno seeks both to theorize and to realize in his philosophy and especially in his aesthetic writings. Indeed, his description of the essay, his most explicit statement on the question of form, offers an acute description both of his own work and of the relationship to one another of the *Star*'s nine central chapters: '[a]ll its concepts are to be presented in such a way that they support one another, that each becomes articulated through its configuration [*Konfigurationen*] with others' (*NL*1, 13; *GS*11, 21).

3   The final and most striking affinity to be drawn between the two thinkers is both religious and ethico-political. The third part of the *Star* describes the

different functions of Judaism ('the eternal life') and Christianity ('the eternal way') in the task of redemption. Rosenzweig's account of the world-historical role of the Jews does much to illuminate Adorno's negative messianism. This role is premised above all on the temporality specific to the Jewish people. Far from seeking a Hegelian reconciliation of time and eternity, Judaism for Rosenzweig consists precisely in holding open the gap between them. In contrast to the infinite time of God, in which ' "I am" is like "I shall be" ', the life of 'man and world' is not eternal; to *know* this difference is to inhabit 'the appropriate time' (*SR*, 272; *SE*, 303) as opposed to the improper time either of the 'sinner' (*SR*, 274; *SE*, 305), whose blindness to any temporality not his own renders his prayer always unfulfilled, or the 'fanatic', whose prayer strives violently to coerce eternity, to appropriate knowledge that is God's alone (*SR*, 274–5; *SE*, 306).

The ethico-political stakes of this distinction between appropriate and improper time are brought out in the closing paragraphs of the *Star*'s chapter on Judaism, in which Rosenzweig contrasts the reality of Jewish eternity with the 'sham' eternity of the State. The eternity of State law is sham because coercive; it subjects the changing forms of 'boisterous life' to an enduring order. Law fails, however, to stay change, because it exists in opposition to life: 'life ... overflows the tablet of hard and fast rules. The law is conserved (*er-hält*) only as long as it is observed by the people' (*SR*, 333; *SE*, 369). In order to stem this overflowing, law must be constantly renewed, and the name of this process of renewal is coercion (*Gewalt*):[14] 'coercion is: the renewal of old law (*Rechts*). In the coercive act, the law must constantly become new law' (*SR*, 333; *SE*, 370). Both Judaism and the State assert the living moment, but the State does so, 'not in the manner of the eternal people, not by eternalizing the moment into custom (*Sitte*) once and for all and into unalterable law (*Gesetz*), but rather by newly and masterfully grasping the moment, and every subsequent moment and shaping it according to its desires and capacities' (*SR*, 333; *SE*, 370). Where the Judaic inalterability of *Gesetz* respects the gap between time and eternity (hence the description of the Jew as 'the only genuine pacifist'), State *Recht* violently assimilates eternity to its own finite, contingent interests: 'Thus', writes Rosenzweig, 'the state turns every moment into eternity' (*SR*, 334; *SE*, 371).

The (almost certainly unconscious) evocation of this distinction between the 'pacifistic' and 'coercive' relationship to eternity in the 'Zum Ende' of *Minima Moralia* is unmistakable. It is in the refusal to coerce redemption into the present by denying the conditionality of thought an experience that Adorno's contemplation of all things 'from the standpoint of redemption' most strikingly echoes Rosenzweig's messianic politics. The state's coercive absorption of eternity into the moment fails to respect the 'impossibility' of 'a standpoint removed ... from the scope of existence', and this failure marks its 'calamitous' deliverance up to the world. Because its every action violates the necessary distance between 'what is' and redemption, the state can never redeem. In short, both Rosenzweig's messianic politics and Adorno's standpoint of redemption begin from the imperative to respect the irreconcilable distance between the present and the redeemed world. For Adorno, however, this distance measures not the distance between this and the next world (this would be his decisive difference from Rosenzweig), but between the hope and actualization of redemption in the present; the possibility of redemption is bound ineluctably to the impossibility of its actualization.

NEGATIVE MESSIANISM: ADORNO, BLOCH, BENJAMIN

Cast in Rosenzweig's light, then, Adorno's politics and aesthetics are revealed as 'Jewish' above all in their passion for the impossible, the fidelity to the ideal of redemption in the form of its refusal. His extreme asceticism toward any type of revealed faith precludes the embrace of Rosenzweig's notably unascetic language of religious experience. However, if Adorno, the half-Jewish professed atheist,[15] balks at positive religious expression, Judaic or otherwise, it is equally the case that those three Rosenzweigian themes just expounded come to the surface of his thought in his essays on those two Jewish contemporaries – Ernst Bloch and Walter Benjamin – whose secularized and coded religious content he is much readier to identify with his own project. The primacy of particulars, configurational or 'constellational' form and above all a negative messianic politics are once again the key points of contact between his own, Bloch's and Benjamin's thought. Adorno's avowed proximity to his Jewish contemporaries increases the more implicitly or negatively the messiaic content of their thought is expressed – hence, perhaps, his near-silence on Rosenzweig, his qualified tributes to Bloch and the very privileged (though to be sure not uncritically so) place given to Benjamin in his thought. Simon Jarvis makes this point differently when he places Adorno in the context of the utopian negativity common to Lukács, Bloch and Benjamin, while characterizing his intervention in this context as an intensification of negativity beyond any of them. Theological motifs are more negative in Adorno's than in Benjamin's writing and 'should never become an appeal to an immanent or positive transcendence'.[16] The Adornian project, then, can be described as driving the truth of religion to the point of most emphatic negativity, pointing up the very impossibility of theology as its truth.

In a late (1965) essay, Bloch's rebellion against the traditional renunciation of thinking the Absolute is identified as the motif which the young Adorno, 'took . . . so much as my own that I do not believe I have ever written anything without reference to it, either implicit or explicit' (*NL2*, 212; *GS*11, 557). In an earlier (1960) essay on Bloch's *Spuren*, this rebellion is read in terms of a lack of respect for the Kantian boundary 'between finite and infinite, phenomenal and noumenal . . .' (*NL*1, 206; *GS*11, 239–40). This will to break through the blockade between 'consciousness and the thing-in-itself', however, is not to lead to the reconciliation of these diremted spheres as in Hegel's speculative idealism. Against the latter, Bloch 'continues to insist . . . on the unreconciled distinction between immanence and transcendence' (*NL* 1, 207; *GS* 11, 241). [17]

In the later essay, Adorno takes up a text from *The Spirit of Utopia* ('An Old Pitcher'), as a means of drawing out the consequence of this breakthrough of a boundary whose two sides remain nevertheless unreconciled, namely an immersion in particulars. Bloch wants to give voice to the mute 'thing-language' of the pitcher, to reveal what that language is 'saying and concealing at the same time'; if we knew this, we would be possessed of a secret which 'would be the opposite of something that has always been and will always be, the opposite of invariance: something that would finally be different (*anders*)' (*NL*2, 219; *GS*11, 566). And yet, Adorno implies, it is only the secret's refractoriness to possession that keeps this ultimate difference intact; exposed to the light of the concept, forced to break its muteness, Bloch's 'thing-language' would fall back into invariance. Concealment belongs to the very structure of the difference promised by Blochian utopianism: 'an exaggerated passion for the possibility lying defeated, an impossibility, in the midst of reality' (*NL*2, 218; *GS*11, 564). [18] Adorno makes this passion for the impossible reverberate throughout his aesthetics: the striving for a 'divine language of creation', blocked to consciousness. His thought is profoundly continuous with Bloch's in its shared striving for a thinking of the absolute which begins from its radical ungraspability to finite experience. It breaks with Bloch in its scepticism towards the conceptual positivity the latter tends to impose upon utopia: 'Bloch's philosophy has to distill utopia that subsumes the concreteness that utopia actually is' (*NL*1, 213; *GS* 11, 247).

This, in fact, is Bloch's difference from Benjamin: '[i]n contrast to Benjamin . . . Bloch does not give himself over to the miniature but instead uses it expressly as a category . . . Bloch declines the fragmentary' (*NL*1, 213; *GS*11, 247). This critique of the assimilation of the utopian to the generalized concept is continuous with a broader critique of positive religion: in question is the claim to apprehend conceptually that which exceeds the grasp of the concept, a claim which must violate the essential negativity of messianic thought. [19]

In contrast, Benjamin's critical gaze continually resists the universalizing concept; its fidelity to the imperative to preserve the particular is perhaps the single strongest affinity between his and Adorno's messianism. As Adorno writes in a late essay on Benjamin, 'he was impelled to break the bounds of a logic which covers over the particular with the universal or merely abstracts the universal from the particular' (*P*, 230; *GS*10.1, 239). This impulse is intimately bound up, as in Rosenzweig, with the development of a configurational form. [20] Adorno repeatedly invokes Benjamin as exemplary in this regard; the latter 'was the unsurpassed master' of the difficult negotiation of contradictory demands: to 'salvage the precision sacrificed when definition is omitted', while avoiding 'betraying the subject matter to the arbitrariness of conceptual meanings decreed once and for all'. This negotiation leads to the 'crystallization' of the elements of the essay 'as a configuration' (*NL*1, 12–13; *GS* 11, 21).

Adorno is quick to recognize the redemptive colour of this impulse to preserve the particular. Benjamin's resistance to classification means that 'the prime image (*Urbild*) of hope for him is the name' (*P*, 231; *GS* 10.1, 240).[21] The name is a repository of hope because it carries the promise of an absolute immediacy, a particular understood without recourse to conceptual abstraction. Benjamin's most sustained meditation on the name, of course, is his early essay 'On Language as Such and On Human Language' ('*Über Sprache überhaupt und über die Sprache des Menschen*'),[22] where the utopian promise of the name is cast as the explicitly religious one of a divine language. To the 'bourgeois conception of language' as the communication of things through words, Benjamin counterposes '[t]he other conception of language' which 'knows no means, no object, and no addressee of communication. It means: *in naming the mental being of man communicates itself to God*'.[22] The 'pure language' of name, or 'the language of language' is of necessity beyond the reach of human language; its communication of man's mental being to God is only an unredeemed promise, an 'image of hope' which forms the horizon of both Benjamin's and Adorno's thought. It is what the latter calls, in reference to the former, 'the paradox of the impossible possibility' (*der Möglichkeit des Unmöglichen*) (*P*, 241; *GS* 10.1, 252), and delineates, as we have seen, in the 'Zum Ende' of *Minima Moralia*.

We will come to see how this paradox – the maintenance of redemption's possibility through its refusal – works itself out in Adorno's aesthetic. For now it is worth noting the extent to which the triad of the particular, configurational form and negative messianicity – find their expression in Adorno via Benjamin. Benjamin, in other words, provides for Adorno the means of articulating negatively the religious truth whose positive expression now lies under a prohibition. In Benjaminian commentary, '[u]topia is honoured through abstinence from all positive meaning. Utopia flees in bitter shame at not yet having succeeded; the expression of utopia is the taboo on its expression' (*NL*2, 331; *GS* 11, 689). Through Benjamin, Adorno's anti-theology is revealed as the despairing *preservation* of theology, since it is only by migrating into the secular, by being 'kept out of sight' that theology can salvage itself from the betrayal of its own promise; hence the importance for Adorno of Benjamin's early 'Theologico-Political Fragment', whose pronouncement that 'the order of the profane assists, through being profane, the coming of the Messianic Kingdom'[23] is echoed in Adorno's 'Introduction to Benjamin's *Schriften*': in the latter's late philosophy is expressed 'the motif of rescuing theology by sacrificing it, by secularizing it mercilessly' (*NL*2, 230; *GS* 11, 579).

Adorno's writings on Bloch and Benjamin, then, should show how the negative messianic politics expressed in Rosenzweig's explicitly religious philosophical vocabulary is to be maintained through an increasing divestment of positive theology. His paradoxically religious task is to take this divestment beyond even Benjamin, such that not even the latter's fragmentary immediacy of the absolute remains possible. Only through the vigilantly sustained negative – exemplified above all in the aesthetic – can the thought of the absolute be kept in reserve. This is why the only explicitly religious imperative invoked throughout Adorno's authorship is the 'ban on images' or prohibition of idolatry; this prohibition, more than any other, speaks the truth of religion as a taboo on its positive expression. It should not be forgotten, moreover, that the prohibition on images is a condition profoundly accentuated by the fact of Auschwitz: 'After Auschwitz there is no word tinged from on high, not even a theological one, that has any right unless it underwent a transformation' (*ND*, 367; *GS* 6, 360). The 'new categorical imperative' is thus inextricable from the prohibition on images. To 'arrange thoughts and actions so that Auschwitz would not repeat itself' would be to refuse the 'calamitous' deliverance of thought to a sham infinite that would violate this prohibition.

THE MORALITY OF CONTRADICTION

We have been concerned thus far with the negative messianic content of Adorno's thought. But how is this tendency to be understood in the context of the social and political dimension of his work? For no account of Adorno's thinking of transcendence can afford to forget that this thinking is always part of a sociological critique of the deformation of collective and individual consciousness in capitalist modernity.

In the preface to their seminal joint work, Adorno and Horkheimer insist that their critique of Enlightenment is no utopian renunciation; on the contrary, 'we are wholly convinced . . . that social freedom is inseparable from enlightened thought' (*DE*, xiii; *GS* 3, 13). However, 'the point is that the Enlightenment must examine itself [*selbst besinnen*], if men are not to be wholly betrayed' *(DE*, xv; *GS* 3, 15). The difficulty is that Enlightenment has come to be characterized precisely by the erosion of the capacity for self-examination. As their well-known thesis contends, Enlightenment is unable to acknowledge its own origins in the very mythic fear it claims to have overcome, and against which it defines itself, for fear of destabilizing its own self-identity. The often murderous excesses of Enlightened modernity – domination of nature, anti-Semitism and racism, mass cultural 'deception' and the 'fungibility' of human beings – are all symptoms of this failure of self-reflection. Modern society seeks everywhere to impose identity upon those concepts and objects – for example the concept of freedom and the experience of unfreedom – whose non-identity it cannot risk examining. Modernity's governing concepts are in this sense without referents, gesturing to ideas – freedom, subjectivity, beauty – not yet realized: '[t]he substance of the contradiction between universal and particular is that individuality is not yet and that, therefore, it is bad [*schlecht*] wherever established' (*ND*, 151; *GS* 6, 154).

Countering the modern logic of identity, however, cannot mean overcoming it, but rather acknowledging the contradictions in which the modern subject is ineluctably entangled. Philosophy, as defined in the final pages of *Dialectic of Enlightenment*, is 'the voice of contradiction, which would otherwise not be heard but triumph mutely' (*DE*, 244; *GS* 3, 281). Far from fulfilling its vocation of fidelity to the law of non-contradiction, which would leave real – social – contradiction unacknowledged and unexamined, philosophy's eminently political task is to refuse this vocation. The more contradiction remains unvoiced, the more violently it will come to impose itself. The self-examination of enlightened consciousness consists above all in inhabiting those contradictions which power would like to disavow. If philosophy is to protest the logic of identity, it must begin by acknowledging its own implication in what it protests against, for there is no position available to the philosopher which is not 'marked . . . by the same distortion and indigence which it seeks to escape' (*MM*, 247; *GS* 4, 283).

It is above all this insistence on the ineluctability of contradiction that distinguishes what Adorno calls his 'revised [*veränderten*] conception of the dialectic' (*H*, xxxvi; *GS* 5, 250). To be sure, his thought wants to open a space for the non-identical, the otherness or difference that escapes the reach of the concept, but as Jarvis points out, this implies not 'a new and non-identificatory kind of thinking, but a demonstration of the insufficiency of identification' (Jarvis, 167). A 'non-identificatory kind of thinking' is oxymoronic insofar as 'to think is to identify' (*denken heist identizieren*); non-identity can never appear as such, but only in the form of contradiction, defined by Adorno as 'non-identity under the aspect of identity' (*ND*, 5; *GS* 6, 17). Only under the aspect of identity can the non-identical maintain itself; posited as a given entity, its constitutive negativity is violated. This is the substance of Adorno's ongoing critique of Heideggerean ontology, wherein 'the inexpressible becomes explicit and compact in the word "Being"' (*ND*, 110; *GS* 6, 116).

What might it mean 'to think in contradictions' (*ND*, 145; *GS* 6, 148)? It would entail first of all thinking through the difficult moral terrain which divides modern consciousness. In a section of the concluding 'Notes and Drafts' (*Aufzeichungen und Entwürfe*) entitled 'Contradictions', Adorno and Horkheimer attempt to elaborate this difficulty by way of 'a discussion between two young people' sparked by the principled refusal of one ('B') to become a doctor. B reasons that doctors objectify 'suffering individuals' as consumers, to whom they behave as 'agents of the establishment'. Asked by A if he believes 'the old quacks should return' he counters that his argument is not meant to be universally prescriptive. The existence of hospitals is better than sick people being left to die, just as the existence of judges and prisons is preferable to unchecked robbery and murder: 'Justice is reasonable. I am not opposed to reason – I simply wish to define the form [*Gestalt*] it has taken'. A objects to the immorality of his argument: B would benefit from those very forces he 'would like to escape', to which B responds, 'I do not deny that, but the contradiction is necessary. It is the answer to the objective component [*den objectiven*] of society' (*DE*, 238; *GS* 3, 273).

The refusal of a fixed moral standpoint induces what Adorno terms a 'vertigo' (*Schwindel*): 'an *index veri*, the shock of inconclusiveness, the negative as which it cannot help appearing in the frame-covered [*Gedeckten*] and never-changing realm . . .' (*ND*, 33; *GS* 6, 43). There is no immediate apprehension of truth in the damaged life of modern society, but only a negative apprehension in the form of a lack of moral security, the necessary refusal of the 'bureaucratic way of thinking' (*Verwaltungsdenken*) which would reduce morality to 'Yes or No answers', in the face of which 'the responsibility of philosophical thought . . . is not to play the game' (*ND*, 32; *GS* 6, 42).

This responsibility returns us to the 'new categorical imperative' with which we began. For if its force, as has been argued, issues from the impossibility of fulfilling the task ('to arrange . . . thoughts and actions so that Auschwitz will not repeat itself') it announces, then thought and action must be heavily invested in 'not playing the game', that is, in resisting the complacency of a fixed and final moral vantage-point. From this perspective, *Minima Moralia*'s 'standpoint of redemption' is a *vertiginous* standpoint: the estranging 'messianic' light such a standpoint casts over the world positions us in a groundless place between 'Yes and No'.

It is in this sense that we should understand Adorno's scattered writings on the ethical dilemmas of post-Nazi Germany. His 1966 radio talk, 'Education After Auschwitz', is one of a series of public contributions to the post-war debate on de-Nazification. Published the same year as *Negative Dialectic*, the essay opens with a stark adaptation of the former's 'new categorical imperative': 'The premier demand on all education is that Auschwitz not happen again' (*CM*, 191; *GS* 10.2, 674). Adorno goes on to suggest that a response to this demand must begin with an inquiry into the conditions of possibility for Auschwitz. How was the participation and collusion of so many individuals and institutions in systematically administrated genocide made possible? The answer is continuous with the thesis of *Dialectic of Enlightenment*: it is 'lack of reflection' which produces the conditions for blind and impassive submission to a collective will; hence 'the most important way to confront the danger of a recurrence is to work against the brute predominance of all collectives . . .' (*CM*, 197; *GS* 10.2, 681).

Dialectic of Enlightenment had offered a more philosophically dense analysis of the relationship between the lack of self-examination and Nazi anti-Semitism in which the Jew figures as a disturbance of the logic of identity (or in the social–psychological language of the later essay, 'the brute predominance of all collectives') on which all racial hatred is premised. Hatred of the Jew is 'the morbid expression of repressed mimesis' (*DE*, 187; *GS* 3, 211–2). The association of Jews with the mimetic,[24] with 'non-manipulated expression' (Adorno and Horkheimer give the example of the grimace) which refuses assimilation to the imperative of 'usefulness', confronts the Enlightenment gaze with an image of its own origins in an irrationality it must forget. This forgetting takes the form of a kind of cannibalization of the mimetic, in which expression is absorbed and regulated by the mechanisms of domination. Rather than simply deny suffering, Nazism forces its expression into the service of domination, and so becomes parasitic on the very otherness it seeks to annihilate.

Against society's unconsciously willed forgetting of the violence by which its rationality has been forged, Adorno seeks to develop a mode of thought and action which always begins from recognition of its implication in that violence. If an adequate response to the moral demands imposed by Auschwitz is to be possible, it must first of all resist collusion with the Yes and No thinking – the denial of the 'vertigo' of modern moral experience – which marks all coercive thought and action.

Nowhere does this vertigo impose itself more forcefully than in the dilemmas arising from German war guilt, as Section 33 of *Minima Moralia* ('Out of the Firing Line' [*Weit vom Schuß*]) suggests. In the context of a discussion of the 'withering of experience' in and by the Second World War, Adorno raises the question of how Germany is to confront its recent past. The ethical aporia is outlined starkly: if Nazism is avenged by violence, 'catastrophe is perpetuated' (*MM*, 55; *GS* 4, 62) in the form of an endless, insitutionalized blood-feud in 'the pre-capitalist pattern of vendettas'. If, however, 'the dead are not avenged, Fascism gets away with its crimes scot-free, and 'having once been shown so easy, will be continued elsewhere'. Adorno continues,

> To the question what is to be done with defeated Germany, I could say only two things in reply. Firstly: at no price, on no conditions, would I wish to be an executioner or to supply legitimations for executioners. Secondly: I should not wish, least of all with legal machinery, to stay the hand of anyone who was avenging past misdeeds. This is a thoroughly unsatisfactory, contradictory answer, one that makes a mockery of both principle and practice. But perhaps the fault lies in the question and not only in me. (*MM*, 56; *GS* 4, 62)

What is 'faulty' about this question? The answer would seem to be that the responses for which it allows – vengeance or mercy, punishment or forgiveness – are legislated in advance by just the kinds of secure ethical categories that Nazism has put in question. The question of 'what is to be done' cannot allow for the complex moral and psychic equivocality which is the condition of thinking after

Auschwitz. Adorno's relentless self-examination, recognizing its own uneasy positioning between renunciation of and implication in violence, figures the ethical task
which follows from his new categorical imperative. Indeed, he brings together
the imperative and the question of German war guilt more explicitly in *Negative
Dialectic*, where the aporetic choice between acquittal and justice, 'the latest stage
of moral dialectics', is invoked only to show that 'contradiction alone is the stage of
morality today' (*ND*, 286; *GS* 6, 282). How are we to make sense of this alignment
of contradiction and morality?

HEGEL CONTRA KANT CONTRA HEGEL

The meaning of the insuperable aporia of morality after Auschwitz can be better
understood by placing it in the context of the debate which has never ceased to
haunt modern philosophy, namely the ongoing controversy between Kant and
Hegel, as well as their respective philosophical progeny. Adorno's complex negotiation of the two philosophers' competing claims structures his entire project. It is
to this negotiation that we now turn, with an eye to its special significance for the
development of a post-Auschwitz aesthetic.

Adorno's negative messianism has been described as a refusal of redemption
in the name of redemption. This doubled movement toward and away from the
Absolute precisely characterizes his treatment of Kant, Hegel and their opposing
relationships to the Absolute. Adorno's critique of this opposition should not be
understood as an attempt to locate truth at a median point between the two. Rather,
he employs the truths and untruths of each to critique the other and so, ultimately,
to disclose the metaphysical aporia they secretly share.

What Kant and Hegel most evidently share is that methodological stance of
German Idealism which became so central to the sociology of the Frankfurt
School, namely a self-critical conception of reason. For both philosophers, reason
is in a state of perpetual self-correction in the face of the illusions and misrecognitions with which it is perpetually confronted by consciousness. But this process of
self-correction in Kant moves in the opposite direction from that of Hegel – that
is, away rather than towards the Absolute.

For both Kant and Hegel, the proper object of Reason, as opposed to the
Understanding, is knowledge of the unconditioned. Kant's *Critique of Pure Reason*,
however, is directed towards demonstrating the insuperable limits which confront
Reason in its attempts to obtain such knowledge. Reason learns, through the process
of self-examination, its ineluctable distance from the unconditioned. The object of
his critique is that of an 'imaginary science' which 'supposes some knowledge
of objects of which no human being has any concept . . . Nothing but the sobriety
of a critique, at once strict and just, can free us from this dogmatic delusion . . .'

(*CPR*, 361; *KR V*, A395).[25] A *sober* critique resists the intoxication of a 'knowledge' which lays illusory claim to the absolute; or to cite Kant's metaphor, it keeps reason on the coast of finitude, 'a coast we cannot leave without venturing upon a shoreless ocean which, after alluring us with ever-deceptive prospects, compels us in the end to abandon as hopeless all this vexatious and tedious endeavour' (*CPR*, 361; *KR V*, A396).

Where self-critical reason for Kant thus guards against the blind leap into the unconditioned, for Hegel it is the necessary means towards attaining knowledge of the Absolute. Indeed the *Phenomenology* as 'the Science of the *experience of consciousness*' (*PS*, 56; *PG*, 81) describes the movement of consciousness through the stages of distortion, misrecognition and illusion which hinder its insight into its own universality. A self-critical phenomenology thus unmasks Kant's limits on knowing the Absolute as a symptom of a consciousness that does not yet know itself. Spirit overcomes the negative (the Kantian 'beyond' of knowledge) not by leapfrogging over it, but by 'looking the negative in the face and tarrying with it [*bei ihm verweilt*]' (*PS*, 19; *PG*, 36).

Both Kant and Hegel, then, infuse reason with a self-critical spirit which Adorno is concerned above all to keep in play. His critique of both philosophers is directed rather against those moments in each thinker in which that spirit exhausts itself, either in the form of a block on thinking the Absolute (Kant) or of the final attainment of it (Hegel). The task of thinking after Auschwitz might be described as a perpetual vigilance against this exhaustion of self-critical reason. Adorno is alluding to this vigilance when he writes in his second Hegel study that 'the debate between Kant and Hegel is not over [*nicht zu Ende*]' (*H*, 86; *GS* 5, 323). For the debate to be over would mean that reason could come to a final resting place, either in finite (Kantian) knowledge or Absolute (Hegelian) Knowledge.

Adorno's intervention in the Kant–Hegel debate turns foremost on the status in each thinker of speculative knowledge of the Absolute. Kant describes such knowledge as that which 'concerns an object, or those concepts of an object, which cannot be reached in any experience' (*CPR*, 527; *KR V*, A634; B662). The first *Critique* rules such knowledge out of court in the realm of theoretical reason.[26] Any assertion of knowledge beyond the reach of experience, however, is not false in the sense that an empirical judgement can be false. To use an example provided by the famous 'Antimonies' chapter, the world's magnitude cannot be known as either finite or infinite; the opposition between these possibilities constitutes not a simple but a *dialectical*, that is, irresolvable, contradiction (*CPR*, 427; *KR V*, A471; B499). Dialectical contradictions are aporetic for Kant insofar as reason cannot achieve their resolution.

For Hegel, in contrast, speculative knowledge reveals this boundary set between finite and infinite knowledge as the misrecognition of an 'unhappy consciousness' (*unglückliche Bewußtsein*) that doesn't yet know itself to be the universal (*PS*, 131;

PG, 168). The Kantian universal, or 'thing-in-itself', precisely because it is determined in advance as the 'void' (*Leeren*) or 'the beyond [*Jenseits*] of consciousness', is condemned to emptiness (*PS*, 88; *PG*, 118). In speculative knowing, the recognition of the limits to consciousness is simultaneously the *overcoming* of those limits. Far from engendering illusion, the speculative proposition lifts it by bringing to light consciousness's identity with the universal.

Part of the complexity of Adorno's working through of these opposed positions lies in the fact that he seems to side with each of them at different points in his corpus. This apparent inconsistency, however, is only the necessary symptom of a deeper consistency which maintains Kant and Hegel in a process of perpetual mutual correction. One way of describing this process would be to say that Adorno accepts Hegel's claim that in grasping the limits to consciousness we have already surpassed them; but that this surpassing itself *reinstates* those limits. This is the doubled movement that occurs in the 'Zum Ende' of *Minima Moralia*, where the (Hegelian) necessity of knowledge from the standpoint of redemption is immediately countered by the (Kantian) impossibility of such knowledge.

Adorno's criticisms of Kant are thus always Hegelian, just as those of Hegel are always Kantian. The process of their mutual critique is figured in the stucture of the third and final part of *Negative Dialectic*, in which the critique of Kant is followed by that of Hegel. The culminating 'Meditations on Metaphysics', in which he attempts to set forth the status and task of philosophy after Auschwitz issues from the conscious non-resolution of this mutual critique.

Three main criticisms of Kant can be identified in *Negative Dialectic*:

1   The first is straightforwardly Hegelian–Marxist, namely that Kant posits freedom as an eternal and invariant Idea and so fails to consider how our concepts
    and experiences of freedom are historically conditioned. Such an insight would
    have shown that history has prevented the realization of the idea of freedom:
    'there is horror because there is no freedom yet' (*ND*, 218; *GS* 6, 217).

2   Kant 'hypostatiz[es] scientific-methodical criteria' such that whatever in
    thought fails to conform to these criteria is expunged: 'theorems which
    cannot be safeguarded from the possibility of their contradictory antithesis
    should be discarded [*abzulegen*] from rational thinking'. In contrast, Hegel
    recognizes that contradiction cannot be eradicated by methodolgical procedure – 'the contradiction may lie in the thing itself' (*ND*, 239; *GS* 6, 238).

3   Perhaps the most equivocal of Adorno's criticisms concerns less Kant himself
    than the fate of his concept of truth. For, if Kantian epistemology rightly sets
    limits to consciousness, nevertheless, '[t]he authority of the Kantian conception of truth turned terroristic with the ban on thinking the Absolute. Irresistibly, it drifts towards a prohibition on all thinking (*Denkverbot*)' (*ND*, 388;
    GS 6, 381). Kant, that is, gives rise to a thinking hostage to what Adorno

calls, in his *Hegel* study, 'the privations of the finite'. The limits of finitude become privative if they block thinking the very possibility of the Absolute. And yet Adorno displays a marked ambivalence towards Kant's scepticism as regards speculative philosophy. If the ban on thinking the Absolute threatens to become terroristic, it is equally true that Kant's doctrine of the 'intelligible character' – that part of consciousness which is the seat of the transcendent moral Law – 'has a touch of the truth of the image ban [*Bilderverbots*] which post-Kantian philosophers – including Marx – extended to all concepts of positivity' (*ND*, 298; *GS* 6, 293). This prohibition on images – the preservation of the Absolute through the block on its expression – is to be the guiding motif of the Adornian aesthetic. Kant's confinement of Reason to finite experience is true insofar as it demonstrates the impossibility of any positive expression of truth, and untrue insofar as it threatens to close truth off to thought altogether. From this perspective, Adorno's imperative is to respond to the dual, contradictory demands that the Absolute imposes on thought after Auschwitz: at once to think the Absolute and to respect the 'image ban' on it. Or, better, to achieve the former through the agency of the latter.

It is these same twin demands that inform Adorno's complex relationship to Hegel. This is why, in spite of the chasm that divides them, the dangers of Kantian and Hegelian thinking converge in his critique. Hegel's speculative achievement of the infinite becomes the mirror image of Kant's prohibition on it, insofar as both moves impose a block upon thinking of the non-identical. Thus, just as the spectre of a 'terroristic' ban on thinking of the Absolute informs his critique of Kant, the threat of an inverse terrorism is at the heart of his complex and ambivalent relationship to Hegel. And, as with Kant, the truth of Hegel's thought is at the same time its untruth.

In the first of his Hegel studies, Adorno points to the undoing of Kant's rigid and abstract methodological oppositions – 'form and content, nature and spirit, theory and praxis, freedom and necessity, the thing-in-itself and the phenomena' by way of the demonstration of their dialectical permeation: 'In order to be thought, and to exist, each inherently requires the other that Kant opposed to it' (*H*, 8; *GS* 5, 257). This mutual permeation is what Hegel famously terms the 'mediation of immediacy', and its significance for Adorno's thought cannot be overestimated. As we have seen, his critical gaze is directed perpetually against the false immediacies – religious, political, aesthetic – towards which a thinking frustrated by its own limits will leap unreflectively.

Nevertheless, the truth of the Hegelian dialectic – the ongoing tension of opposed terms – is also its falsehood. For in recognizing itself as its other, the difference that inheres in each term is negated or 'sublated'. It is at precisely this point where the permeation of differences becomes their dissolution that Adorno wants to distance himself from Hegel. Kant's sedimented subject–object opposition threatens to pass into its equally abstract contrary whereby 'subject–object is subject'. The subject that comes to know its universality absorbs into itself all that was other to it, and in the process misses the 'ultimate truth' of the dialectic: 'that of its impossibility ... its unresolved and vulnerable quality, even if as the theodicy of self-consciousness, it has no awareness of this' (*H*, 13; *GS* 5, 261). The theodicy of self-consciousness is the enforced reconciliation of the irreconcilable, and it is to this theodicy that Adorno counterposes a negative messianism that vigilantly maintains the impossibility of reconciliation, or rather, the impossible as reconciliation's very possibility.

Negative Dialectic, Adorno's most systematic philosophical text, can be described as an extended attempt to expunge this theodicical content from the dialectic. Precisely because of its indebtedness to Hegel, the negative dialectic is invested in demonstrating its decisive difference from the former's speculative dialectic. In the pivotal section of the book, Adorno expresses this difference in terms of the status of the negative in Hegel's and his own thought. In the former, famously, the dialectical 'negation of negation' produces a positive *Resultat*; self-consciousness recognizes its actual identity with what appears other to it, and in so doing renders otherness a moment of itself. Whereas for Adorno, '[t]o negate a negation does not bring about its reversal (*macht diese nicht rückgängig*): it proves, rather, that the negation was not negative enough' (*ND*, 159–60; *GS* 6, 162). Negation is thus not the positing of the identity of subject and object (or identity and non-identity), but the maintenance of the object's irreconcilable difference from the subject (the *non*-identity of identity and non-identity). 'This', continues Adorno,

> is the decisive break with Hegel. To use identity as a palliative for dialectical contradiction, for the expression of the insolubly nonidentical, is to ignore what the contradiction means ... the thesis that the negation of a negation is something positive can only be upheld by one who presupposes positivity as all-conceptuality (*Allbegrifflichkeit*) from the beginning. (*ND*, 160; *GS* 6, 162)

Dialectical sublation, in enforcing the reconcilation of identity and non-identity, betrays the very idea of reconciliation: 'Irreconcilably the idea of reconcilement bans its affirmation in a concept' (*ND*, 160; *GS* 6, 162). Hegel's dialectic falls on its inability to tolerate anything that exceeds the reach of the concept, any otherness that refuses assimilation to subjective totality. This is the Kantian objection to Hegel which must always attend the Hegelian objection to Kant: the dialectic is not to be an instrument for conceptualizing the Absolute, but for illuminating the Absolute's irreducibility to the concept. Adorno is clear about the religious entailments of this 'revised conception of the dialectic': '[t]he idealist doctrine of the Absolute would absorb theological transcendence ... would bring it to an immanence that tolerates no absoluteness, no independence of ontical conditions' (*ND*, 201; *GS* 6, 201). The Judaic impulse at the heart of Adorno's thinking resurfaces here: theological transcendence is destroyed by its conceptual articulation, hence its survival depends on its 'being kept out of sight'.

These opposed relationships to the Absolute, then, end in the same stasis of thinking: Kant's insistence on the inaccessibility of the intelligible realm to theoretical reason, framed as an invariant condition of all thought, threatens to impose an eternal block upon thinking the non-identical which would disturb the Understanding's self-certainty. Hegel's thought, on the other hand, rigidifies because it comes to rest in an Absolute Knowledge which recognizes nothing outside it. The meaning of the negative dialectic lies in the unstinting refusal of this coming to rest. Thinking after Auschwitz is bound to keep in sight *both* the Absolute blocked by Kant and the block violated by Hegel. To reframe this in terms introduced at the outset of this chapter, thinking involves the (Kantian) renunciation of reconciliation in the (Hegelian) name of reconciliation.

AUSCHWITZ AND REPRESENTATION: ADORNO, LYOTARD AND ROSE

Adorno's negotiation of the Kant–Hegel controversy is thus more than an intervention in the interpretative history of those philosophers; it is at the heart of the urgent imperative to 'arrange . . . thoughts and actions so that Auschwitz will not repeat itself'. The contemporary force of this twin critique can be drawn out by putting it to work against two of the most significant interventions in the philosophical debate over the meaning of Auschwitz: those of Jean-François Lyotard and Gillian Rose, representatives respectively of Kantian and Hegelian poles of this theoretical space.[27] The question of the aesthetic – more specifically of the representability or otherwise of Auschwitz to consciousness – is the terrain on which this debate is played out.

Lyotard approaches Auschwitz via a range of philosophical–theoretical motifs: Freudian *Nachträglichkeit*, Levinasian obligation, Adorno's negative dialectic, and above all the Kantianism of the *Critique of Judgment*. 'Auschwitz' becomes the name of an unnamable or sublime terror, inassimilable to consciousness or memory, which can be adequated to no concept or representation:[28] 'when the sublime is "there" (where?), the mind is not there' (*Hj*, 32).[29] The mind's inability to conceptualize this intuition of the Absolute is above all a crisis of representation, most famously described by Lyotard in this passage from *The Differend*:

Suppose that an earthquake destroys not only lives, buildings and objects, but also the instruments used to measure earthquakes directly or indirectly. The impossibility of quantatively measuring does not prohibit, but rather imposes in the minds of the survivors the idea of a very great seismic force. The scholar claims to know nothing about it, but the common person has a complex feeling, the one avowed by the negative presentation of the indeterminate.[30]

To think Auschwitz is thus to think its implacable resistance to thought, just as to remember it is to recognize it as 'something that never ceases to be forgotten' (*Hj*, 3; 17). Put another way, Auschwitz is the Kantian disturbance of the Hegelian machine which would 'put to work' every negativity, every otherness: 'It would be a name without a speculative "name", not sublatable [*irrelevable*] into a concept' (*D*, 88; 133). It is in this section of *The Differend* that Lyotard takes up Adorno's negative dialectic. The latter announces the ruin of the speculative dialectic, as Lyotard attempts to show through the analysis of different 'language games', specifically the command to die. When, for example, the members of the Paris Commune execute the 'command' to 'die rather than be defeated', the authority behind the command is one 'freely' submitted to by those who obey it: addressor and addressee of the command thus form a cohesive 'we' (*D*, 98; 149). Lyotard takes this impossibility as the condition for a new conception of the 'we' of ethics and politics, one founded in a disjunction, rather than identification, between addressor and addressee:

> This we is certainly not the totality of the I's, you's, and the s/he's in play under the name of 'Auschwitz', for it is true that this name designates the impossibility of such a totalization. Instead, it is the reflective movement of this impossibility. (*D*, 101; 152)

The proximity of this thought to Adorno's is undeniable: for both thinkers, Auschwitz is the ruin of the metaphysical faculty,[31] the exhaustion of every available theology, ethics and aesthetics. Indeed, in *Heidegger and 'the Jews'*, Adorno becomes the exemplar of this 'writing of the ruins' (*Hj*, 43; 76), the only possible form philosophy can now take. However, these undoubted affinities obscure a subtle but decisive difference between the two thinkers, namely that for Lyotard, Auschwitz appears to take thought altogether beyond the reach of the concept, and into a politics whose claimed aconceptuality threatens to reify the non-identical.

While *Heidgger and 'the Jews'* is careful to insist that there is no means of bringing the sublime horror of Auschwitz into positive expression, Lyotard's political thought in particular tends to violate the negativity of non-identity not in the Hegelian form of sublation, but by invoking the non-identical as the name of a distinct and describable practice of consciousness and social organization – variously 'figural', 'paganist', 'micronarrative', or 'Jewish' according to the particular stage in his corpus. This tendency is especially evident in Lyotard's early critique of Adorno,

'Adorno as the Devil', which takes issue with the residual Hegelianism of the nega-tive dialectic. Adorno's negative dialectic performs what Lyotard calls 'a satanic parody' of the reconciliation of subject and object, in which Adorno is cast as the devil (the figure is taken from Mann's *Dr Faustus*, in Chapter 25 of which the devil delivers passages from the *Philosophy of Modern Music*), internal Adversary in the divine system, rupturing its logic from within. Lyotard's compact summary and critique of this 'diabolism' runs thus:

> Totality is missing = there is no god to reconcile = all reconciliation can only be represented in its impossibility, parodied = it is a satanic work. You wasted your time replacing God with the devil, the prefix super- with the old subter-ranean mole, you remain in the same theological deployment. You pass from shamefaced nihilism to flaunted nihilism. Adorno's work, just as Mann's and Schönberg's, is marked by nostalgia. The devil is nostalgia of God, impossible god, therefore possible precisely as a god. ('AD', 132–3)

A diabolist dialectic, then, is still a dialectic, still operating within the 'theologi-cal deployment' legislated by Hegel. To be brought out of capital and 'art' (as theol-ogy) requires not 'criticism' in the Frankfurt sense, but 'a deployment of libidinal investment ... [w]e do not *desire* to possess, to work, to dominate ... [w]hat can they do about that?' ('AD', 136). The libidinal investment divests us of the will to dominate:

> To cease composing in politics is to cease conserving *in absentia* the idea of the totality, the military, industrial, clerical organization which represents totality, to cease constructing a 'party'. In place of the *politica ficta fingens* a *politica figura*. What can an affirmative politics be, which does not look for support in a repre-sentative (a party) of the negative, etc.? That is the question left, abandoned by Adorno. ('AD', 137)

The 'politica figura' is the refusal and disruption of representation, of the sub-sumption of the diversity of political intensities under the sign of an organizing political mechanism like the Party. The 'figure' is the central term in Lyotard's *Discours, Figure*,[32] and describes that which interrupts the ordering logic of the discursive, introducing into it that which exceeds perspectival representation and so revealing the concealed 'openness' within it.

As Samuel Weber has argued with acuity, Lyotard's persistent disavowal of domination, the claim to have overcome every desire to 'possess', 'work', 'repre-sent' in favour of releasing a limitless multiplicity of incommensurable language games obscures a powerful proscriptive impulse all the more dangerous for being unacknowledged: 'By prescribing that no game, especially that of prescription, should dominate the others, one is doing exactly what is simultaneously claimed is being avoided: one is dominating the other games in order to protect them from domination'.[33] In other words, it is precisely at the point that Lyotard expresses his impatience with Adorno – the lingering 'theological deployment' of the negative dialectic – that the blind-spots of his own thinking come to light. For even though Lyotard's later work is more sympathetic to the Adornian dialectic, the difference that the early essay insists upon is evident throughout the former's authorship. Lyotard renders Auschwitz the sublime Other of the concept, with the consequence that he conceives the task of thought and action very differently from Adorno. Thought is to escape the domination of the concept, to expunge it from its mechanisms. In this hastiness to overcome domination, Lyotard misses one of Adorno's pivotal insights, namely that 'the nonidentical is not to be obtained directly' (*ND*, 158; *GS*6, 161), inasmuch as it is always implicated in the logic of identity, marked by the very rationality it resists. Lyotard's figural politics and aesthetics cannot acknowledge its implication in this rationality; its insistent affirmations of its own non-identity (and criticism of Adorno for having left behind the 'affirmative question') are symptoms of this disavowal.[34]

It is in this regard that an Adornian critique of Lyotard would be in accord with Gillian Rose's Hegelian polemic against postmodernism's post-Holocaust ethics and aesthetics. For Rose, the trope of unrepresentability pervasive in postmodern theory is haunted by its own 'bad conscience'; for it marshalls in the service of its arguments the very methods of critical reason it finally wishes to abolish. Revealing Auschwitz as the dark heart of 'the history, methods and results hitherto of reason', it must disavow its own implication in that very history. Athens' postmodern citizens have abandoned the irredeemably scandalized city in which they grew up, and 'have set off on a pilgrimage to the New Jerusalem, where they seek to dedicate themselves to difference, to otherness, to love – to a new ethics, which overcomes the fusion of knowledge and power in the old Athens'.[35]

Against this perceived demonization of reason, Rose's philosophical project begins from the injunction to inhabit reason's contradictions, 'to take on the difficulties and injustices of the existing city' (Rose, 36). To imagine a space dedicated to the pure affirmation of difference, which isn't implicated in these same difficulties and injustices, is itself a kind of violence: a violent evasion of the risks of action, in the guise of unconditioned and unconditional ethics.

The same unacknowledged violence informs the aesthetic of 'Holocaust piety' so pervasive in the representation of the Nazi genocide. Rose's critique is directed specifically against the positioning of the viewer/reader as traumatized, passive witness. To take up the standpoint of 'silence, prayer . . . the witness of "ineffability" ' is to block inquiry into the historical conditions that made Auschwitz possible, or '*to mystify something we dare not understand*, because we fear it may be all too understandable, all too continuous with what we are – human, all too human' (Rose, 43, Rose's emphasis).

Rose contrasts two texts – Spielberg's *Schindler's List* and *The Remains of the Day* (both Ishiguro's novel and its Merchant Ivory adaptation) as exemplars of, respectively, Holocaust piety and its implicit critique. Where Spielberg's film encourages silence before the atrocities represented, providing us with a chain of stable and unambiguous points of ethical identification, the latter implicates us in the violence tacitly represented, forcing us to confront the stark question, '[c]ould I have done this?'.[36] *The Remains of the Day* takes the reader/viewer beyond the unassailable security of witness, and implicates her in the consequences of Stevens' (the butler) inviolable loyalty to his 'master' Lord Darlington, when the latter attempts to forge an alliance with the Nazis. Positioned with Stevens, we cannot disown his disastrous collusions.

Forced to confront this collusive logic, in herself as well as Stevens, the viewer is denied the ethical security produced by *Schindler's List*. But she is given instead '*the remains of the day* – "dignity" minimally reassembled out of the ruins of ideals, out of the pieces of the broken heart' (Rose, 53, Rose's emphasis). Alive to her own implication in 'the ruins of ideals', she is ready to participate once more in the existing city, 'released for the perilous adventures in the always precarious configurations of rationalized domination' (Rose, 58). Only by inhabiting these 'precarious configurations' can the attitude of silent witness before Auschwitz be overcome, the specific political conditions which enabled it illuminated:

> If fascism is the triumph of civil society, the triumph of enraged particular interests, then the subject of representation does not need to be superseded: the danger of its experience needs to be exposed. And that same danger will be the means of exposition. (Rose, 58)

If Lyotard seeks overhastily to drag us out of representation, Rose is too sanguine about exposing us to its dangers. The reading of *Remains of the Day* seeks to draw Auschwitz back into the concept, rendering determinate its social and psychological meanings. Where both Adorno and Rose are thinkers of complicity, the former sees its demand as maintaining all possible distance between Auschwitz and the violence of representation. For Rose, however, it is the thought of complicity which precisely makes Auschwitz available to the violence of representation. In the account of the Holocaust as 'all too continuous with what we are', with civil society's 'enraged particular interests', it is precisely the *absence* of 'rational' interests driving the genocide which is elided.

In other words, and contra Lyotard, to argue that Auschwitz ruins historical determination is not to abandon, but to lend greater precision to, the historical understanding of the Nazi genocide. For the historical specificity of the Nazi war crimes consists in their excess of every available rationality, economic, territorial or political. This is Hannah Arendt's point in her 'Epilogue' to *Eichmann in Jerusalem*: the genocide of the Jews throws up insurmountable problems in the field of

international law because it is unprecedented, 'not only in degree but in essence'.[37]
The Nazi regime's attempt 'to make the entire Jewish people disappear from the
face of the earth' constitutes a crime not against 'fellow-nations' but 'against
the very nature of mankind' (Arendt, 268). At the heart of this distinction is a
problem of determination: the essential difference of the Nazi genocide is that
unlike legalized discriminations, expulsions and large-scale murders practised, for
example, in Balkan countries prior to the Second World War, it is 'a crime that
could not be explained by any utilitarian purpose; Jews had been murdered all
over Europe, not only in the East, and their annihilation was not due to any
desire to gain territory that "could be used for colonization by the Germans"'
(Arendt, 275). It is this excess of determination that Rose's Hegelian critique
leaves out of account, and which makes sense of her insistence on the continued
need for a representational aesthetic after Auschwitz. Where Adorno's aesthetic
teaches that Auschwitz ruins representation, Rose's seems to return to representation its lost efficacity, to draw Auschwitz back into the order of historical and
psychic intelligibility.

   Both Adorno and Rose, to be sure, would trouble, rather than stabilize the
reader or viewer's ethical security, implicating her in the very violence she would
protest against. But the experience of this implication would be different for each
thinker. For Adorno, the inescapability of representation's violence demands precisely the recognition of its limits, of the danger of seeking adequation between the
event and its representation. Rose, in contrast, seems to insist on just such adequation; if Auschwitz is 'all too understandable, all too continuous with what we are',
then its representation becomes that of us – our enraged investments, our disavowed complicities – to ourselves. This claimed continuity of Nazi with quotidian violence blocks recognition of its non-identity, its relentless negation of the
concepts which we must nonetheless employ; for Auschwitz would in fact be
brought within our orders of knowledge and representation.

   Thus, Rose offers a kind of perverse immanentist mirror image to Lyotard's claim
that Auschwitz transcends all systems of knowledge. Adorno's diagnosis of the
twin errors of these modes of thinking is pertinent here: 'if stubbornly immanent
contemplation threatens to revert to idealism, to the illusion of the self-sufficient
mind in contemplation of both itself and of reality, transcendent contemplation
threatens to forget the effort of conceptualization' (P, 33; GS 10.1, 28). Adorno's
aesthetic, as shall presently be shown, is an ongoing attempt to think a mode of art
that would vigilantly resist these polarities.

ART AGAINST ITSELF: RETHINKING THE AESTHETIC

We should not be surprised, then, that the debate between Kant and Hegel continues to rage through the pages of *Aesthetic Theory*. A new aesthetic must 'go

beyond [*über*]' this controversy, though 'without leveling it through a synthesis' (*AT*, 355;[38] *GS*7, 528). Is not to move 'beyond' Kant and Hegel without synthesizing them to render their controversy interminable, and even to make of this interminability a philosophical project? This is what is suggested by the text's consistent criticisms of each thinker in the name of the other. Thus to Kant's insistence on the autonomy of art, the need to free it from 'the avaricious philistinism that always wants to touch it and taste it', Adorno puts the Hegelian objection that this condition should not be, as in Kant, 'transcendentally arrested [*stillgestelt*]' but recognized as 'a historical process' (*AT*, 10; *GS*7, 23). 'The artwork's autonomy', he goes on, 'is … not a priori but the sedimentation [*Gewordenes*] of a historical process that constitutes its concept' (*AT*, 17; *GS*7, 34). This criticism of Kant's rendering of conditioned experience as transcendent is of course familiar from *Negative Dialectic*, where it is his concept of freedom rather than aesthetic autonomy which is charged with ahistoricality.

Arguably, however, the criticisms of Hegel in *Aesthetic Theory* are stronger and more decisive. Once again, Adorno's break with Hegel is announced at the point of their near convergence: the latter is the first philosopher to reveal the 'overarching process of spiritualization' to which 'the spirit of artworks' is subjected across the history of consciousness. This process consists in its 'division from nature', and demands the expunging of 'everything sensually pleasing in art, every charm of the material' (*AT*, 91–2; *GS*7, 142). Hegel's hostility to the late romantic artwork is directed against its resistance to spiritualization, its scandalous embrace of 'finitude and mutability', an 'entanglement in the relative'[39] which prevents it from realizing its own universality. In particular, the romanticism of his Jena contemporaries, the circle of writers and philosophers around the Schlegel brothers, could approach the universal only via the fragmentary and transient illuminations of *Witz* and irony, that is, through means necessarily inadequate to a realized universality.

At one level, Hegel's account of the diremption of natuer and spirit, inner and outer, provides Adorno with a potent account of the development of aesthetic autonomy – for this autonomy attests precisely to the failure of Spirit to realize its own universality. For Adorno, however, this 'failure' signifies not, as for Hegel, modern art's state of misrecognition but on the contrary, its truth. Art gives expression to Spirit's constitutive insubstantiality, to the impossibility of its own actualization: 'In no artwork is the element of spirit something that exists [*ein Seiendes*]; rather, it is something in a process of development and formation [*ein Werdenes, sich Bildendes*]' (*AT*, 92; *GS*7, 142). The artwork does not seek to attain its own achievement (which would also be its 'dissolution') as fully realized spirit. The spiritual artwork as *Seiende* would violate the truth of art, whose character as *Werdene* – as processual and incomplete – is not a temporary condition to be superseded, but its constitutive mode of (non)being.[40] Put another way, what Adorno refuses in the Hegelian aesthetic is its ambition to 'redeem' the other of spirit, an ambition which works to 'exclud[e] the heterogeneous and strengthen its image character' (*Bildcharakter*) (*AT*, 92; *GS*7, 142). The Adornian artwork is marked rather by its resistance to *Bildcharakter*, which in its drive to make present the infinite in the form of an image, would draw transcendence into an immanence that 'tolerates . . . no independence of ontical conditions' (*ND*, 201; *GS*6, 201). The constitutive impossibility of redeeming the artwork is its paradoxical fidelity to redemption.

If Adorno attributes greater truth to the Kantian than to the Hegelian aesthetic, it is not an indication that he has finally come down on one side of the controversy. Rather, it attests to the greater fidelity of the former to aesthetic experience after Auschwitz. The final telos of the Hegelian artwork – the reconciliation of matter and spirit – remains unachieved and unachievable for Kant. The truth of the Kantian position is revealed even in its inconsistencies. Thus, the judgement of taste as elaborated by the third *Critique* is simultaneously a 'logical function' and 'extralogical' insofar as it presents itself ' "without a concept" ': 'This contradiction, however, is inherent in art itself, as the contradiction between its spiritual and mimetic constitution (*Wesens*)' (*AT*, 97; *GS*7, 149). Art can be described as the site of the unending irreconcilability of the spiritual and mimetic, of the 'constructive' labour of the concept and the 'expressive' play of the aconceptual.[41] The imperative of art's realization and dissolution at the heart of Hegel's *Aesthetics* can now be thought of only in its impossibility: 'Kant's theory is more apposite to the contemporary situation, for his aesthetics attempts to bind together consciousness of what is necessary with consciousness that what is necessary is itself blocked to consciousness' (*AT*, 343; *GS*7, 511). The 'contemporary situation' dictates that redemption, the necessary task of thought, take the form of its own blockage. The history of aesthetic experience has ended not in art's sublation by a realized philosophy, but in the endless antagonism of its constitutive elements.

What separates Adorno from any unproblematic affirmation of Kantian aesthetics, however, is his refusal to see redemption and its impossibility as opposed terms. This, in a sense, is Hegel's error; for while he 'was the first to realize that the end of art is implicit in its concept', he identified that end with the realization of the absolute Idea. Adorno agrees that art's end is implicit in its concept: 'art must be and wants to be utopia . . .'; yet the end of art (or 'utopia') is not to be conflated with its 'temporal end' (*AT*, 32; *GS*7, 55). The sense of the end developed here is very close to that of Maurice Blanchot in his essay 'Slow Obsequies': 'when philosophy lays claim to its end, it is to a *measureless* [*démesurée*] end that it lays claim'.[42] The Adornian utopia of art can be described by just this measurelessness. His figure for 'the new' – 'a child at the piano searching for a chord never previously heard' – compacts the experience of the end as an unfulfilled longing. Insofar as 'the chord . . . was always there', the end of art is contained within its concept; but the achievement of this end would not be the hearing of the chord: 'The new is the longing (*Sehnsucht*) for the new, not the new itself' (*A T*, 32; *GS*7, 55). Adorno here introduces a kind of homonymy into the new; the term at one and the same time signifies and negates itself; if the new is not 'the new itself', then fidelity to its demand must take the form of an infidelity, a failure to redeem its promise.

This is why Adorno begins *Aesthetic Theory* by announcing that '[a]rt must turn against itself, in opposition to its own concept, and thus become uncertain of itself right into its innermost fiber' (*A T*, 2; *GS*7, 10). Art's own concept is its 'inescapable affirmative essence', the promise of its 'end' in utopian reconciliation. In order to keep faith with itself – *to be art* – art must thus negate its own essence or *not be art*. Art shares the homonymous logic of the new, signifying both itself and something other than (even opposed to) itself. And – at least in the current age, when 'the real possibility of utopia . . . converges with the possibility of total catastrophe' (*A T*, 33; *GS*7, 56) – it is in this mode of otherness to itself that it is most itself.

INTERRUPTING HEGEL: HÖLDERLIN

Art is not the fulfilment but the maintenance of its promise; this is the crucial point of divergence from Hegel. But how, according to Adorno, does art stage this philosophical difference? The most sustained response to this question is to be found in perhaps his most important literary essay, 'Parataxis: On Hölderlin's Late Poetry'. The poetry of Hölderlin, Hegel's friend and contemporary, serves in this essay as both counterpart and antagonist to the latter's philosophy, and as such reveals the stakes of the Adornian break with it.

Hölderlin's poetry diverges from Hegel's philosophy at the point of their closest convergence. Hölderlin's gaze, like Shelley's and Baudelaire's 'sees correspondences between ideas and particular existents everywhere'. These correspondences are the means through which the poet seeks to fulfil the supreme ambition of language itself: 'to convey names, which the Absolute does not have and in which alone it could exist, across the concept' (*NL*2, 122; *GS*11, 462). The name is the promise of pure singularity which language, bound inextricably to the generality of the concept, must always betray. The name has always barred in advance the possibility of its own expression, insofar as it signifies precisely what language cannot disclose other than through its concealment in a given utterance. The Absolute thus 'does not have names' because the name is what must always exceed possession, what refuses subsumption to the rule of the universal: in names, 'there always remains an excess of what is desired but not attained' (*NL*2, 123; *GS*11, 463). At the same time, it exists only through names, because the Absolute is itself that which is never brought into the full presence of the concept.

This desire to 'convey the name . . . across the concept' is not alien to Hegel, for he too wants the particular to subsist as a moment of the Absolute, rather than simply to subsume it in 'a higher-order concept'. Both thinkers, then, are faced with the necessary failure of language to maintain difference *as* difference. In Hölderlin, 'the poetic gesture tells the living, as does Hegel's philosophy, that they are mere signs. They do not want to be that; it is a death sentence for them' (*NL*2, 122–3; *GS* 11, 463). But it is just at this moment of affinity that the poet and philosopher diverge; if, for Hegel, 'the negation of the existing entities' is a necessary and so affirmative moment in the progress of Spirit, Hölderlin's poetry 'by virtue of the detachment of its formal law from empirical reality, laments the sacrifice it requires'. Hölderlin's poetics are clearly being made to stage the Adornian revision of the dialectic here. For Hölderlin, as for Adorno, there is no positive means of expressing the 'living being', for positive expression carries language into the order of the concept which kills it. But this death is also what allows the living being to appear negatively, in the form of the lament over its sacrifice: 'The difference between the name and the Absolute, which Hölderlin does not conceal and which runs through his work as an allegorical cleft [*Brechung*], is the medium of his critique of the false life in which the soul is not granted its divine right' (*NL* 2, 123; *GS* 11, 463). The break with Hegel is thus the insinuation into the Absolute of the difference promised by the name, a break that takes the form of a poetic strategy: parataxis.

Adorno describes parataxes as 'artificial disturbances that evade the logical hierarchy of a subordinating syntax' (*NL*2, 131; *GS* 11, 471). Parataxis draws poetry towards the aconceptual language of great music, as Adorno attempts to show in his commentary on these lines from 'Brot und Wein':

> Warum schweigen auch sie, die alten heilgen Theater?
> Warum freuet sich denn nicht der geweihete Tanz?
> Drückt den Stempel, wie sonst, nicht dem Getroffenen auf?
> Oder er kam auch selbst und nahm des Menschen Gestalt an
> Und vollendet' und schloss tröstend das himmlische Fest.

> [Why are they silent, even the ancient holy theaters?
> Why has the joy disappeared out of the sacred dance?
> Why does a god no longer, as once, on the brow of a man
> Stamp his mark to declare: this is the target I choose.
> Or a god himself came with the form and features of manhood,
> Bringing the heavenly feast comfortingly to an end.] (*NL*2, 132;
> *GS* 11, 472)

Adorno identifies a paratactic interruption in the form of the 'oder', the point at which 'what is most specific, the catastrophe, is named' (the fall of antiquity, conjoined with the appearance of Christ). The 'or' which draws Christ into the poem does not take the form of 'predicative assertion'; rather, the promise of reconciliation opened up by the union of human and divine is 'suggested, like a possibility'.

Hölderlin refuses the hubris which would impose Christianity as the necessary and incontestable redemption of the fall of antiquity, acceding instead to the impossibility of guaranteeing the meaning of this historical relationship. In thus dispensing with 'fixed propositional form', he 'causes the rhythm to approach musical development, (*Verlauf*)[43] just as it softens the identity claims of speculative thought, which undertakes to dissolve history into its identity with spirit' (*NL2*, 132; *GS*11, 472–3). Parataxis is thus the mode through which redemption is maintained as possibility rather than fulfilment, showing up an otherness which cannot be sublated in the speculative proposition.

The paratactical interruption thus speaks for the autonomy of poetry itself. Because the poem refuses to guarantee the fulfilment of redemption's promise, it cannot be subordinated to theology. This is 'what is eminently modern in him': 'The relation of his poetry to theology is the relation to an ideal; the poetry is not a surrogate for theology' (*NL2*, 137; *GS*11, 478). It is difficult to avoid the sense of displaced self-description on Adorno's part, for this sentence describes with uncanny precision the relation his aesthetic sets up between the artwork and theology. Art is not secularized theology; it does not do theology's work in a different guise. Rather, it lets theology appear negatively (an 'ideal' cannot be brought into language), in the form of its impossibility: 'Hölderlin's aesthetic *coups de main* [*Handstreiche*], from the quasi-quantitative stanzaic divisions of the great elegies to the triadic constructions, are witnesses to an impossibility at the very core [*Innersten*]' (*NL2*, 139; *GS*11, 480). Precisely because it has no substantial existence of its own, the 'stylistic principle', the parataxes concealed in the manifest content of the poem, is alone able to carry the promise of utopia. Hölderlin must continually resist the temptation to substantialize utopia in language, as these two lines from 'Mnemosyne' attest: 'Vorwärts aber und ruckwärts wollen wir/Nicht sehn. Uns wiegen lassen, wie/Auf schwankem Kahne See' ['But forward and back we will/Not look. Be rocked as/On swaying skiff of the sea']. Adorno comments: 'Not forward: under the law of the present, which in Hölderlin is the law of poetry, with a taboo against abstract utopia, a taboo in which the theological ban on graven images, which Hölderlin shares with Hegel and Marx, lives on' (*NL2*, 142; *GS*11, 483). The identification here of 'the law of poetry' with the Judaic *Bilderverbot* compacts in a few words the complex relationship of art to religion in Adorno. The poem is here the site of fidelity to the present, to the ineluctable finitude which philosophy longs impotently to overcome. It is entrusted with preserving the truth content of religion by vigilantly enforcing the prohibition on its positive expression.

To reiterate, Adorno's counterposing of Hölderlin to Hegel should not be read as a simple decision 'against' the Hegelian and 'for' the Kantian aesthetic. Jay Bernstein's situating of Adorno's aesthetic writings in relation to the third *Critique* is illuminating here. Bernstein argues that Kant's aesthetic enacts the 'expulsion of

art from modern societies and their cognitive and practical mechanisms'.[44] In carrying art beyond the reach of the concept, Kant effectively divests it of its power to
speak the truth, and especially the political truth. Art either adapts itself to Kant's
discursive concept of truth, and so betrays its potential to speak a truth beyond the
discursive, or it abandons the discursive, and so 'necessarily falls silent' (Bernstein,
10). Bernstein argues that Adorno's aesthetic begins from this aporia of the discursive, from whence derives also its political content. Art, as the only means through
which a truth beyond cognition can be articulated, is the cipher for an absent, idea-
lized politics: 'Speculatively, art and politcs are one. Beauty bereaved is politics
bereaved' (Bernstein, 13).

Bernstein is perhaps too quick to insist on the speculative identity of art and
politics – we have seen that 'the law of poetry' is its refusal to be subordinated to
a speculative future. Nevertheless, he is right to stress that the Hegelian horizon of
reconciliation continues to haunt – negatively – Adorno's apparently Kantian
aesthetic. Hölderlin is a privileged name for this doubled motion in which reconciliation is thought through its negation.

MIMESIS: THE SEMBLANCE OF REDEMPTION

Shierry Weber Nicholsen has argued persuasively that Adorno's aesthetic resistance to Hegel's totalizing dialectic consists above all in the assertion of language
in the face of its unthinking effacement. Citing the former's charge in the third of
his Hegel studies ('Skoteinos, or How to Read Hegel' [Skoteinos oder wie zu lesen sei]),
of 'a sovereignly indifferent attitude toward language', Nicholsen comments: 'This
failure with regard to language is the failure of Hegel's philosophy'.[45] Language
names the irreducible difference between Hegel and Adorno, between the dialectic
that sublates and the dialectic that maintains otherness. This is not to suggest that
language serves as the hypostatized other of the concept, but to insist on its necessarily *doubled* character; for language is both at the service of the concept, in the form
of communication, and other to the concept in the form of what Adorno will call
mimesis. If language is the co-presence of these conceptual and aconceptual elements, poetry is that form in which the latter struggles painfully against the
former. In the poem, language strives towards a 'necessarily indistinct and ungraspable otherness' (Nicholsen, 74), that is, towards the absolute immediacy which it
longs even in the knowledge of its impossibility. Poetic language is that space in
which the forgotten mimetic impulse buried within the sedimented language of
communication is recalled.

Adorno gestures to this mimetic impulse when he writes, in a clear invocation of
Benjamin's 'The Task of the Translator', 'no work of art, regardless of what its

maker (*Hervorbringende*) thinks of it, is directed toward an observer, not even toward a transcendental subject of apperception; no artwork is to be described or explained in terms of the categories of communication' (*A T*, 109; *GS*7, 167).[46] Like Benjamin in the 'Translator' essay, Adorno sees the true artwork as the always unfulfilled desire to bring to light what the former calls 'pure language' and the latter 'nonexistent' or 'impossible' language (*NL2*, 197; *GS*11, 541).[47] Adorno continues:

> Artworks are semblance [*Schein*] in that they help what they themselves cannot be to a type of second-order, modified existence; they are appearance [*Erscheinung*] because by virtue of aesthetic realization the nonexistent [*Nichtseiende*] in them, for whose sake they exist, achieves an existence [*Dasein*], however refracted [*gebrochenen*]. (*A T*, 109; *GS*7, 167)

Concentrated in this sentence is not only his thought of the negative or 'refracted' existence of the non-existent in the artwork, but also his singular understanding of mimesis as *semblance* of the impossible, of 'language itself'.[48] This is what is meant by Adorno's apparently opaque statement that '[t]he mimesis of artworks is their resemblance [*Ähnlichkeit*] to themselves' (*A T*, 104; *GS*7, 159). Against the Platonic conception of mimesis as copy or representation (in an essay on Valéry, he claims rather that in mimetic behaviour the artwork 'rid[s] itself of any likeness to objects' [*NL1*, 170; *GS*11, 198]), Adornian mimesis is resemblance to the work's own 'objective ideal' (*A T*, 104; *GS*7, 159). In what does this objective ideal consist? The discussion of the Hölderlinian name offered one response to this question. The poetic invocation of the name is a striving towards a language of language, prior to any communication. But this gesture towards the name is parasitic on the very communicative abstraction it wants to escape, such that the gesture is always also the 'lament' over its necessary failure.

In the concept of mimesis, this lament becomes the very site of hope in the work. The mimetic comportment disallows in advance any attempt to give positive expression to the non-existent, instead preserving and maintaining it in its constitutive impossibility; for the law of the artwork's self-resemblance endows it with an inviolable autonomy which is its guarantee against 'incorporating' the Absolute: 'by the autonomy of their form, artworks forbid the incorporation of the Absolute as if they were symbols. Aesthetic images stand under the prohibition on graven images. To this extent aesthetic semblance, even its ultimate form in the hermetic artwork, is truth' (*A T*, 104; *GS*7, 159). The truth of aesthetic semblance is its vigilantly non-violent relation to the Absolute, which is also its fidelity to the interdiction of idolatry. The doubled motion whereby the artwork speaks and conceals (or better, speaks by concealing) truth is what Adorno calls its 'enigmaticalness' (*Rätselcharakter*): 'Through form, artworks gain their resemblance to language [*sprachähnlich*], seeming at every point to say [*bekunden*] just this and only this, and at the same time whatever it is slips away [*entwischt*]' (*A T*, 120; *GS*7, 182). Because the artwork is constitutively semblance, it is only ever *sprachähnlich*, 'language-like'. If it could stop at the point of saying or showing (another meaning of *bekunden*) 'just this and only this', it would have attained the impossible state of language itself. But the moment it *seems* to expose the impossible is also the moment at which the impossible withdraws from its grasp, 'slips away'. In the artwork, truth speaks by revoking its own expression.

The enigma of the language of art is elaborated most fully in the essays on poetry, of which his 1967 essay on Rudolf Borchardt, 'Charmed Language' ('*Die beschworene Sprache*'), is exemplary. Nicholsen rightly identifies the interpretative key to the reading of Borchardt in his 'incomparable line, "Ich habe nicht als Rauschen" ["I have nothing but murmuring"]' (*NL*2, 193; *GS*11, 536). Adorno's commentary on this line is as follows:

Language murmurs and rustles through him like a stream. He reaches for language and learns to deploy it in order to serve it; he made his work an arena for language. He was borne by the experience his whole literary oeuvre was striving for the experience of language itself speaking . . .' (*NL*2, 193; *GS*11, 536)

The striving for 'language itself' (and it is worth noting that a few lines on language itself is compared to 'the authentic language Jewish mysticism speaks of') is what endows Borchardt's poetry with its 'persistent enigmatic character' (*NL*2, 193; *GS*11, 536). This enigmatic character, in full conformity to its definition in *Aesthetic Theory*, is the twin movement of speaking and concealing which characterizes Borchardt's entire oeuvre. 'In Borchardt', writes Adorno, 'irretrievability becomes a technique'; that is, if the transcendence to which history has irreversibly closed us is to remain unachieved, this non-achievement is not to be seen as a failure – even a heroic one – but as the substantial form of the poetry itself. Poetry's 'failure' to incorporate the Absolute symbolically becomes its achievement. Again and again, Borchardt attests to this (non-)achievement. His poetic speech 'calls, as if across the abyss, to the Other, who has become indistinct and is in the process of vanishing. Spun on and on indefatigably, it bears witness to the difficulty of getting through to that Other, as though the impossible could be attained through repeated attempts' (*NL*2, 200; *GS*11, 543). The paradoxical character of Borchardt's poetry – that in seeking to grasp the Other it merely accentuates its ungraspability – attests to its philosophical and historical truth, for the aporetic relation to the Other is the condition of modernity itself: 'That it [his poetry] gave artistic form to its own impossibility is the seal [*Echtheitssiegel*] of its modernity' (*NL2*, 208; *GS* 11, 553). Only the fulfilment of the poem's yearning for language itself could betray its truth.

MICROLOGICAL READING: PROUST AND THEOLOGY

We should by now be closer to understanding the privileged place of art in Adorno's thought. Only in art can language articulate the promise of redemption without traducing it. Where, as we have seen, modern positive religion can think redemption only by way of its violent incorporation into language, art – and especially 'radical art up to Beckett' (*NL2*, 207; *GS* 11, 552) – gives form to the impossible as unfulfilled possibility and so avoids 'velleity or violence'. For this reason, art should never be seen as simply another name for mimesis, for the mimetic comportment 'survives only through its antithesis, the works' rational control over everything heterogeneous to them' (*AT*, 96; *GS* 7, 148). Art, that is, is always marked by the very conceptuality from which it yearns to break free; its task thus cannot be to disavow conceptuality, but to give voice to the mute language of the Other which subtends conceptual language. Hence, '[a]rt is rationality that criticizes rationality without withdrawing from it' (*AT*, 55; *GS* 7, 87); again, Adorno requires us to be attentive to the doubling of a single term. In art, rationality is made to confront its own otherness to itself, the very otherness against which it defined itself. If art disavowed rationality, it would merely invert its logic – instead, it must show rationality the mutual inherence of itself and its other: 'The inextricability of reification and mimesis is the aporia of artistic expression'. If art is 'the plenipotentiary [*Statthalter*] of an undamaged life in the midst of mutilated life' (*AT*, 117; *GS* 7, 179), its promise cannot be presented in immediate form without betraying it. The necessary constructive element in the artwork – compositional form, technique, stylistic or generic convention – attests to the inescapable rational moment in the work through which alone the promise of rationality's other can be transiently glimpsed.

For Adorno, the task of an aesthetic must be to draw out this promise without on the one hand fetishizing its aconceptuality or, on the other, subsuming it under the concept. These twin dangers – which we might call 'Kantian' and 'Hegelian' – are alluded to in the citation from Schlegel which, the editors of *Aesthetic Theory* tell us, was to be the book's epigraph: 'What is called the philosophy of art usually lacks one of two things: either the philosophy or the art' (*AT*, 366; *GS* 7, 544). As Adorno does not tire of reminding us, only a micrological criticism, one that begins from immersion in the work's particulars rather than overarching conceptual categories, is in a position to refuse these polarized terms. Criticism should be animated by the same impulse that makes itself felt throughout the text which, he avows, 'has played a central role in my intellectual economy for decades' (*NL2*, 312; *GS* 11, 669), namely Proust's *À La Recherche du Temps Perdu*. 'In Proust', he writes, 'the relationship of the whole to the detail is not that of an overall architectonic plan to the specifics that fill it in: it is against precisely that, against the brutal untruth of a subsuming form forced on from above, that Proust revolted' (*NL1*, 174; *GS* 11, 203).

Proust's text provides an exemplary lesson not only in how to write but equally in how to read, as Adorno's invocation of and commentary upon one passage suggests:

> At one point Proust extols the medieval masters who introduced ornaments in their cathedrals so hidden that they must have known no human being would every set eyes on them. Such unity is not one arranged for the human eye but rather an invisible unity in the midst of dispersion, and it would be evident only to a divine observer. Proust should be read with the idea of those cathedrals in mind, dwelling on the concrete without grasping prematurely at something that yields itself not directly but only through its thousand facets. (*NL1*, 175; *GS* 11, 204)

Proust's cathedrals enact uncannily the complex relation between particular and universal which the literary text and the experience of reading it put in play. If the universal is present in the particular, it is so not in the Hegelian sense of their identity in the former. The Proustian model of this relation shows rather that the universal can come to light only by *refusing* to impose its identity with the particular upon it. Adorno's language is misleading in this respect, for its talk of 'an invisible unity in the midst of dispersion' suggests a kind of negative theological guarantee of the ultimate harmony of the dispersed elements. But this 'invisible unity' is not one that could ever be made present outside the ineluctable disunity of the text. It 'exists' only as a promise that haunts the text, and as such exacerbates rather than remedies its dispersion. Adorno thus turns the conventional vocabulary of the aesthetic against itself: unity achieves itself only by failing to do so, by becoming other than itself.

A criticism that leaps over the work's particulars with the ambition of apprehending its unity directly can only fall into the error of modern positive religion, namely a falsely immediate expression of the universal. A further allusion to Proust in the 'Theses on Art and Religion Today' is revealing here. The seventh and last of the theses is an attempt to specify precisely the peculiar character of the art–religion relation. How, Adorno asks, can the artwork express the universal if it is in a dichotomous relation to religion? In responding, he appeals to the Leibnizian figure of the monad, the windowless space whose structure reproduces that of the universal yet which 'has no immediate access to universality'. The internalized universality of the monad finds a correlative in the artwork, insofar as both are intensified by their distance from the true universal: 'The relationship of the work and the universal becomes more profound the less the work copes explicitly with universalities, the more it becomes infatuated with its own detached world, its material, its problems, its consistency, its way of expression' (*NL2*, 297; *GS*11, 652). The exemplary artist in this regard is Proust, in whom is realized 'a truly theological idea, that of immortality'. He approaches this idea, however, in the paradoxical gesture of turning away from it, that is, by embracing the extremes of concretion. The obsessive exactitude with which Proust seeks to render the singular details of lived experience – 'the taste of a madeleine or the color of the shoes of a lady' – becomes the carrier of a desire 'to salvage life, as an image, from the throes of death ... by giving himself up to the most futile, the most insignificant, the most fugitive traces of memory' (*NL2*, 297–8; *GS*11, 653). Adorno's description of a universality approached by way of its opposite cannot fail to recall the strange movement of the profane in Benjamin's 'Theologico-Political Fragment', which comes closer to the messianic as it moves 'in the opposite direction': 'the profane assists, through being profane, the coming of the Messianic Kingdom'.[49] Proust's immersion in the profane is certainly not secularized theology – that is, it does not involve investing the objects of sensory memory with some intimation of the sacred. He approaches religious truth rather by retreating ever more deeply into the order of the profane. As such, he illuminates the unspoken and unspeakable religious itinerary of art, its paradoxical fidelity to religious in the form of 'an almost ascetic abstinence from any religious claim' (*NL2*, 294; *GS*11, 649).

This play of fidelity and abstinence is one of the most consistent threads of thought running through *Aesthetic Theory*. It is compacted in the term Adorno uses to describe the truth content of aesthetic experience: *Sehnsucht*, or longing – the very term Horkheimer employs to describe the latent religious content of the Critical Theory project. But if the artwork is a form of longing, does it do no more than articulate a melancholy impotence in the face of unredeemed life? Such a conclusion would rest on a fundamental misconstrual of how longing functions in the artwork. This function is characteristically paradoxical, even self-contradictory: 'Artworks would be powerless if they were no more than longing, though there is no valid artwork without longing'. The sentence appears to impose two conflicting demands on art – to transcend longing, and to sustain it. How might the artwork be 'more than longing' while resisting the lure of a false reconciliation? Adorno goes on: 'Not for-itself, with regard to consciousness, but in-itself, what is wants the other; the artwork is the language of this wanting, and the artwork's content [*Gehalt*] is as substantial as this wanting' (*AT*, 132; *GS*7, 199). If these terms consciously evoke Hegelian aesthetics, their use turns them against Hegel, for Adorno gives substance to longing – the very 'unhappy consciousness' that for

Hegel cannot yet be substance. In consciousness, longing merely mourns impotently the truth it fails to attain; but as content, longing transcends itself without thereby negating itself, or 'concretizes utopia without betraying it to existence' (*AT*, 132; *GS*7, 200).

The paradox of a substantial longing is elaborated more explicitly in the reading of Eichendorff's poem '*Sehnsucht*' at the end of Adorno's essay on the late romantic poet. The speaker of the poem, standing 'alone at the window', hearing a posthorn in the distance, speaks of a feverish desire to 'journey alone/in the magnificent summer night [*mitreisen .../In der prächtige Sommernacht*]' (*NL*1, 71; *GS*11, 85). Adorno points to the circular structure of the poem as the means by which *Sehnsucht* is both transcended and maintained. In the reappearance of the '*prächtige Sommernacht*' within the poet's ecstatically imagined journeying, longing is fulfilled by remaining itself: 'longing opens out onto itself as its proper goal, just as the one who yearns [*der Sehnsüchtige*] experiences his own situation in the infinity of longing, its transcendence beyond all specificity; just as love is always directed to love itself as much as the beloved'. Longing, then, fulfils itself in suspending its own fulfilment; indeed, fulfilment reveals itself as longing, 'the eternal contemplation of the godhead' (*NL*1, 72; *GS*11, 86).

The '*Sommernacht*' of Eichendorff's poem exemplifies what *Aesthetic Theory* calls the convergence in the artwork of the 'not-yet-existing' and remembrance. In an undisguised allusion to Proust, the irretrievable fullness of past experience becomes the figure for the unrealized utopia of the future: 'The object of art's longing, the reality of what is not, is metamorphosed in art as remembrance' (*AT*, 132; *GS*7, 200). This convergence of the irretrievable past and the unrealized future converge in Eichendorff's poem above all in its 'demonstrably derivative' language.

The apparently worn romantic tropes of nature transcend their overfamiliarity through transformation from 'a confirmed goal of the senses' into 'an allegory of longing' (*NL*1, 72; *GS*11, 86). Eichendorff's employment of a sedimented romantic rhetoric is not a failure of linguistic or perceptual precision, but an illumination of the gap between the ideal that rhetoric distantly evokes and the historical fate of real sensory experience. The remembrance of a nature prior to domination figures simultaneously an immemorial past and an unachieved future. Commenting on a line from Borchardt in *Aesthetic Theory*, Adorno describes this doubled temporal movement: 'The image of what is oldest in nature reverses dialectically into the cipher [*Chiffre*] of the not-yet-existing, the possible ...' (*AT*, 73; *GS*7, 115).

Aesthetic experience is nothing but this passion for the not-yet, for 'the ever-broken promise of happiness' (*AT*, 136; *GS* 7, 205), and as such in greater proximity to the truth claims of religion than modern positive religion. It is in terms of this proximity – which is also a distance – that we can understand the centrality of the second commandment as an organizing motif in *Aesthetic Theory* and across Adorno's later corpus. The interdiction of the graven image expresses not only a theological but equally an aesthetic truth: 'That one should make no image, which means no image of anything whatsoever, expresses at the same time that no such image is possible' (*AT*, 67; *GS*7, 115).[50] In revealing the theological truth about the impregnable resistance of transcendence to its integration, the prohibition on images simultaneously sheds light on the truth of art, and especially modern art; as Adorno notes, '[f]rom Rimbaud to contemporary avant-garde art, the obstinacy of this prohibition is unflagging' (*AT*, 22; *GS*7, 40). If modernity gives rise to a 'catastrophe of meaning', art must continually attest to this catastrophe by withholding meaning, by shattering the graven image which claims 'to have the infinite at its disposal' (*ND*, 13; *GS*6, 25). This shattering, precisely because it denies to consciousness any positive experience of the divine, is a profoundly though unspeakably religious act, perhaps the only possible religious act that can remain true for the modern subject. The passage cited at the outset of this chapter is testimony to this migration of religious truth into art; let us recall it:

> The total subjective elaboration [*Durchbildung*] of art as a nonconceptual [*nichtbegrifflichen*] language is the only figure, at the contemporary stage of rationality, in which something like the language of divine creation [*Sprache der Schöpfung*] is reflected, with the paradox that what is reflected is blocked. (*AT*, 78; *GS*7, 121)

If the structure of the sentence appears to separate these moments of reflection and blockage,[51] it is all the more important to insist on their inextricability; in the modern artwork, divine language is reflected only *in* this blockage, in its own impossibility.

Modern aesthetic experience thus realizes the governing imperative of Adorno's philosophy: 'For the sake of reconciliation [*Versöhnung*], authentic works must blot out every memory-trace [*Erinnerungsspur*] of reconciliation' (*AT*, 234; *GS*7, 348).[52]

Art remembers reconciliation in forgetting it, in abandoning any claim to its achievement. It is the privileged executor of the new categorical imperative because in it alone does the figure of utopia converge with its unrelenting renunciation. Modern positive religion, tethered to an illusory language which speaks as if the absolute were in its grasp, is fated to betray the promise of religion. It is the modern artwork's vigilant refusal of this language of illusion that renders it the sole possible bearer of this promise. The artwork worthy of the name works by way of the perpetual deferral of its resolution, its repeated restatement of itself as a question: 'Artworks that unfold to contemplation and thought without any remainder are not artworks' (*AT*, 121; *GS*7, 184). The artwork is thus subject to an aesthetic, ethical and – in the displaced sense we have set out here – religious imperative to maintain itself as a question. The task of art after Auschwitz is to submit itself unconditionally to this imperative.

ART AFTER AUSCHWITZ: BECKETT

But what might such an art look like? And, as importantly, given the prohibition of images, what must it refuse to look like? Adorno's overcited and under-interpreted pronouncement that '[t]o write poetry after Auschwitz is barbaric' (*P*, 34; *GS* 10.1, 30) points to a response to both questions. For Adorno's judgement on poetry after Auschwitz demands not that art be abandoned, but that it recognize the inescapable barbarism of its continued existence. In the wake of genocide, the very fact of art comes under suspicion: 'In its disproportion [*Misverhältnis*] to the horror that has transpired and threatens, it is condemned to cynicism; even where it directly faces the horror, it diverts attention from it' (*A T*, 234; *GS* 7, 348).

This disproportion gives rise to at least two possible future for the artwork. The first is to seek to minimize or disavow the horror by assimilating it to the space of representation, creating what Adorno scathingly calls 'a photograph of the disaster [*Unheils*]' (*A T*, 19; *GS* 7, 35). The second – the new aesthetic itinerary mapped out in *Aesthetic Theory* – is to make this very disproportion the condition and substance of the artwork, to expose itself to its own necessary failure. After Auschwitz, art labours under the burden of its 'inescapable affirmative essence'. If it is to maintain its own truth, we recall, 'it must turn against itself, in opposition to its own con-cept, and thus become uncertain of itself right into its innermost fiber' (*A T*, 2; *GS* 7, 10). *Aesthetic Theory* can be read as the attempt to reorient the classical voca-bulary of aesthetics towards this self-inversion. History itself has annihilated the conditions for the artwork's self-certainty, and it is in the form of this annihilation that it enters the artwork. Any attempt at representational adequation between the artwork and suffering violates the truth of the latter, which lies precisely in its strangeness to any possible knowledge. Art must absorb into itself the experience of its own collapse as a form of knowldge; hence its recurring description through-out *Aesthetic Theory* as 'uncertain', 'a question' or 'a failure'.

Through Adorno's late writings, the self-inversion of the artwork attached to one proper name in particular: Samuel Beckett. Beckett's authorship presupposes that thought and experience after Auschwitz go on under the shadow of 'the destruction of meaning'. Yet his plays' significance lie in their pushing 'beyond meaning's abstract negation', beyond, that is, a mere 'absence of any meaning' which would render them 'simply irrelevant'. Rather than signalling the end of all conceptual and aesthetic categories, 'they force traditional categories to undergo this experience [of the destruction of meaning] . . . they put meaning on trial; they unfold its history' (*A T*, 153; *GS* 7, 230). Rather than abandoning traditional cate-gories (which would only leave them intact), Beckett subjects them to their own crisis, and makes this crisis the very substance of his writing. Thus, the emancipa-tion of the plays becomes 'aesthetically meaningful . . . precisely because aesthetic meaning is not immediately one with theological meaning'. The non-coincidence of aesthetic and theological meaning allows meaninglessness to articulate itself 'with the same determinacy as traditional artworks enunciate their positive meaning' (*A T*, 153; *GS* 7, 230). Beckett's oeuvre is not other to meaning, knowledge or conceptuality; rather, it enacts their disintegration under the unbearable weight of history. Under Beckett's gaze, the negation of meaning becomes the means through which the artwork gains its content (*Gehalt*). The fulfilment of meaning has become one with its impossibility.

The difficult convergence of meaning and its negation is elaborated in Adorno's famous extended reading of Beckett's *Endgame*. The title of the essay – 'Trying to Understand *Endgame*' ('*Versuch, das Endspiel zu verstehen*') – compacts the plays doubled relation to the understanding, which Adorno characterizes thus: 'Understanding it can mean only understanding its unintelligibility [*Unverständlichkeit*], concretely reconstructing the meaning of the fact that it has no meaning' (*NL*1, 243; *GS* 11, 283). The play's unnamed and indeterminate post-apocalyptic landscape is the figure for this 'positive nothingness' (*A T*, 153; *GS* 7, 230). In postwar Europe, 'everything, including a resurrected culture, has been destroyed without realizing it; humankind continues to vegetate, creeping along after events that even the survivors [*Überlebenden*] cannot really survive, on a rubbish heap that has made even reflection on one's own damaged state [*Zerschlagenheit*] useless' (*NL*1, 244; *GS* 11, 285). The survivor – the one who 'lives on' (*lebt über*) – cannot really live on. Experience can no longer be reconciled with the concepts that would render it meaningful. 'Everything' is 'destroyed without realizing it'; that is, our faculty for imposing meaning – for 'realizing' – is a part of the 'everything' that has been destroyed. From this perspective, the understanding of Adorno's title can be read as the Kantian Understanding that brings intuitions under concepts. This faculty 'tries' to operate in the face of *Endgame*, only to find itself put on trial by a language and imagery which refuses conceptual subsumption, exposing the understanding to its own extinction.

Endgame is Adorno's exemplary post-Auschwitz text because in it this crisis of the understanding is given substantial form. It dramatizes this crisis not abstractly, in the form of some external perspective on the condition of its characters, but through the internal life of its language, both verbal and gestural. Language in the play gives voice not to the life but the death of the individual subject: the tortuously repetitive exchanges, wearisome tales, lame jokes, along with the ritually purposeless sequences of movement all attest to the prising apart of language from subjective intention. Clov, Hamm, Nell and Nagg's words give the lie to 'the individual's claim to autonomy and being [*Seinanspruch*]' (*NL*1, 249; *GS* 11, 291); the insubstantiality of their talk is that of subjectivity itself. The unnamed and unnamable apocalypse that precedes the play is the figure for an experience which has shattered the very substantiality of consciousness. Meaning, 'the discursive element in language', is transformed 'into an instrument of its own absurdity, following the ritual of the clown, whose babbling becomes nonsense by being presented as sense' (*NL*1, 262; *GS* 11, 306). This – the clownishness of language in the face of an experience that exceeds it – is the source of the play's privileged mode of expression: laughter. Laughter is the carrier of the final irreconcilability of subject and experience. It functions as a means of survival, of living on after life has ceased to live. It affirms universal bonds only in the form of their disintegration. Laughter occurs 'without a canon for what should be laughed about, without a place of reconciliation from which one could laugh' (*NL*1, 257; *GS* 11, 300).

When Adorno writes of Beckett's sense of the convergence of 'aesthetic transcendence and disenchantment' (*AT*, 79; *GS* 7, 123), he might be alluding to the function – or functionlessness – of laughter. Transcendence is made visible by being kept resolutely out of sight, fatally obscured by the laughter that speaks its terminal impossibility – an impossibility that is yet its only possibility.

If Beckett's writing reveals the truth of aesthetic experience after Auschwitz, it does not do so alone. In a more fragmentary and allusive way, *Aesthetic Theory* suggests that this truth may find a different but no less authentic voice in Paul Celan – poet and Jewish survivor.

CODA: CELAN

Despite his ambitions for a fuller study, Adorno had made only a few general references to Celan in his writings before his untimely death in 1969. The most extensive of these is one of the 'Paralipomena' to *Aesthetic Theory*. The paragraph opens with a reflection on the meaning of 'hermetic' poetry today. In a reprisal of an argument of his well-known 'Commitment' essay, he suggests that the hermetic work is the only mode through which art can now approach politics. In the face of a dominant 'pseudo-scientific' ideology that depends on 'communication' for its efficacy, 'art is integral only when it refuses to play along with communication' (*AT*, 321; *GS* 7, 476). The post-Mallarméan hermetic poem was not without its own ideological traps, however, inasmuch as it was prone to the lure of an 'art religion' which 'convinced itself that that the world was created for the sake of a beautiful verse or a well-turned phrase'. The hermeticism of Celan's poetry represents the inversion of this self-affirming aestheticism, and in this sense exemplifies the movement whereby art 'turns against itself'. Its monadic self-enclosure is the expression not of aesthetic rapture but of 'the shame of art in the face of suffering that escapes both experience and sublimation'. Adorno goes on to describe the way in which this shame insinuates itself into the poetry:

> Celan's poems want to speak of the most extreme horror through silence. Their truth content itself becomes negative. They imitate a language beneath the

helpless language of human beings, indeed beneath all organic language: it is
that of the dead speaking of stones and stars ... The infinite discretion with
which his radicalism proceeds compounds its force. The language of the lifeless
becomes the last possible comfort for a death that is deprived of all meaning.
(*AT*, 322; *GS 7*, 477)

Adorno's description reveals the inversion that the Kantian sublime undergoes
when exposed to the memory of the death camps; the awesome majesty of sublime
nature in Kant's 'Analytic' gives way to what Lacoue-Labarthe terms, 'the sublime of destitution'.[53] Adorno's fragmentary commentary confronts poetry with
the question of how it can articulate itself through silence and death? The readings
of two Celan poems – 'With A Changing Key' ('*Mit Wechselndem Schlüssel*') and
'A Rumbling' ('*Ein Dröhnen*') – that follow are an attempt to imagine an Adornian
response to this question. Let us begin by quoting the first poem in full:

> Mit wechselndem Schlüssel
> shließt du das Haus auf, darin
> der Schnee des Verschwiegenen treibt.
> Je nach dem Blut, das dir quillt
> aus Aug oder Mund oder Ohr,
> wechselt dein Schlüssel.
> Wechselt dein Schlüssel, wechselt das Wort,
> das treiben darf mit den Flocken.
> Je nach dem Wind, der dich forstößt,
> ballt um das Word sich der Schnee. (*SP*, 91)

> [With a changing key
> you unlock the house in which
> drifts the snow of the unspoken.
> Your key changes
> depending on the blood that gushes
> from your eye or mouth or ear.
> Your key changes, the word changes,
> that may drift with the flakes.
> What snowball forms around the word.
> Depends on the wind that rebuffs you.][54]

The poem speaks to Adorno's remarks in a number of telling ways. First, it
thematizes its own impossible desire to speak through silence, in the form of a
'lifeless' language of the elements. In the first three lines, the '*wechselndem Schlüssel*'
promises to bring the '*Verschwiegenen*' – literally discreet or secret – language of
night into the light of day. But this promise is haunted from the very beginning
by a philological ambiguity in the word '*aufschliesen*', which in the transitive form

used by Celan does indeed mean 'unlock'. Given the lines that follow, however, it is difficult to avoid hearing an echo of the verb's intransitive form, which translates as 'to close up' or lock. Certainly the poem appears to mime this doubleness, for what the key unlocks is not meaning, but a refusal to mean – unlocking in this sense falls into its opposite: the 'snow' of the unspoken seals itself off from communication.

In 'The Meridian', his 1960 speech on the occasion of receiving the Büchner prize, Celan speaks of '*Gegenworte*', literally 'counter-words' or 'a word against the grain'.[55] The *Gegenwort* is 'the word that cuts the "string", which does not bow to the "bystanders and old warhorses of history"'. It is an act of freedom. It is a step'.[56] From what does the *Gegenwort* set the poem free? Following Adorno, we might respond: from the strictures of 'communication', from the sedimented meanings legislated by the 'old warhorses of history'. *Aufschliesen* is a counter-word not only in the sense of its homonymous meaning, but in terms of its movement within the poem; the unspoken turns unlocking against itself, refusing it fulfilment. The sense of counter-movement is enforced by its being the only verb in the poem to take second-person form: the '*du*' of the second line is subject of the act of unlocking, but once performed, the act divests '*du*' of subjectivity. What occurs after the key turns is no longer in her grasp. Changes of key (ll4–6) depend not on the intentions of the '*du*', but on the involuntary and unforeseeable gushes of blood from 'eye', 'mouth' or 'ear'. The spark of traumatic memory may be ignited by seeing, speaking or hearing; each modality unlocks differently the space of the unspoken.

Writing of a different Celan poem ('*Engführung*'), Peter Szondi[57] points to an inversion of the poetic function of death which has immeasurable consequences for language. When the poem speaks of the dead as 'at home', this is not because, as the history of this trope might have us believe, death is 'the harbor to which one returned, because life is considered a journey; now it is so because Celan's poetry has its origin in death, in memory of the dead, in "remembrance"' (Szondi, 234). If the poem's origin is the memory of the dead, its language must always be a radical interruption of the living word. The insinuation of death into the poem destroys in advance the possibility of meaning's fulfilment, for death, in Adorno's words, is 'deprived of all meaning'. The promise opened up in the opening lines of '*Mit Wechselndem Schlüssel*', of unlocking the secrets of silence, is fated to be broken – the turn of the key reveals only the resistance of the unspoken to speech. The gush of blood is thus the figure for a 'shame' that engenders both the desire to make speak the unspoken, and the refusal of the unspoken to be drawn into language.

The poem's second stanza further unfolds this failure to release the meaning of the unspoken. The key or word which promised to clear the snow to reveal a concealed truth, instead succumbs to the same concealment, finding itself free to 'drift with the flakes'. The key-word that wanted to distinguish itself from the snow has become part of it, approaching the same unreadable condition of whiteness, until, in the poem's concluding lines, a snowball has formed around it. The shape of this snowball cannot be foreseen, however, for there is no telling just how the wind – the poem's second *Gegenwort* – will rebuff the seeker after the secret. Every act of speech after Auschwitz, and especially of poetic speech, tells the story of this rebuff in its own singular way, to form a different snowball. Each poem attests anew to its failure to fulfil its own intention.

For Celan, then, the poem is the space in which the possibility of approaching the unspoken is expressed as its impossibility: truth is the block on truth. This experience of truth as its own accessibility takes on new form in '*Ein Dröhnen*'. The poem's six short lines read thus:

> EIN DRÖHNEN: es ist
> die Wahrheit selbst
> unter die Menschen
> getreten,
> mitten ins
> Metapherngestöber. (SP, 270)

> [A RUMBLING: it is
> Truth itself
> appeared
> among humankind,
> in the middle of their
> flurrying metaphors.][58]

Truth cannot appear apart from that which prevents its appearance; the poem presents us with the essential dilemma of poetry, its dependence on the very language it wishes to silence in order to let truth emerge in its immediacy. '*Dröhnen*' – variously, according to the dictionary, rumbling, ringing, the roaring of a motor – echoes Borchardt's '*Rauschen*', the murmuring of language itself, but equally the noise of '*Metapherngestöber*', quotidian language. The rumbling of one is indistinguishable (or barely distinguishable) from the other; the noise of truth is also the noise that drowns it out. The word '*getreten*' occupies a line of its own, miming its separateness from '*Wahrheit selbst*': truth is separated from its appearance by '*die Menschen*' among whom it appears, sandwiched imperceptibly between them and their worn metaphors.

In revealing the radical concealment of truth, then, Celan's poetry reveals the blocked religious content of art after Auschwitz. If art today is the 'sole task of thought', that of thinking from the standpoint of redemption, it is because it alone is able to approach truth without traducing it; for its mode of approach is also the experience of a block, of truth 'rebuffing' the word. Holding to this task, Celan renounces redemption; but only this renunciation keeps open its possibility.

CHAPTER 3

'Absolute Insomnia':
Interrupting Religion, or Levinas

Towards the end of his 1975 Talmudic reading, 'Damages Due to Fire', Emmanuel Levinas draws from his chosen text (*Baba Kama*, 60a–b) the revelation of a disquieting continuum between peace, war and holocaust. Warning of the angel of death who, deprived of the liberty granted him by war, 'slinks along in hiding' when the city is at peace, the text augurs a condition in which, writes Levinas:

> Everywhere war and murder lie concealed, assassination lurks in every corner, killings go on on the sly. There would be no radical difference between peace and Auschwitz. I do not think pessimism can go much beyond this. Evil suppresses human responsibility and leaves no corner intact where reason could collect itself.
>
> But perhaps this thesis is precisely a call to man's infinite responsibility, to an untiring [*inlassable*] wakefulness, to an absolute insomnia. (*NTR*, 193; *DSS*, 174)[1]

While Levinas' post-war corpus is scattered with intimations of the demand Auschwitz has imposed on his life and thought,[2] nowhere is the nature of this demand more explicitly specified than in these lines of commentary.

What relationship do these lines forge between the war-like peace they describe and the imperative to 'absolute insomnia' they subsequently announce? It is tempting to read off them a kind of ethical theodicy whereby evil is justified by the good it awakens. Yet Levinas' language is directed with some precision against such a reading; he suggests not that the thesis of ubiquitous murder engenders a posterior call to responsibility, but this thesis *is* (or 'perhaps' is – an essential tentativeness attaches to every one of Levinas' attempts to specify the event of the ethical) this call. The distinction is more than pedantic; just as fidelity to Adorno's 'new categorical imperative' demands a suspension of the claim to have fulfilled it, so Levinas' 'call to infinite responsibility' can be heard only as the experience of evil rather than its overcoming. Responsibility cannot annul evil without thereby annulling itself, curbing its infinity, putting its insomnia to sleep. Indeed the very vocabulary of responsibility – 'untiring wakefulness, absolute insomnia' – attests to its essential irredeemability. To be responsible is perhaps to undergo the very suffering responsibility seeks in vain to redeem.

Levinas' ethical philosophy, and in particular his near-contemporary work *Otherwise Than Being, or Beyond Essence* (*Autrement qu'être ou au-delà de l'essence*) teaches the *unassumability* of such a responsibility, its anteriority to any choice or decision I might make. A debt 'older' than any contract, increasing the more it is paid, Levinasian responsibility names an ethics which refuses its own fulfilment; it 'takes place' only in the form of a vigilantly maintained failure to take place. If Auschwitz imposes a task upon thought and action, it is one that takes its force from a resistance either to assumption or accomplishment, and whose accomplishment, paradoxically, *is* this resistance.

In what form does this task come to us? If the question is difficult to answer, it is because the 'form' of the Levinasian task is the dissolution of every form, the erasure of every statement of itself. Thus if, as we inevitably must, we name this task an 'ethics', we will be pointing not to a set of particular and identifiable moral prescriptions, but, to use Jacques Derrida's phrase, to 'an ethics of ethics',[3] that is, a thinking of the conditions of possibility (or, perhaps, of impossibility) of any ethics whatever. This 'ethicity' is a relation with the Other in his or her absolute immediacy, a 'relation without relation' which ' "absolves" [the Other's absolute exteriority] from the relation in which it presents itself' (*TaI*, 50; *TeI*, 21).

As his commentators have not ceased to insist, such a relation is defined by the very impossibility of its appearing or taking place *as such*, by what Maurice Blanchot calls the impossible experience of immediacy, 'the infinite presence of what remains radically absent' (*IC*, 38; *EI*, 54). But is this impossibility to be thought of only negatively, as that which ruins itself? Does it not name at the same time a passion, an infinite demand? This chapter will identify this demand in what Levinas names religion, with a gesture which turns the very term against itself. Religion for Levinas signifies not the struggle for the reconciliation of finite being and the Absolute but their untiringly preserved non-reconciliation: 'Religion, where relationship subsists between the same and the other despite the impossibility of the Whole – the idea of Infinity – is the ultimate structure' (*TaI*, 80; *TeI*, 53).[4]

How does this 'ultimate structure' insinuate itself into finite human experience? This chapter will develop a number of possible responses to this question – the ethical relation, 'the extraordinary proname' of God, and finally, the imperative of political justice. It will identify in Levinas' Judaism – as articulated through the 'confessional' essays and Talmudic readings – a privileged structure for maintaining these questions. Religion, in short, will be read as the carrier of the insomniac task of responsibility to which Auschwitz calls us.

Yet the ultimacy Levinas confers on religion gives rise to the question of another, more ambiguous mode of transcendence to which he insistently returns with a profound and instructive ambivalence: the question of art.

ETHICS CONTRA ART

Levinas' writings on art do not yield a coherent and unified aesthetic. Taken together, they read rather as an ongoing interrogation of the aesthetic's troubling relation to the ethical; troubling because of what seems to be their simultaneous affinity to and suspicion of one another. The distance Levinas interposes between art and ethics is shadowed by a proximity which he seems at times to want to disavow and at others to expose.

Certainly, Levinas' earliest writings on art, most notably his 1948 essay 'Reality and Its Shadow', are marked by a note of intense suspicion, if not hostility. What is it that sets Levinas against art in these early texts? 'Reality and Its Shadow' provides at least two related responses:

1 Art is the modality through which the spurious infinity of the *il y a* (*there is*) reveals itself. The *il y a* is the term Levinas develops in his short book of the previous year, *From Existence to Existents*.[5] It names a horror before the irremissibility of being, an impossibility of nothingness that takes the form, or non-form, of an obscure, nocturnal Something preceding and haunting the world of 'economy'. It is an elemental materiality, 'a content obtained through the negation of all content ... like a density of the void, like a murmur of silence' (*EE*, 63; *DEE*, 104). If art's element is the *il y a*, it is because it is the very event of obscuring, of 'a descent [*tombée*] into the night, an invasion of shadow' ('RS', 132; 'RO', 773) which neutralizes the concept–object relation and gives rise to the dangerous sovereignty of the image, that is, of the object withdrawn from the order of the real. In the image, reality appears not against the horizon of a world, but 'in its exotic nakedness as a worldless reality' (*EE*, 55; *DEE*, 88). To be subjected to the image is to be possessed by its essential *musicality*, to yield up one's initiative and freedom to the nocturnal disorder of rhythm. Aesthetic experience is the exemplary form of what Levinas, after the anthropologist Levy-Bruhl, calls participation,[6] the passive fusion of the self with the mythical or pagan divinity of the elements.

It is hard to avoid hearing the resonance of the early Nietzsche in this description of aesthetic experience, and more particularly of *The Birth of Tragedy*'s thesis of the essential musicality of the artwork. For Nietzsche, music symbolizes a sphere which is earlier than appearance and beyond it'.[7] The Dionysian musician is the dissolution of every determinate form, exposing us to 'the horror of individual existence' (Nietzsche, 102; 114); 'himself imageless', he 'is nothing but original pain and reverberation of the image' (Nietzsche, 39; 41). Levinas' account of the artwork points up the same reversion to nothingness, the withdrawal of objects from the world which would confer determinate meaning on them, yielding to that 'imageless' music through which 'a quality can divest itself of objectivity – and consequently of all subjectivity …' (*EE*, 53; *DEE*, 86). The avowed hostility of 'Reality and Its Shadow' to art is thrown into relief by this Nietzschean reverberation, for, as will be seen, Levinas' ethics is heavily staked in the sober renunciation of ecstatic Dionysiac intoxication.

2   Levinas' second objection to art evokes the other side of Nietzschean art, the ordered domain of Appolonian form. If the obscurity of the image reveals its essential musicality, its withdrawal from the 'real' world of language and concepts discloses its essential *plasticity*. In an unashamedly Platonic move, Levinas describes the artwork as 'a semblance of existing', a 'lifeless life, a derisory life which is not master of itself, a caricature of life' ('RS', 137–8; 'RO', 781–2). The idolatrous nature of art stems from this divestment of the life, and more specifically the *time* of being. If 'every artwork is in the end a statue' ('RS', 137; 'RO', 782), it is because it freezes being in an 'immobile instant' it is powerless to move beyond: 'this present, impotent to force the future, is fate itself, that fate refractory to the will of the pagan gods, stronger than the rational necessity of natural laws' ('RS', 138; 'RO', 783). Because fate strips human will of the capacity to assume its future, rendering it passive and immobile, it is the very contrary of ethical existence – 'irresponsible', 'wicked', 'egoist' and 'cowardly'.

At this point in his authorship, then, Levinas seems unable to think art apart from myth, from the sham infinity of the pagan elements which paralyses the moral will. Nevertheless, it is worth observing that the terms he invokes to describe the ethical – freedom, initiative, assumption[8] – are the key terms of ethics as thought by tradition, that is, as a secondary region of philosophy, and as such the very terms *against which* Levinas' mature philosophy will think the ethical. It should be further noted that the terms which he invokes to impugn the aesthetic – passivity, impotence, obscurity – will be the very terms through which he elaborates his account of ethical subjectivity in his second major work, *Otherwise Than Being, or Beyond Essence*.

Nevertheless, *Totality and Infinity* continues, thirteen years after 'Reality and Its Shadow', to be invested in rigorously distinguishing the language of art and the *il y a* from that of ethics. Here, the critique of participation and the nocturnal universe of the *il y a* is integrated into Levinas' ethical metaphysics. Participation is here associated with 'enrootedness', a mode of 'primordial preconnection' which 'would maintain participation as one of the sovereign categories of being, whereas the notion of truth marks the end of this reign' (*TaI*, 60–1; *TeI*, 32). The truth gestured towards by participation is that of elemental infinity of being, and as such always falls short of truth. Levinas is signalling, of course, his designation of the ethical as a truth 'beyond being', outside of the purview of existence. Tethered to the obscure, impersonal and faceless gods of myth, the transcendence of the *il y a* is that of a 'transdescendence', a degraded absolute of the below, in contrast to the infinite height of the 'transascendance' of the ethical relation.[9] These spatialized terms intimate an ominous *neutrality* at the heart of transcendence which will become increasingly significant for his treatment of the question of evil. Transcendence – that which refuses all conceptual mediation – is not synonymous with the Good, but lends itself to the service of both the heights *and* depths of the ethical.

Thus, set in the context of Levinas' corpus, the apparent urgency of this distinction between two modes of transcendence would seem to arise from the very difficulty of sustaining it. Both ethical and poetic speech are defined by a 'pure experience' of signification, an immediacy of language prior to any content. As Jill Robbins argues, at this level of the 'quasi-transcendental' condition of language, such distinctions, in attempting to give a determination – whether ethical or aesthetic – to what is refractory to any determination, becomes impossible to sustain. Can we consistently oppose bad to good exteriority, false to true transcendence without doing violence to exteriority itself? 'Can we be sure that the two do not communicate with each other, interpenetrate and contaminate one another . . .?'.[10] If pure signification or, to use Levinas' term 'signification *kath' auto* [out of itself]' is what evades capture by a theme, how can we determine it as purely ethical or impurely aesthetic without falling into the very thematization we sought to escape?

LANGUAGE, ART AND EVIL: AFTER BLANCHOT

Yet one very significant thread running through Levinas' life and thought sees this apparently rigid distinction called into question: his friendship and ongoing conversation with Maurice Blanchot. In his periodic essays on the writer and critic (collected in the 1976 volume *Sur Maurice Blanchot*), the distance at which he elsewhere holds poetic and ethical signification apart seems to contract. The Blanchotian poetic reveals an ineluctable proximity of the horror of the *il y a* to ethical Desire, a proximity which Blanchot himself draws out in his successive writings on Levinas.

Levinas' 1956 essay 'The Poet's Vision', a commentary on Blanchot's *L'Espace Littéraire* (published the previous year), attests to an awareness, five years prior to *Totality and Infinity*, of the curious and complex kinship of Blanchot's poetic language to his own pre-significative language of ethics. Paraphrasing Blanchot, he writes, 'literature lets speak and be accomplished that which is most radically non-world: the being of beings, the very presence of their disappearance' (*PN*, 131; *SMB*, 15). The 'fundamental experience' of literature is one of 'absolute exteriority', an exposure to an absence prior to any presence–absence opposition, an absence which is the necessary condition of any possible presence: 'a prior [*préalable*] transcendence . . . is required in order for things to be able to be perceived as images' (*PN*, 130; *SMB*, 13).

Levinas' essay, like all of his writing on Blanchot, seems to fight shy of any explicit statement of affinity with or divergence from the latter. Yet an implicit avowal of their affinity is undoubtedly audible in his attempt, towards the end of the essay, to draw the Blanchotian away from the Heideggerian poetic (even as he acknowledges their 'high degree of proximity').[11] If the Heideggerian poem is 'a primordial disclosure' it is nevertheless a ' "disclosure of being" ', a drawing of the obscurity of experience into the light of 'unconcealment'; whereas, 'In Blanchot, *the work uncovers, in an uncovering that is not truth*, a darkness' (*PN*, 136, Levinas' emphasis; *SMB*, 22). Exactly what is at stake for Levinas in this distinction? The primordial darkness of Blanchot's poetic language signals 'an uprooting [of] the Heideggerian universe', that is, of a thought for which being is the ultimate horizon. In the movement of 'uncovering' which yields no truth, which discloses only darkness, is intimated the suspicion of an Outside which ruins the totality of consciousness.

It is worth pausing to observe that the terms which in this later essay augur a break-up of totality and a departure from the horizon of beings – withdrawal, obscurity, non-truth – are the very same ones which in 'Reality and Its Shadow' were turned against the artwork. Between the earlier, general critique of art and the later appreciation of Blanchot, two turns appear to have been taken in Levinas' thought: first, rather than enacting a necessary evasion of or withdrawal from responsibility, the artwork – at least as conceived by Blanchot – may in fact open us to the Other by exposing us to what escapes the reach of consciousness. Second, Levinas' thinking of the ethical has surrendered the language of initiative and assumption which gave the earlier essay such an anachronistically moralizing tone.

Blanchot's two sustained meditations on Levinas – the first comprising three consecutive essays in *The Infinite Conversation*, the second a series of fragments initially published separately, and later integrated into the first part of *The Writing of the Disaster* – respond, respectively, to *Totality and Infinity* and *Otherwise Than Being*.[12] Both texts push Levinas' 'relation without relation' towards a term to which he frequently appears antagonistic: writing. Rather than force this affinity, however, Blanchot allows it to emerge via an acknowledgement of Levinas' suspicion of poetry.

Indeed, the three essays from *The Infinite Conversation*, written in the form of conversation between two anonymous interlocutors, hinge on just this suspicion. In the first of the three pieces, 'Knowledge of the Unknown', one of the interlocutors wonders whether the asymmetrical and insatiable desire for the Other that Levinas describes might be fittingly characterized by the poet René Char's 'superb words': 'The poem is the realized love of desire that has remained desire'. The other speaker replies, 'Levinas mistrusts poems and poetic activity, but when

Simone Weil writes "Desire is impossible" – which we commented upon by saying "Desire is precisely this relation to the impossible, it is impossibility become relation" – perhaps such a manner of speaking would not be out of place' (*IC*, 53; *EI*, 76). The exchange is revealing because the mistrust of poetry the second speaker recognizes in Levinas fails to erase the affinity between the latter and Char insinuated by the first speaker. Instead, the relation between an impossible desire and the poetic is simultaneously suggested and suspended, maintaining the two in a precarious mode of contact.

It is this contact which looms behind the questions Blanchot goes on to put to Levinas' key term: ethics. The first question, even while acknowledging the unexpectedness and courage of Levinas' defence of morality 'in a time when no one expects anything "good" to come of morals' (*IC*, 54; *EI*, 78), questions whether 'the general name "ethics" [is] in keeping with the impossible relation that is revealed in the relation of *autrui*, which far from being a particular case, precedes any relation of knowledge?' (*IC*, 55; *EI*, 55).

Blanchot's question points up those moments within Levinas' thought where exteriority is put under threat by a secondary or derivative language which is insufficiently conscious of itself. The threat is most intensified in *Totality and Infinity* in the privileging of speech over writing, a privilege that helps illuminate its hostile treatment of art. For Levinas, the pre-significative language of ethics expresses not a particular content, but the very fact of relationality itself. As exposure to absolute alterity, language manifests 'the coinciding of revealer and revealed', that is, a word without mediation. This immediacy is repeatedly named in the text as '*droiture*', rightness or, as his English translator has it, 'straightforwardness'. It is in the light of this *droiture* that the artwork's distance from the ethical discloses itself, for as we have seen, art is inscribed by a doubleness which contaminates *droiture* with an ineradicable obscurity: if '[t]o be good is to be *kath' auto*' (*TeI*, 183; *TaI*, 158), then the artwork cannot be good. Here, then, is the source of the book's insistent phonocentrism – where language enables the attendance of the signified by the one signifying, written language has always already reverted to the secondary status of the sign: 'Signs are a mute language, a language impeded' (*TeI*, 182; *TaI*, 157).

Blanchot responds to this phonocentrism by consciously inverting its terms, suggesting that far from maintaining the Other, speech as Levinas describes it threatens to reapproprate it. If oral discourse is 'a manifestation without peer', it is because of the attendance of speech by its speaker, who 'is always ready to answer for it, to justify and clarify it, contrary to what happens when it is written. Let us for a moment admit this, though I hardly believe it. We see, in any case, that the privilege of spoken language belongs *equally* to the Other and to the Self, and thus makes them equal . . .' (*IC*, 56; *EI*, 81). It is the very 'advantages' of speech, in other words – clarity, answerability, sincerity – that, in being extended to all speakers, compromise the radical asymmetry, indeed impossibility, of the relation to the Other: 'The thought that recognizes in the Other this dimension of radical exteriority with respect to the Self cannot at the same time ask of interiority that it furnish a common denominator between the Self and the Other' (*IC*, 57; *EI*, 81).

To a speech which expresses the 'coinciding of revealer and revealed . . .' (*TaI*, 67; *TeI*, 38), Blanchot counterposes a speech which perpetually withdraws from the signified, a speech which in a self-conscious paradox which, of course, anticipates Derrida, is identified in the third of the essays on Levinas ('The Relation of the Third Kind: Man without Horizon') as *writing*. Writing, as that which dispossesses the writer of selfhood, exposing him to that space in which he becomes other; as that which forever 'denies the substance of what it represents' (*WF*, 310; *PF*, 314) and which places us at an infinite distance from what we would comprehend, is for Blanchot the exemplary access to the Levinasian relation without relation: '*Language, the experience of language – writing – is what leads us to sense a relation entirely other* . . .' (*IC*, 73, Blanchot's emphasis; *EI*, 103). Blanchot thus insists on the very affinity between writing and primordial signification which Levinas seems so intent on refusing. Indeed, he seems to suggest that it is *ethics*, and not poetry, which threatens to relativize the absoluteness of exteriority.

Though he never responds explicitly to Blanchot's questions, their ongoing mutual commentary undoubtedly provides Levinas with a space in which to deepen his thinking of the relationship between poetic and ethical language. This rethinking is made most explicit in his 1971 'Conversation with André Dalmas', in which *the il y a* is displaced from its position at the opposite pole of the Other. In response to Dalmas' suggestion that writing 'disrupts, shakes and disperses the *said*', Levinas points to 'two directions' in which interpretation of Blanchot can lead. The fist takes us to the revocation of meaning engendered by the *il y a*, whereby '[w]e are delivered up to the inhuman, to the frightfulness [*l'effrayant*] of the neuter' (*PN*, 154; *SMB*, 51). Yet what Levinas calls the 'second direction' is not in any sense the positive departure from the first that we might expect. There is no intimation of a positive Infinite in Blanchot, but rather a negative critique of the ordered, indifferent totality of the world:

> Blanchot reminds that world that its totality is not total – that the coherent discourse it vaunts does not catch up with another discourse with it fails to silence. That other discourse is troubled by an uninterrupted noise. A difference that does not let the world sleep, and troubles the order in which being and nonbeing are ordered in a dialectic. (*PN*, 154–5; *SMB*, 51–2)

Where in *Totality and Infinity* the inhumanity of the Neuter is directly opposed to the height of the Other, Blanchot seems to point to a different relation between the two, in which the one is the opening onto the other. It is the same relation we identified at the outset of this chapter in Levinas' 1975 Talmudic reading: exposure

to the inhuman is to be understood not as a transitional moment in the progress to
the ethical. Rather, the two must be thought of in their difficult simultaneity.

What is it that induces this subtle yet decisive shift in Levinas' thought? How do
art and the elemental terror it exposes come to insinuate themselves at the heart of
the very ethical experience to which they were once opposed? Reading across his
later writings, this shift seems indissociable from the 'Nazi horror' whose 'presentiment and memory' (DF, 291; DL, 374) has dominated his life and work. The final
contribution to the Blanchot collection, 'Exercises on "The Madness of the Day"'
(published the same year as 'Damages Due to Fire'), directly identifies Auschwitz as
the thought behind this intrication of writing and ethics. 'The Madness of the Day',
Blanchot's brutally compacted anti-narrative 'written shortly after the Liberation',
describes a world withdrawn from sense, a descent of the clarity of day into the
hellish indeterminacy of madness: 'the light was going mad' writes its anonymous
narrator, 'the brightness had lost all reason, it assailed me irrationally, without
control, without purpose'.[13] The light of Blanchot's 'mad' day is wrenched from
its illuminating function, placed in a relation of radical proximity to darkness.
Juxtaposed against Levinas' Talmudic reading of 1975, its irrational brightness
anticipates disquietingly that state of war-like peace in which evil 'leaves no
corner intact where reason could collect itself' (NTR, 194; DSS, 173). The affinity
of the texts underscores Levinas' suggestion as to the historical source of this
total (and in Blanchot's case literal) eclipse of reason. In this 'hellish unfreedom' of
irrational malevolence ('an unfreedom less free than any determinism and any
tragedy'), he locates

> [a] movement maintained in a maintenance that, in a human Self, is suffocation
> in self. The madness of the now, the madness of the day. The madness of Ausch-
> witz, which does not succeed in passing (qui n'arrive pas à passer). Is the structure
> of the present – the actual, the Today – like this? The infernal. The infernal that
> shows itself in the temporality of time, maintaining it. (PN, 159; SMB, 60)

The Auschwitz intimated without reference in Blanchot's narrative exposes an
infernal consignment to a time without progress, an instant that never releases the
subject from its grip.[14] This irremissible present ruins the clarity of distinctions,
drawing good and evil into a zone of terrifying indistinction, dramatized potently
in one of the text's key episodes.

The incident, in the context of the récit's infernal landscape, appears almost
tauntingly trivial: the narrator witnesses, a few steps away, a woman manoeuvring
a baby carriage through a door. A man walking through the same door at that
moment steps back, enabling the woman to lift the carriage and enter the house.
'Seized by joy', the narrator walks to the house and looks through the opening,
where he sees 'the black edge of a courtyard ... As the cold wrapped around

me from head to foot I slowly felt my great height take on the dimensions of this boundless cold'.[15]

Levinas' gloss on this passage seems at first to assimilate it unproblematically to his own project: 'something abnormal ensues: one person withdraws before the other, one *is* for the other. Whence the narrator's lightheartedness, which seems to lift him above being' (*PN*, 166, Levinas' emphasis; *SMB*, 68). Ethical transcendence, then, has broken through the brutal anonymity of being; and yet, as Levinas goes on to remark, this event is far from being free of ambiguity: 'A misleading event, which is immediately confused with the dark chill of anonymity – with the cosmic coldness chilling the narrator, who looks into the depths of a dark [*obscur*] courtyard, to the bone. The silence of those infinite spaces . . .' (*PN*, 166; *SMB*, 68). The madness of the day – of Auschwitz – divests the encounter with the Other of its *droiture*, consigning it to an obscurity from which it cannot escape unmarked.

Auschwitz marks the infinite distance between art as conceived in 'Reality and Its Shadow', and in Blanchot. As Paul Davies argues, where the earlier Levinas saw in art's withdrawal from the real a self-interested distraction from responsibility, the Levinas of the Blanchot essays sees art lose its 'protective naiveté'.[16] This risky self-exposure is the infinite burden placed on art by the Nazi horror; '. . . when Levinas does speak positively about art', observes Jill Robbins, '. . . art always has a relation to the Holocaust' (Robbins, 133).

A number of other essays in *Proper Names* confirm Robbins' observation. Those poets whose language has been formed by the experience (Celan) or memory (Jabés) of Auschwitz enact the very rupture of being which characterizes the ethical relation. In Celan, '[t]he fact of speaking to the other – the poem – precedes all thematization' (*PN*, 44; *NP*, 63), while in Jabès, the 'true poet . . . is that which, in the eminent sense of the term, *loses its place*, ceases occupation, precisely, and is thus the very opening of space' (*PN*, 63, Levinas' emphasis; *NP*, 93). No longer enclosed within its own privileged language, poetry for Celan names the very condition of possibility of relation; unable to take refuge in the eternal and invulnerable safe-house of art, the poet in Jabès has become rather the impossibility of refuge. Auschwitz, in short, forces art's passage from self-gratifying aestheticism to the vulnerability of responsibility.

Nowhere, moreover, is this intrication of writing and Auschwitz more passionately interrogated than in Blanchot's final response to Levinas in *The Writing of the Disaster*. The book comprises a series of mutually interruptive fragments, in which 'disaster' figures as that which destines writing to its measureless self-erasure. As the experience which 'escapes [*soustrait*] the very possibility of experience' (*WD*, 7; *ED*, 17) – that is of conceptuality, intelligibility, positive meaning – Auschwitz introduces into writing its own impossibility. It is Levinas' *Otherwise Than Being* that provides Blanchot with a language for this impossibility. Two terms from Levinas' book in particular resurface obsessively in *The Writing of the*

Disaster: passivity and responsibility. For Levinas, passivity is the impossible experience of exposure to an obligation I have not chosen and which is anterior to any choice: 'an offering oneself which is not even assumed by its own generosity, an offering oneself that is a suffering, a goodness despite oneself' (*OB*, 54; *AE*, 70). Goodness is that precarious condition in which I find myself – passively, without assumption – as soon as I acknowledge my primordial exposure to the Other's command. In the passivity of 'goodness despite oneself', the self's possession of itself – *its selfhood* – discovers itself always already ruined. As recast by Blanchot, passivity becomes the very impossibility of writing as willed activity: 'To want to write: what an absurdity. Writing is the decay of will, just as it is the loss of power' (*WD*, 11; *ED*, 24).

Levinas' intimately related term responsibility, in turn, names the infinite unassumability of my obligation to the Other, inasmuch as responsibility is constitutively insatiable, perhaps insatiability itself, for the pre-original 'debt' of responsibility is increased the more I seek to fulfil it. Blanchot finds in this term a radical estrangement of its sedimented bourgeois associations – responsibility, far from the undertaking of a determinate and finite duty, is a term that can only annul itself, for '[i]t requires . . . that I answer for the impossibility of being responsible – to which this responsibility without measure has already consigned me by holding me accountable and also discounting me altogether [*me dévouant et me dévoyant*]' (*WD*, 25; *ED*, 46).[17] This 'discounting' of self – the withdrawal of language from both action and revelation – is that movement of dispossession which Blanchot has insistently named 'writing'. A double annihilation, literary speech denies the existence of both speech and speaker: 'if my speech reveals being in its nonexistence [*inexistence*], it also affirms that this revelation is being made on the basis of the nonexistence of the person making it, out of his power to remove himself from himself, to be other than his being'.[18] To write is to expose the self's otherness to itself which everyday or dialectical speech can only disavow.

It is at this moment of dispossession or 'denucleation', then, that Blanchotian writing and Levinasian ethics converge – that is, at the point of disaster. The ethical itinerary to which Auschwitz consigns us is in this sense an inescapably *writerly* itinerary; not, of course, in the sense that ethics would be subsumed under or dissolved into writing, but rather that it comes to assume writing's constitutively paradoxical structure.

LANGUAGE, TIME AND THE IMPOSSIBLE

The ambivalent status of art in Levinas' authorship can be ascribed to an irreducible ambiguity introduced by Auschwitz into thought. Auschwitz marks the point at which those distinctions made in *Totality and Infinity* between clarity and obscurity, frankness and dissimulation, indeed between good and evil, come under insupportable strain. Nowhere is the effect of this strain more evident than in the changes to which Levinas subjects his thinking of language in the thirteen years between *Totality and Infinity* and *Otherwise Than Being*. Language in the former text, as has been shown, is characterized by an uncontaminated immediacy expressing, prior to any content, the very fact of relationality as signified in the face. The interruptive approach of the Other's face accomplishes 'the coincidence of the revealer and the revealed' (*TaI*, 67; *TeI*, 38), liberating the Other in advance from the thematization or comprehension to which my gaze would subject her.[19] As will presently be shown, the subsequent course of Levinas' thought sees language increasingly divested of this pure immediacy by means of its exposure to time or 'diachrony'. Language, by the time of his late work, can no longer be unambiguously opposed as ethical clarity to art's irresponsible obscurity, and the erosion of this opposition has significant implications for Levinas' ethics and politics.

Totality and Infinity, however, seems to draw back from the radical implications of its own conception of language. As Blanchot revealed, rather than develop the paradox of impossibility in which the idea of linguistic immediacy is always already caught, Levinas attempts to resolve it by appealing to the *droiture* which the speaker's attendance of his speech brings to the word. It would seem that in speech, at least as *Totality and Infinity* conceives it, *droiture appears* – is coerced into phenomenality – and it is in this appearance that Blanchot perceives a threat to the Other's radical exteriority.

The 1961 text, then, preserves the immediacy of language from its own impossibility, or put another way, from time as diachrony – time's irreducible non-coincidence with itself – inasmuch as it is diachrony which *prevents* the Other from appearing, protects him from the light of phenomenality. As will presently be shown, the discourse of temporality in *Totality and Infinity* persistently undermines the text's claims for the immediacy of speech. The chapter entitled 'The Ethical Relation and Time' defines temporality as a logic of postponement, where, contra Heidegger, the mortal being's relation to death is experienced as an unrelieved 'not-yet': 'Time is precisely the fact that the whole existence of the mortal being – exposed to [*offert à*] violence – is not being for death, but the "not-yet" which is a way of being against death, a retreat before death in the very midst of its inexorable approach' (*TaI*, 224; *TeI*, 199). Death – Heidegger's ownmost possibility of being[20] – is for Levinas being's exposure to its *im*possibility, inasmuch as its approach can only ever be experienced as a retreat, as what exceeds the horizon of my possibilities the more I attempt to grasp it.[21] The infinite time of death *is* this ungraspability, 'maintained', as Dennis Keenan puts it, 'at a distance from itself . . . in the interval of the not yet . . .'.[22]

Earlier in the book, Levinas takes pains to distinguish this thought of death as inassimilable alterity from death as conceived by the historiographer, for whom death renders intelligible and objectifiable the meaning of a life. '[T]he common time of history' annuls the 'dead' or postponed time of the not-yet, drawing the deceased being into the totality of a continuous narrative: 'In the totality of a historiographer the death of the other is an end, the point at which the separated being is cast into the totality, and at which, consequently, *dying* can be passed through [*dépassé*] and past [*passé*] ...' (*TaI*, 56; *TeI*, 27). But the time of interiority or 'psychism' exposes this Hegelianized narrative to its impossibility; the 'agony' of the dying being consists precisely in the inability to apprehend and appropriate this end for itself, for this end is what approaches my comprehension only by retreating; for this reason, 'death is ... not reducible to the end of a being ... Dying is an agony [*angoisse*] because in dying a being does not come to an end while coming to an end ...]' (*TaI*, 56; *TeI*, 27). The mortal being can experience his own end only in the paradoxical mode of a non-experience, a withdrawal from revelation that places an insuperable block between dying and death: 'In the impossibility of knowing the after my death resides the essence of the last moment [*l'instant suprême*]' (*TaI*, 234; *TeI*, 211).

Levinas' temporality of postponement thus casts an ambiguous light on his conception of language as absolute immediacy or 'the coincidence of the revealer and the revealed'. The distinction between historical and interior time suggests that only in the former is such a coincidence possible. Language could effect the appearance of the face *kath' auto* only with an illusory leap across the unbridgeable gap between mortality and infinity, dying and death.[23] *Otherwise Than Being* is perhaps nothing but the acknowledgment and unfolding of this impossibility of immediacy.

If language is defined by *droiture* in the earlier text, the later text renders it, to the contrary, the site of *enigma* (literally 'dark saying'). To be sure, this shift does not imply the abandonment of the idea of a pre-original language prior and irreducible to any communication; rather this speech (the *Dire*, or Saying) now signifies only as what refuses signification *as such*, and is thus discernible only by way of its trace in empirical language (the *Dit*, or Said).[24] Consigned to the unavoidable detour of enigma, the Other is revealed only in the form of its own erasure. Obscurity, once the preserve of the pagan infinity of the *il y a*, has become 'an inalienable power in saying and a modality of transcendence' (*OB*, 10; *AE*, 11).

The trace names the equivocal structure through which transcendence signifies itself. Levinas describes it thus:

The trace left by the infinite is not the residue of a presence; its very glow is ambiguous. Otherwise, its positivity would not preserve the infinity of the infinite any more than negativity would. The Infinite wipes out its trace not in order to trick him who obeys, but because it transcends the present in which it commands me, and because I cannot deduce it from this command. (*OB*, 12; *AE*, 15)

Neither residue – the lost plenitude of an irrecoverable past, nor trick – the dissimulation of an ultimate Presence awaiting disclosure in a redeemed future, the trace signifies what has neither been nor will be made present to being other than in the form of its own perpetual withdrawal. Comprehended in the present, the infinite could command me only to a particular content, to this or that moral prescription; its capacity to obligate me absolutely, prior to any assumption on my part, is the effect of its immemoriality: 'The immemorial is not an effect of a weakness of memory, an incapacity to cross large intervals of time, to resuscitate pasts too deep. It is the impossibility of the dispersion of time to assemble itself in the present, the insurmountable diachrony of time, a beyond the said' (*OB*, 38; *A E*, 48).

The immemorial is thus that to which human language – the said – is exposed by diachrony, by time's resistance to any synthetic apprehension. As the force of this resistance, diachrony ruins the coincidence of revealer and revealed, consigning language to an ineluctable ambiguity. Yet diachrony is not to be characterized merely negatively, as the Said's inadequacy to the saying, but equally as the enabling condition of the command of the Other. Only the perpetual erasure of its tracks – its 'ab-solution' – maintains the Other's infinity. Always and insuperably ahead of me, yet to be comprehended, the command is my very exposure to diachrony.

To be in language is to undergo diachrony, an experience Levinas renders profoundly ambiguous if not contradictory. The temporal dislocation effected by my responsibility to the Other is, in the language of *Otherwise Than Being*, a persecution, an obsession, a being-hostage, an 'extreme passivity' that is *simultaneously and inextricably* a glory and inspiration. My insuperable separation from the Other, the meanwhile [*entretemps*] or 'interval of difference' (*OB*, 141, Levinas' emphasis; *A E*, 180) which prevents our reconciliatory communion is nothing other than this doubled experience in which suffering and revelation, hell and utopia – in short, evil and the Good – fall into a zone of indistinction. The responsibility to which Auschwitz assigns us must be understood in terms of this indistinction if Levinas' ethics is not to be assimilated to the theodicy it everywhere seeks to resist. Glory is never the redemption of my suffering for the Other; it is this very suffering in its ethical significance.

RESTLESS RESPONSIBILITY

The term that best describes this doubled experience of persecution and inspiration is *restlessness* (*inquiétude*). The term appears, among other places, in a section of *Otherwise Than Being* in which Levinas describes the procedure of 'reduction'[25] by which the 'saying beyond the logos' is allowed to resonate within the Said. 'The reduction', writes Levinas, '. . . is reduction to signification, to the one-for-the-other involved in responsibility (or more exactly in substitution), to the locus or non-lieu, locus and non-lieu, the utopia, of the human. It is the reduction to rest-lessness in the literal sense of the term' (*OB*, 45; *AE*, 58).

The term recurs in Chapter 3 ('Sensibility and Proximity'), in a discussion of maternity. Maternity is here an exemplary modality of responsibility, 'a bearing par excellence', in which is concentrated the very essence of sensibility. Sensibility, prior to its integration into intentional consciousness, is a pre-original 'exposedness to the other': 'sensibility is being affected by a non-phenomenon, a being put in question by the alterity of the other . . . It is a pre-original not resting in oneself, the restlessness of someone persecuted . . . , a writhing in the tight dimensions of pain . . . Is not the restlessness of someone persecuted but a modification of mater-nity, the groaning of the wounded entrails by those it will bear or has borne?' (*OB*, 75; *AE*, 95).

Taken together, these passages reveal restlessness as the point at which trans-cendence and evil converge. Both a synonym for 'the utopia of the human' and 'a writhing in the tight dimensions of pain', it is the signification of the ethical in its essential ambiguity. In restlessness, language and the body in their everyday being are awakened to the immemorial beyond of being. Speech as the said of commu-nication is exposed to an infinite saying prior to and ahead of any communicable content; the body as apprehension and intention to an infinite vulnerability that conditions it. Restlessness alerts the speaking, sensible being to the constitutive paradox of responsibility: that it is 'mine' only in the measure that it dispossesses me. To assume responsibility is to do violence (though perhaps, as we shall see, a necessary violence) to its measurelessness, for 'my' responsibility limits itself as soon as it differentiates itself from 'yours'.

The concept of substitution (for Levinas the 'centerpiece' [xlvii; ix] of the book), yoking responsibility to an impossibility of assumption, or *denucleation*, is an unrelenting resistance to such ethical pragmatism. Levinas is careful not to con-flate substitution with the 'alienation' of the subject; on the contrary, it is the restless assignation to the Other, in which identity is found 'gnawing away at itself [*se rongeant*]' (*OB*, 114; *AE*, 145), that I am most inalienably – irreplaceably – myself ('*Ich bin du, wenn ich ich bin*' as the chapter's epigraph from Celan has it). Where the alienated subject recalls and seeks to recover its lost integrity, the substituted subject is 'forgetful of itself, forgetful in biting in upon itself' (*OB*, 115; *AE*, 147). This forgetfulness is what we have cautiously alluded to, following Blanchot as the 'writerly' logic of ethical subjectivity, where 'writing is the decay of will, just as it is the loss of power' (*WD*, 11; *ED*, 24). Forgetting here is not an act but 'a passivity more passive still than the passivity conjoined with action' (*OB*, 115; *AE*, 146).

Both responsibility and writing are synonyms for substitution, for the insatiate demand to which the Other assigns me without my consent: 'To be oneself, the state of being a hostage, is always to have one degree of responsibility more, the responsibility for the responsibility for the other' (*OB*, 117; *AE*, 150). Substitution thus unravels an infinite chain of responsibility. Enclosed within myself, the limits of my responsibility are clearly demarcated; departing myself for the Other, these limits are erased as soon as they are set down, for this departure is the unending discovery of my act's incapacity to fulfil my responsibility, of the 'one degree more' that always escapes my grasp.

In spite of his aversion to what he perceives as the subject-centred logic of psychoanalysis,[26] Levinas' use of the figure of trauma to describe this condition of infinite vulnerability accords quite precisely with that of the later Freud. In *Beyond the Pleasure Principle*, the latter writes: 'We describe as "traumatic" any excitations from outside which are powerful enough to break through the protective shield',[27] that is, through consciousness's apparatus for staving off those stimuli it is unable to absorb, destabilizing the equilibrium of its self-enclosure.

Levinas' affinity to Freud on the question of trauma is disclosed in the former's account of 'affection': 'the blow of the affection makes an impact traumatically, in a past more profound than all that I can reassemble by memory, by historiography, all that I can dominate by the a priori – in a time before the beginning' (*OB*, 88; *AE*, 111). Responsibility is traumatic in the strict psychoanalytic sense that it resists working-through, 'reassembling' in memory, and is thus always to be confronted anew. Like the traumatic dream, the demand of the Other interrupts the slumber of consciousness into which we fall not only during our night's sleep but especially in our waking day; this is what Levinas alludes to when he speaks of 'a wakefulness without intentionality, but awakened ceaselessly from its very state of wakefulness' (*OGW*, 26; *DDQ*, 51). Intentional consciousness, enclosing me within its limits (Freud's 'protective shield'), is at rest even when it apprehends and acts.[28]

The evident sobriety of such a consciousness belies a secret intoxication with its own projects, its own 'persistence in being'. It is a sobriety that has become *substantive*, that is, caught in 'the amphibology of Being and entities' (*OB*, 38; *AE*, 49) by which the diachrony of an infinite process is assimilated to the synchrony of the noun-form. As a nomination, a determinate attribute of a being 'sobriety' is divested of its essential *verbality*, 'is fixed, assembled in a tale, is synchronized, presented, lends itself to a noun, receives a title' (*OB*, 42; *AE*, 54). In responsibility, this denomination undergoes its own dissolution; no longer a fixed state of being, sobriety is returned to its essential verbality, its constitutive incompletion: 'The *living* [*vivacité*] of life – an incessant bursting of identification ... A sobering up [*Dégrisement*] always yet to be further sobered, a wakefulness watchful for a new awakening, the Same always awaking from itself – Reason' (*OGW*, 30, Levinas' emphasis; *DDQ*, 57).

Restlessness, trauma, a sobering 'yet to be further sobered': Levinas' language does not merely describe a suffering – it is itself a suffering, a speech perpetually awakened to the 'one degree more' which prevents its coming to rest. In this sense, the Said's exposure to the saying and the body's 'experience' of an infinite vulnerability stand in a literal rather than metaphorical relation to one another; sensibility is the experience beyond experience of the body in language, of pain signifying in speech.

If the impossible relation to the Good is a suffering, it is a suffering neither ennobling nor redemptive. The Good is not an end that redeems and justifies suffering, nor is it the means through which I attain grace. Both conceptions return suffering to an economy which annuls its essential excess, its radical 'dis-inter-estedness'. To suffer *for* the Good is to suffer interestedly, to assume an attainable end. In responsibility, my suffering is, on the contrary, always unassumed, radically passive: the very condition of being towards the Other. It is worth remarking once more the affinity of this structure of responsibility to the experience of writing; writing, like responsibility, enacts the dispossession of the self's power of assumption. The assumed responsibility to which Levinas had opposed art in 'Reality and Its Shadow' gives way to the unassumable responsibility which *describes* art.

SUFFERING THE IMMEMORIAL

That the intrication of being for the Other and suffering is elaborated in the book that Levinas dedicates '[t]o the memory of those who were closest among the six million assassinated by the National Socialists' can be no coincidence.[29] Does not *Otherwise Than Being* describe a trauma 'more profound than all that I can assemble by memory?' (*OB*, 88; *AE*, 111). If Levinas' dedication haunts the book's pages, it is because the memory it invokes is precisely not one 'I can reassemble by memory', but which remains always to be remembered, perpetually calling us to 'one degree of responsibility more', to an 'untiring wakefulness, an absolute insomnia'. The memory of suffering is a memory that suffers.[30]

Otherwise Than Being leaves open the question of its dedication's relationship to the pages which follow, as if any explicit reflection of this kind would fix the dead in a theme, laying their memory to rest. In an number of later essays, however, most notably his 1982 'Useless Suffering', Levinas casts his phenomenology in the shadow of Auschwitz, 'the paradigm of gratuitous human suffering, in which evil appears in its diabolical horror' (*EN*, 97; 107).[31] The essay's opening description of suffering evokes *Otherwise Than Being*'s account of the enigma of language – suffering is both 'a *datum* in consciousness, a certain "psychological consciousness"' (a said) and, 'in this very "content", an in-spite-of-consciousness, the unassumable' (*EN*, 91/100) (the trace of the saying).

Neither inside nor outside experience, suffering is the experience of what exceeds experience, 'the way in which, within a consciousness, the unbearable [*l'insupportable*] is precisely not borne, the manner of this not-being-borne; which, paradoxically, is a sensation or a datum' (*EN*, 91–2; 100). Suffering, in other words, is *constitutively* useless, its meaning deriving, like Beckett's *Endgame* as read by Adorno, from 'the fact that it has no meaning' (*NTL* 1, 243; *GS* 11, 283). For Levinas, as for Adorno, suffering takes meaning and meaninglessness out of a relationship of opposition. The meaningless signifies without thereby being sublated into a higher-order meaning, insofar as it can signify only by *maintaining* its un-meaning. Thus, when Levinas goes on to suggest that it is only in 'my own experience of suffering' and never in the Other's that suffering's 'congenital useless-ness can take on a meaning' (*EN*, 94; 104), he is not arguing that this uselessness is ever annulled or superseded. If only my suffering can take on meaning it is, on the contrary, because only as mine can uselessness signify as uselessness, take on mean-ing without thereby being relieved of its meaninglessness.

The meaning of my suffering lies of course in responsibility, in 'becoming a suffering for the suffering' (*EN*, 94; 104). But the meaning of this 'suffering for the suffering' can never be reduced to a representable content. Rather, suffering for the Other is infinitely unredeemed, destined to a restlessness that leaves it per-petually behind any fulfilled meaning. To ascribe meaning to the Other's suffering is always and necessarily to fall into theodicy, to justify it in the name of a higher order or purpose. Levinas emphatically refuses this 'political teleology of suffering' (*EN*, 95; 105) in which the pain of others takes on pedagogic, regenerative or other 'usable' meanings,[32] even as he recognizes 'the profundity of the empire it exerts over humankind' (*EN*, 96; 106). The meaning of my suffering is thus the only possible meaning suffering can bear; it escapes theodicy because it is intimately bound to its meaninglessness, that is, to a responsibility or persecution I have never chosen. In this sense my suffering is never 'mine', never an end I have assumed or aimed at and so could hope to overcome.

To bear suffering without assuming it, as a 'not-being-borne', might well be described as the meaning of religion after Auschwitz, a religion stripped of any intimation of theodicy (even while alive to its temptations). Where theodicy would bring thought to rest, Levinasian religion is its unceasing awakening, not only from sleep but from the 'slumber' of a wakefulness not wakeful enough. In his essay 'Transcendence and Evil', a reading of Philippe Nemo's *Job et l'excès du Mal*, Levinas names this bearing of the unbearable *evil* (*mal* − we should be attentive to the comparative diffuseness of the French term, which can of course mean wrong, trouble or sickness as well as evil). Evil as Job undergoes it is 'excess', a term which must be dissociated from 'the quantitative idea of intensity' and read rather as 'excess in its very quiddity … suffering as suffering is but a concrete and quasi-sensible manifestation of the nonintegratable, or the unjustifiable. The "quality" of evil is this *non-integratableness* itself . . .' (*OGW*, 128; *DDQ*, 197, Levinas' emphasis). And yet, Levinas continues, evil – monstrous, 'disturbing', 'foreign' – is '*in this sense transcendence!*' (*OGW*, 128; *DDQ*, 198, Levinas' emphasis).

The transcendence of evil is not, in other words, a transformative negation in which evil passes into its other. Transcendence is not the integration but the *maintenance* of evil's non-integratability (it may be helpful at this point to remind ourselves of the other meanings of *mal*), and is only '*in this sense*' transcendent; as long as thought seeks to annul or overcome this non-integratability, it is complicit with theodicy. In this distinction lies Levinas' decisive point of contention with Nemo, whose reading of Job he finds otherwise 'so personal, so new, and so mature' (*OGW*, 133; *DDQ*, 205). Nemo seems to find in Job a narrative progression 'leading from the "horror of evil" to the discovery of the Good'. Does not this movement, asks Levinas, 'lead only to the opposite of evil and to a goodness of simple pleasures, however great this might be?' (*OGW*, 134; *DDQ*, 204). To identify such a movement is to smuggle in, even if unwittingly, a theodicy which overcomes and redeems evil.

To this residual theodicy, Levinas puts the question whether the Good does not 'maintain a relationship less distant with the evil that suggests it, while differing from it with a difference more different than opposition' (*OGW*, 134; *DDQ*, 204). In Nemo's reading of Job's redemption, the Good is both too far from and too near to evil; too far because it places the two terms in opposition, too near because the relation of opposition cannot do justice to the profundity of Good's distance from evil.[33] This distance is best described with deliberate paradox by one of the key terms from *Otherwise Than Being*: proximity.

Proximity is a relation to the Other which exceeds every spatial or conceptual construal of relation, troubling the opposition of contact and separation: 'In contact itself the touching and the touched separate, as though the touched moved off, [*s'éloignant*] was always already other, did not have anything *in common* with me' (*OB*, 86, Levinas' emphasis; *AE*, 109). The proximity of evil to Good as 'Transcendence and Evil' describes it partakes of just this difficult logic. Contact with evil is always already an awakening to its other: 'The excess of evil by which it is in surplus to the world is also the impossibility of our accepting it. The experience of evil would thus also be our waiting for the good – the love of God' (*OGW*, 131; *DDQ*, 203). The Good is never experienced as such, but only in its consignment to evil, for evil is always also 'hatred of evil', an insomniac 'waiting for the good'.

In this respect, Levinas' familiar gesture of distancing himself from Heidegger takes on a new significance, for when he writes that 'The ontological difference is preceded by the difference of good and evil' (*OGW*, 130; *DDQ*, 201), he draws attention as much to their shared structure as to the priority of the latter. This structure is what Heidegger names *In-sein* (Being-in), that is Being's necessary consignment to the world, such that it can only appear in and as Dasein: ' "*Being-in*" *is*

*thus the formal existential expression for the Being of Dasein, which has Being-in-the-world
as its essential state*' (Heidegger, 80, Heidegger's emphasis; 54). For Levinas as for
Heidegger, and in spite of their very real differences, transcendence cannot be
thought apart from what it transcends. If '*Being is the transcendens pure and simple
[schlechtin]*' (Heidegger, 62, Heidegger's emphasis; 38, Heidegger's emphasis) it is
so above all in the impossibility of appearing as such. Heidegger's ontological and
Levinas' ethical difference are inadequately described by the structure of opposition: the absoluteness of the difference they each name demands thinking rather
in terms of a radical proximity, a separation as 'being-in' or 'contact'.

From this perspective, Levinas' critique of Nemo for remaining in Heidegger's
categories – the God or 'You' 'summoned in evil, is interpreted by way of recourse
to being' (*OGW*, 131; *DDQ*, 202), obscures his implicitly 'Heideggerean' objection
to Nemo's ethics. Nemo, he argues, will not escape the temptation of theodicy as
long as he thinks the Good as an overcoming and superseding of evil. The absoluteness of the Good can remain absolute only if it is thought in its proximity – its
contact–separation – to evil: 'A breakthrough of the Good which is not a simple
inversion of Evil, but an elevation. A Good that is not pleasant, which commands
and prescribes' (*OGW*, 134; *DDQ*, 206). Where the inversion of evil would merely
leave it intact, its elevation awakens us to the call of its absolute other, 'to an untiring wakefulness'.

Entitled 'Ambiguity', the concluding paragraph of 'Transcendence and Evil'
describes briefly the 'alternation' which constitutes 'our modernity': 'Recovery
and Rupture, Knowledge and Sociality'. These terms are synonyms, of course,
for Being and its Beyond, and their alternation performs 'time itself, time in its
enigmatic diachrony' (*OGW*, 134; *DDQ*, 206). This is the diachrony we have seen
unfold in the trace, the very ambiguity of the saying which prevents the Good from
appearing as such, apart from the evil which awakens it: 'It would signify the
ambiguity of an incessant adjournment or the progression of holding and possession. But it also signifies the approach of an infinite God, an approach that is His
proximity' (*OGW*, 134; *DDQ*, 206). With this approach, we are returned to that
'ultimate structure' of Levinas' thought of which Blanchotian writing, the trace
of the saying, and unassumable suffering are displaced descriptions: religion.

UNPRESENTABLE RELIGION: ADIEU

Religion, let us recall, is what maintains a relation to the Other in spite of 'the
impossibility of the Whole' (*TaI*, 80; *TeI*, 53); that is, it is what prevents this relation from coming to rest or completion. It is thus 'ultimate' only as the refusal of
every ultimacy. In Levinas' mature philosophy, the term increasingly invoked to

signify this refusal is 'the extraordinary name of God' (*OGW*, xii; *DDQ*, 8). As that which is revealed by withdrawing from every revelation, God is that very impossibility of the Whole which conditions every relation.

Section 1B of *Totality and Infinity* describes the irreducible structure of separation which opens and maintains the Other's absolute distance from me. Neither spatial nor conceptual, this distance is that paradoxical movement of contact in separation we have seen described in *Otherwise Than Being* by the name of proximity. In the earlier work, it is religion which provides phenomenological description with the most potent resources for thinking this paradox. The relation to God – a relation 'without relation', that is, without knowledge, conceptuality or reciprocity – is conditioned by an ineradicable *atheism*, for only atheism can purify this relation of 'the violence of the sacred' (*TaI*, 77; *TeI*, 49). In sacred myth, the approach to God must culminate in an annihilatory mystical fusion which 'would hold the I in its invisible meshes [*filets*]' (*TaI*, 77; *TeI*, 49). In holy religion (the title of Levinas' second volume of Talmudic readings, *From the Sacred to the Holy*, intimates just what is at stake in this distinction), in contrast, this approach never overcomes my separateness: 'Only an atheist being can relate himself to the other and already *absolve himself* from this relation' (*TaI*, 77; *TeI*, 49, Levinas' emphasis). The most urgent imperative of religion is to maintain a relation to the Absolute which would not traduce it, which continuously ab-solves or revokes itself; only 'metaphysical atheism',[34] as that which has always already refused any conceptual relation to God, can be adequate to this demand. Atheism guarantees that radical otherness of God to being that finds itself forever betrayed in 'the concept of God possessed by the believers of positive religions ...' (*TaI*, 77; *TeI*, 50).

Otherwise Than Being, as its title indicates, continues and deepens this wresting of God from the grasp of positive religion or theology. The always-unassumed responsibility we have elaborated above cannot be dissociated from the relation to a God that tolerates no assumption and ruins every will. I am in relation to God only in the form of a being-affected, an exposure to a command that obligates me before any contract – in short, in the form of witness, 'this way for a command to sound in the mouth of the one that obeys, of being "revealed" before all appearing, before all "presentation before a subject" ...'[35] (*OB*, 147; *AE*, 187). In bearing witness, a 'plot' unfolds that refuses integration into noematic, causal or anamnesiac knowledge, a plot which 'connects to what detaches itself absolutely, to the Absolute ... One is tempted to call this plot religious; it is not stated in terms of certainty or uncertainty, and does not rest on any positive theology' (*OB*, 147; *AE*, 188).

The language of 'certainty or uncertainty', faith or doubt, presupposes an ontology of the divine, drawing God into an order of conceptuality which would guarantee the meaning of human experience. A thought of God which ruins this order, which puts in question rather than resolves the meaning of experience would alone be worthy of the name religion.

The religious witness attests to a revelation which signifies in the form of its own revocation, its refractoriness to presence. This is why God's name is absent from the exemplary prophetic attestation: '*Hineini*', 'Here I am' ('*Me voici*'). To bear witness to God is to state the bare fact of my exposure to the Other, to the primordial condition of responsibility in which I find myself 'without having anything to identify myself with, but the sound of my voice or the figure of my gesture – the saying itself' (*OB*, 149; *A E*, 190). To be in the 'presence' of God is precisely to find myself exposed to the 'outside, or on the "other side" of presence' (*OB*, 149; *A E*, 190), in a space where discursive language experiences its own ruin, reduced to saying nothing – no thing or 'said' – but 'saying itself'.

Levinas' account of the prophetic 'Hineini' both follows and radicalizes Rosenzweig's interpretation of the same word.[36] For the latter too, 'Here I am!' is the exemplary affirmation of revelation, of the soul 'called by his name . . . all unlocked, all spread apart, all ready all-soul: "Here I am." . . . Here is the I, the individual human I, as yet wholly receptive, as yet only unlocked, only empty, without content, without nature, pure readiness, pure obedience, all ears' (*SR*, 176; *SE*, 196).

For Levinas, as for Rosenzweig, the experience of witness is conditioned by a pure receptivity anterior to any content. In Rosenzweig, however, the purely obedient I's reception of a content – the command to love the Lover, God – draws revelation into the immanence of experience, a pure present. As the awakening of the soul to his createdness, to his being beloved of God, revelation is the instant of absolute immediacy: 'The creation which becomes invisible in revelation is creation of the revelation. At this point the experiential and presentive character [*der Erlebnis- und Gegenswartscharararakter*] is immovably fixed . . .' (*SR*, 183; *SE*, 203). If *Totality and Infinity* carries over something of this 'presentive character' of revelation in its thought of the coincidence of revealer and revealed in speech, in *Otherwise Than Being* this coincidence is thinkable only in its impossibility, an impossibility which is the very essence of religiosity as distinguished from theology.

It is precisely the absence of the word God – its *non*-presentive character – from the 'Here I am' – 'the phrase in which God is for the first time involved [*se mêler*] in words' (*OB*, 149; *A E*, 190), that renders it religious. The more positive religion seeks to overcome this unpresentability, the more it will traduce its own truth:

> Thus theological language destroys the religious situation of transcendence. The infinite 'presents' itself anarchically, but thematization loses the anarchy which alone can accredit it. Language about God rings false or becomes a myth, that is, can never be taken literally. (*OB*,197; *A E*, 155)

There is no language of God '*à la lettre*' because God's immediacy tolerates no linguistic mediation. An unrelenting refusal of experience or presentation is what enables language to approach God without 'destroying the religious situation of transcendence'.

This approach in the form of withdrawal is signified in the single term which concentrates the entirety of Levinas' religious philosophy: adieu.[37] The unhyphenated word, of course, signifies a leave-taking (but also, in certain circumstances, a greeting); by interposing a hyphen, Levinas doubles the word, restoring its literal meaning without thereby annulling its more conventional sense. The effect of this gesture is to render the approach to God (à-Dieu) indissociable from a retreat (adieu).

Levinas' collection *Of God Who Comes To Mind* (*De Dieu qui vient a l'idée*) can be read as a kind of interminable unfolding of this doubled gesture; interminable because it consigns 'the thinking of God [*penser à-Dieu*]' to a '"deportation" or transcendence beyond every end and every finality' (*OGW*, xiii; *DDQ*, 10). This deportation points to a further doubling, for the adieu takes leave of both being and the Beyond-being. Thus in one essay, the adieu is addressed 'to the world, to the firm ground, to presence and to ess*a*nce' (*OGW*, 50; *DDQ*, 87) – to enter into a relation with the Good is to be carried away from the interestedness of the self and towards – *à-Dieu*.

And yet in 'God and Philosophy', perhaps Levinas' most sustained interrogation of 'the extraordinary word God', this adieu to the world also destines the self to an interminable adieu to God and the Good: 'The goodness of the Good – of the Good that neither sleeps nor slumbers – inclines the movement it calls forth to turn it away from the Good and orient it toward the other, and only thus toward the Good' (*OGW*, 69; *DDQ*, 114). To be drawn towards the Good is to be turned away from it: this is the constitutive paradox that structures the religious relation. The approach to the Absolute – God or the Good – takes the form on an infinite detour towards the other human being; responsibility is what opens me to the Absolute and what, in interposing the 'one degree more', sends me away from it.

Read alongside Adorno, Levinas' adieu reads like an attempt to forge a religious language that resists the conceptual violence which according to the former has so irrevocably contaminated positive religion.[38] It is a language which, like Adornian art, turns religion against itself, invoking and revoking simultaneously the divine Name. If Adorno finds in positive religion an intoxication by a sham transcendence, Levinas' doubled movement of divine approach and withdrawal is the vigilant refusal of such intoxication. In the face of its constant temptation to intoxication, religion must perpetually sober itself up, with a sobriety 'always yet to be further sobered' (*OGW*, 30; *DDQ*, 57).

THE SOBER MESSIAH: JUDAISM

If Levinas finds in Judaism religion's exemplary articulation, it is because its legal and hermeneutic forms perpetually enact this infinite sobering. In a short essay from *Difficult Freedom*, he identifies this intimacy of Judaism and sobriety in the paradigmatic figure of the pharisee, or rabbinic hermeneut. For the pharisee, '[e]nthusiasm is not the purest way to enter into a relationship with God' (*DF*, 28; *DL*, 47–8). The rabbinic relation with the divine is premised not on mythic fusion (or 'participation'), but on a contact in separation which leaves intact the other term of the relation.

Levinas invokes two rabbinic pronouncements on the life of Torah learning to elaborate this distinction. The first, from Rabbi Eliezer, claims that ' "If all the seas were ink, reeds pens, the heavens parchment, and all men writers, they would not suffice to write down the Torah I have learned, and the Torah itself would be diminished only by the amount drawn out of it by the tip of a paintbrush dipped in the sea" ' (*DF*, 29; *DL*, 48). The apparently intoxicated 'audacity' of the initial claim is sobered by the humility of the second – the infinity of pens, ink, parchment and writers extracts barely a drop from its oceanic source. Yet Rabbi Akiva's response further sobers even this modest calculus: 'They [his masters] managed to extract their part from the Torah. For me, I have broached it purely like the man who breathes in the perfume of the cedar tree – his joy takes nothing away from the cedar. Or like the man who draws water from a spring. Or like the man who lights his flame from a flame' (*DF*, 29; *DL*, 48).

The effect of Akiva's response is to remove every intimation of diminution from the image of the source: tree, spring and flame are 'infinitely renewable', their abundance indifferent to those that draw from it. Akiva's subtle but decisive revision of the image restores to transcendence its inviolable exteriority. The pharisee draws from the source, but 'he does not merge with it':

> He is not possessed by the forces that range and alter and dissolve self-presence. The liquid he drinks quenches his thirst without causing drunkenness. Everything remains in its place. God is outside and is God for that very reason … To have an outside, to listen for what comes from outside – oh, miracle of exteriority! That is what is called knowledge [*connaisance*] or Torah. (*DF*, 29; *DL*, 49)

To the knowledge acquired by way of pagan fusion on the one hand and the active, appropriative intellect on the other, Levinas counterposes a 'knowledge' which is neither possessed nor possessing, which annihilates neither self nor other but keeps their difference intact. Torah vigilantly resists – sobers – both the mystic intoxication of the other and the conceptual intoxication of the self, maintaining itself in relation with what is outside – what ab-solves itself from – every relation.

Levinas' expansive body of writings on Judaism subjects all of its key terms to this sobering, wresting from them every association with eschatological finality or resolution. Nowhere is this dissociation more striking than in his scattered writings on the question of the messianic. Levinas offers a clear summation of his thought on this question in an interview with Richard Kearney: 'I could not accept a messianism that would terminate the need for discussion, that would end our watchfulness' (FEL, 31). The first of two of the Talmudic readings, published in *Difficult Freedom* under the title 'Messianic Texts' (delivered to the third and fourth colloquia of Franco-Jewish intellectuals in 1960 and 1961), can be read as an attempt to excavate from rabbinic tradition's wealth of voices a messianism of interminable watchfulness.

One of the messianic texts discussed in theses readings is a dialogue from Tractate *Sanhedrin* (97b–98a) concerning the necessary conditions for the coming of the Messiah. Levinas begins by distinguishing two positions; the first, Rab's, states that ' "[a]ll the predestined dates [for redemption] have passed, and the matter [now] depends only on repentance and good deeds" ' (DF, 69; DL, 95). Levinas interprets this statement as a kind of proto-Hegelianism, whereby the objective conditions for the end of history have passed, leaving the destiny of a messianic coming to the work of individuals – good deeds bring about redemption.

The second position, Samuel's, is more ambiguous; he says simply that '[i]t is sufficient for a mourner to keep his [period of] mourning' (DF, 69/DL, 96). As Levinas points out, this pronouncement immediately begs the question as to just who is said to be in mourning. Three responses to this question are recorded: the first states that God is the mourner, and that it is only at the end of His period of mourning – that is, at a point of objective historical necessity rather than by individual action – that the Messiah can come. The second identifies the mourner as Israel, and sees the suffering of the nation as the condition for its redemption – a position which harmonizes Rab's voluntarism with the objectivism of the first interpretation of Samuel's statement. A third opinion from the sixteenth-century Talmudist Maharshah (frequently invoked by Levinas) agrees that Israel must be identified as the mourner but is disturbed by the christological motif of suffering as redemption. Suffering according to this position is not a good in itself, but a condition for a redemptive repentance – 'it is through suffering that a *freedom may be aroused*' (DF, 71; DL, 98, Levinas' emphasis).

Rather than choose among these options, Levinas points to a different Talmudic passage which identifies the mourner differently again as the Messiah himself. The passage in question is one of the Talmud's most famous, an encounter between Rabbi Joshua and the prophet Elijah. The rabbi asks Elijah when the Messiah will come, to which the prophet responds by sending him to the lepers among whom the Messiah is sitting to ' "ask him himself" '. The Messiah is distinguished by Rabbi Joshua as the only one tending each leprous sore separately rather than untying all bandages at once; for 'at any moment he might be called upon to appear, at any moment the "coming of Messiah" may occur [*peut se produire*] . . .[39] He must not be delayed by the time it takes to perform one medical act' (DF, 71; DL, 98–9). When Joshua asks him when he will come, the response is 'Today'. Joshua returns

to Elijah to question whether this 'today' is not false; the latter completes the
Messiah's response by invoking Psalm 95: ' "Today, if ye will hear his voice" '.
Levinas glosses the encounter thus:

> What we have here, therefore, is a Messiah who suffers. But salvation cannot
> ensue [*se produire*] from the pure virtue of suffering. None the less, the whole
> of history has been crossed, every time completed. The Messiah is ready to
> come this very day, but everything depends on man. And the suffering of the
> Messiah and, consequently, the suffering of humanity which suffers in the Mes-
> siah and the suffering of the humanity for whom the Messiah suffers, are not
> enough to save humanity. (*DF*, 71–2; *DL*, 99)

Read in the context of our earlier discussion of suffering, the leprous Messiah
emerges as the very embodiment of an 'untiring wakefulness'. If his leprosy is destined to remain unhealed – his vigilance prevents the fulfilment of the medical act
that could cure him – that is, if his redemptive potential is to remain unrealized, it is
because suffering is not in itself salvational. Suffering remains, on the contrary,
stubbornly excessive, useless; theodicy fails to redeem it. The Messiah's readiness
to come can be made good only by the humanity for whom he suffers, and who
suffer for him.

This messianism of the interminable is further developed by a discussion a few
pages on of *Sanhedrin* 98b–99a, centring on the heretical claim of Rabbi Hillel
(a minor Tanna rather than the great Elder whose rulings form the basis for the
entirety of Jewish legal practice) that no Messiah is to come for Israel 'since they
have already enjoyed him during the reign of Hezekiah' (*DF*, 81; *DL*, 111). The
rabbis pronounce their astonishment at this 'fantastic idea of a messianism that has
been superseded', for which they ask God to forgive Hillel. Yet this apparent rejection does not annul the suggestive force of Hillel's affirmation. Under Levinas'
interpretative eye, his opinion is tied to a suspicion of 'redemption through the
Messiah' in favour of a 'higher aspiration' (*DF*, 82; *DL*, 112). What might this
curious 'surpassing of the messianic idea' be? Levinas offers the following response:

> One could do worse than adopt Jankélévitch's view that if the moral order
> is incessantly improving [*dans son perfectionnement incessant*], this is because it is
> always on the move and never provides an outcome [*jamais aboutissement*].
> A moral outcome is immoral. The notion of morality having an outcome is as
> absurd as the immobilization of time which it assumes. Deliverance by God
> coinicides with the sovereignty of a living morality that is open to infinite pro-
> gress. (*DF*, 82–3; *DL*, 112)

The immorality of a moral outcome is tied here to an 'immobilization of time',
that is, to a coming to rest. Returning to the discussion of 'verbality' in *Otherwise*

Than Being, we might say that a moral outcome would render morality substantive – 'fixed, assembled in a tale ..., synchronized, presented' (*OB*, 42; *AE*, 54). The messianic, far from signifying a substantive being or event, would be precisely that which prevents morality's assembling into a narrative, which gives morality over to what Levinas will call, in a much later Talmudic reading, 'an eschatology paradoxically endless or precisely infinite' (*ITN*, 60; *ALH*, 72). 'Messianism', then, 'is therefore not the certainty of the coming of a man who stops History. It is my power to bear the suffering of all' (*DF*, 90; *DL*, 120). This power is the condition for what Levinas will later call a religion that 'does not begin in promise', a religion 'impossible to preach', in which we may recognize 'the difficult piety – all the certainties and personal risks – of the twentieth century, after the horrors of its genocides and its Holocaust' (*EN*, 177; 183–84).

SHATTERING THE IDOLATROUS WORD: TALMUDIC HERMENEUTICS

We are, perhaps, coming closer to understanding the inextricability of the ethical and the hermeneutic in Levinas' religious thought.[40] Judaism's struggle against idolatry – against the coercion of infinite responsibility into finite act, of saying into said – is staged above all in the interpretative practices of rabbinism. The Talmudic hermeneutic, at least as Levinas reads it, is an awakening of language to what perpetually exceeds its reach, drawing reading and writing into a mode of infinition, of constitutive incompletion. Invoking and provoking Heidegger, Marc-Alain Ouaknin coins the term '*différence herméneutique*' to describe this interpretative orientation; Talmudic language is the perpetual insinuation of this internal difference, of a '*pouvoir-dire*' – an infinite potential to mean – that both falls into and exceeds – *dépasse* – its '*vouloir-dire*' or meaning.[41]

One of Levinas' most sustained explorations of this hermeneutic difference is to be found in his 1969 essay, 'The Name of God According to a Few Talmudic Texts'. When the Talmud wishes to invoke that which Western languages designate as 'Theos' 'Dieu', 'Gott', 'God' etc., it employs the term '*Ha Kadosh Baruchu*' – 'the Holy One Blessed Be He'. The Hebrew word *kedusha* – holiness – also designates that which is separated, 'like', Levinas observes, 'our word "absolute"', a doubleness which confers on this 'name' of God a profoundly paradoxical status: 'The term names – and this is quite remarkable – a mode of being or a beyond of being rather than a quiddity' (*BV*, 119; *AV*, 147). Rather than nominalizing God, in other words, the Talmudic 'Name' merely signifies His refractoriness to naming. Naming in the Talmud enacts a theo-logy which only ever speaks its own impossibility, the insufficiency of its *logos* to the *theos* it approaches. To invoke the divine Name is 'to understand revelation both as a modality which paradoxically preserves transcendence from what is revealed, and consequently as something that goes beyond the capacity of an 'intuition, even of a concept' (*BV*, 120; *A V*, 148). Levinas' affinity to Blanchotian writing finds its full if implicit articulation here: revelation and its revocation, writing and its erasure, are rendered simultaneous in Talmudic theology. Thus '[t]he square letters are a precarious dwelling from which the revealed name is already withdrawn' (*BV*, 121; *A V*, 149). The approach *à Dieu*, if it is not to traduce its own truth, cannot escape its own diversion, its perpetual *adieu*. It is only this diversion which assigns us to responsibility for the human other: 'The transcendence of God is his actual effacement, but this obligates us to men' (*BV*, 125; *A V*, 153). Ethics is the perpetual detour to which God assigns human beings in withdrawing from them. Responsibility is not an experience of transcendence, then, but of its radical inaccessibility to experience.

Levinas offers a more general account of the rabbinic hermeneutic in his 1985 Talmudic reading, 'Contempt for the Torah as Idolatry'. Here, Torah (in this context the Hebrew Bible) is named 'the book of anti-idolatry', not in reference to its specific interdictions and prescriptions, but first of all as 'being a force warding off idolatry by its essence as Book, that is, by its very writing, signifying precisely prescription, and by the permanent reading it calls for – permanent reading or interpretation and reinterpretation and study; a book destined from the start for its Talmudic life' (*ITN*, 58; *ALH*, 70–1). The Torah's destining to its own measureless interpretative afterlife is no a fortiori contingency, but is inscribed into its very meaning. Exegesis carries the responsibility for the Torah's infinite renewal, such that its every act is an awakening to 'one degree more' of exegesis. This infinition of exegesis enacts the '[i]ncompleteness that is the law of love: it is the future itself, the coming of a world that never ceases coming . . .' (*ITN*, 59; *ALH*, 72). The 'eschatology paradoxically endless' (*ITN*, 60; *ALH*, 72) that characterizes Jewish messianism for Levinas is the effect above all of an interpretative practice which prevents any final coincidence of revealer and revealed.

This practice engenders a critique of both sacred and profane idolatry; that is, of the sacral 'immanentizing' of transcendence (in the form of pagan ecstasy or Spinozist pantheism), but also of the 'demystifying' annihilation of transcendence in the form of modern scepticism, exemplified in this case by the nineteenth-century *Wissenschaft des Judentum*, the German scholarly movement which subjected the Bible to thoroughgoing historicist criticism. Levinas finds an anticipatory critique of the latter in a *baraita* – a teaching not included in the *Mishnah* – in his chosen passage (*Sanhedrin* 99a–b – part of a sequence of pages to which he repeatedly returns), which condemns as idolatrous the one who says ' "The Torah is not from heaven" ' (*ITN*, 64; *ALH*, 76). At first glance, little more than support for a Biblical fundamentalism can be gleaned from this pronouncement, 'a condemnation in advance of all critical exploration of the biblical text on the grounds of idolatry' (*ITN*, 64; *ALH*, 77). Levinas' interpretation, however, steers the *baraita* away from this anti-critical stance; set in the context of a rabbinic hermeneutic, the denial of Torah's heavenly origin is impugned not for opening but for *closing* the text to reading, that is, for reducing the infinite fullness of interpretative revelation to a set of determinate 'histories and anecdotes':

> Idolatry would be the reduction of these sources to the histories and anecdotes lived by the individuals of the past, instead of sensing in them the prophecy of persons and the genius of a people, and hearing in them the birth of the message for all, and the voice of God in its extreme straightness through the appearance of the tortuous paths it follows. (*ITN*, 65; *ALH*, 77)

The *baraita* has insisted on the absolute straightness – *droiture*, in the language of *Totality and Infinity* – of God's voice, its freedom from any admixture of finitude (not even one verse, it goes on, should be attributed to Moses ' "on his own initiative" '). For Levinas, however, this straightness can 'appear' only through 'the tortuous paths it takes'. That is, the divine voice can never be heard as such, but only by way of the unending detour of human exegesis, 'the very locus of interrogation and response' (*ITN*, 64; *ALH*, 77). Historical criticism is what puts an end to this detour, by collapsing without remainder the *droiture* of an incommunicable saying into the history of a finite said.

The difficult path of true reading, then, demands an unrelenting refusal of determinism, whether in the name of religion or rationalism. One of the sequence of teaching further on in the text, on the 'sins of reading', affirms this refusal explicitly: 'Rabbi Yehoshua ben Korha said: "Whoever studies the Torah without repeating the lesson is like a sower who does not reap" '. This failure to repeat, suggests Levinas, 'means denying what the first reading – which opens but at the same time covers up – has already hidden' (*ITN*, 67; *ALH*, 79). Repetition is thus the solicitation of the text's irreducible internal difference, without which the text is reduced to 'first-level truths'. Repetition ruins literalism, 'the source of all idolatry', by unfolding the text's interminable difference from itself, its doubled movement of concealment and revelation.

In Judaism, then, we are awakened to the ineradicable *difficulty* of the relation to the absolute. Nor is this difficulty confined to the ethical terrain of the interpersonal relation; the essays and readings in Judaism and its textual sources are, more than any other of his writings, the space in which the infinite demand of the ethical is confronted by the urgently practical demands of the social and political. Levinas' Jewish writings, in short, read as responses to a key question in the phenomenological texts not yet broached: how can the ethical relation be just? And, reciprocally, how can justice remain ethical?

ETHICS AND JUSTICE, ISRAEL AND THE STATE

This is a question that seems to draw Levinas some distance from the Blanchotian concern with language and writing addressed above. And yet what has been termed the 'writerly' structure of the ethical bears directly on the question of justice. How is justice, as the systematic negotiation of the demands of many others, to be born of the infinite demand of the Other that refuses every system? Put another way, how can the writerly structure of ethics maintain itself in the readability of justice? Levinas poses the question in an explicitly religious register in a 1988 interview. How, he asks, is the 'rigor and strict impartiality of justice demanded by God in Deuteronomy 10:17 to be reconciled with the luminosity of 'the Face of God turned toward the man undergoing judgment in Numbers 6:25?' (EN, 230; 243).[42] What happens when the immediacy of the relation to the Other (figured in the face of God) is troubled by the appearance of the third party – 'other than the neighbour, but also another neighbour' (OB, 157; AE, 200). The title of the third section of Chapter 5 in Otherwise Than Being – 'From Saying to the Said, or the Wisdom of Desire' compacts the 'contradiction' that the appearance of the third party insinuates into the ethical relation, for if the latter commands one to infinite responsibility, the third signals 'the limit of responsibility and the birth of the question: What do I have to do with justice?' (OB, 157; AE, 200). The passage from responsibility to justice – to 'comparison, coexistence, contemporaneousness, assembling, order, thematization, the *visibility* of faces and thus intentionality and the intellect, and in intentionality and the intellect, the intelligibility of a system and thence also a copresence on an equal footing before a court of justice' (OB, 157; AE, 200)[43] – is thus a necessary one, a desire rendered 'wise'. Nor should we see this wisdom as posterior to responsibility, for the third does not come after the fact of the Other, but is, as Derrida observes (in the most recent of his commentaries on Levinas), there from the first. '. . . the third does not wait; it comes at the origin of the face, and of the face to face' (AEL, 31; 63). The command of responsibility – of the other – has always been haunted by the demand of justice – of other others.[44]

Religion is the perpetual and vigilant negotiation of these competing and irreconcilable claims. Its task is not to effect some synthesis or compromise between them, but to make each insistently audible to the other. Levinas' earlier definition on justice in the 'Conclusions' to *Totality and Infinity* – that in the face of the anonymous and universal narrative of the State, '[j]ustice is a right to speak' (TaI, 298; TeI, 274) – helps specify this task. For if 'comparison, coexistence, contemporaneousness, assembly' are necessary if ethics is not to collapse into the (unethical) solitude or 'concupiscence' of the Two, their necessity must be exposed to the counter-necessity of the Other's unassumability, that is, to the Other's 'right to speak'. It is in this mutual exposure of irreconcilable demands, Levinas goes on to suggest, 'that the perspective of a religion opens' (*TaI*, 298; *TeI*, 274).

The questions addressed across the Jewish writings – assimilation, technology, human rights, war guilt, revolution, feminism – repeatedly stage this mutual exposure, bringing the ethical up against its limits while destabilizing those limits in the name of the ethical. Nowhere is this dynamic more explicitly played out than in the writings on Zionism – the modern movement in which Hebrew and Greek, ethics and politics, the State and its other, are brought face to face in their irreducible difference. The significance of the State of Israel consists in the very irreconcilability of its two terms: the State, 'the ultimate refuge of idolatry' (*BV*, 183; *AV*, 216), the violent totality in which the self becomes a reified object of 'the virile judgment of history' (*TaI*, 243; *TeI*, 221), of the regime of light which reduces the individual life to its works; and Israel, the possibility of a truth beyond and refractory to the State, 'separated from any historical, national, local or racial notion' (*DF*, 22; *DL*, 39) as from 'the fascinating hallucination' of 'political determinism' (*DF*, 240; *DL*, 310–11).

Zionism is the promise of the State's subjection to, and transformation by, Israel, of a politics that is 'already non-political, epic and Passion, irrepressible energy and extreme vulnerability' (*BV*, 191; *AV*, 225). Commenting on this sentence, Derrida asks, 'What does "already" mean in the expression "and already non-political"? How might this "and already non-" eat into [*mordre sur*] what it still is, namely "political"? Or how might it let itself be eaten into by what it no longer is, that is "political", by what is still eating into it?' (*AEL*, 82; 148–9).

The task of Zionism is to respond incessantly to the question of how Israel can interrupt ('eat into') the State, while giving itself over to (being 'eaten into' by) it. How would a State, 'freed from the fascinating hallucination' of political determinism function? How to conceive an Israel as judge of universal history once it becomes a player in that history? Levinas' ongoing response to this question involves the imagining, or, to use Derrida's term, 'invention', of a state which alienates every conventional understanding of the term, a political structure conditioned by the irreducibly non-political. Writing early in the State's history (1961), he is unabashedly utopian about the possibility of realizing this promise: '. . . the State of Israel is the first opportunity to move into history by bringing about a just world. It is therefore a search for the absolute and for purity' (*DF*, 164; *DL*, 215).

In spite of their apparent contrast, Levinas is not so far from Rosenzweig on the question of the Jewish relationship to history and the state. The 'move into history' he describes is no Fackenheimian 'return into history'. For Fackenheim, the State of Israel sacralizes history by drawing together messianic futurity and the present, signifying the return of its people to the world-historical stage.[45] Levinas, in contrast, sees this 'return' in more paradoxical terms, whereby the 'move into history' is simultaneously a move *against* history, a confrontation of the totalizing logic of the political by the 'absolute' and 'pure' demand of justice. Notwithstanding their crucial difference on the viability of the State as a structure which could realize this task (a difference in large part conditioned, of course, by the unbridgeable historical gap of both Auschwitz and the establishment of the State itself), Levinas' historical move against history closely resembles Rosenzweig's 'messianic politics'. For Rosenzweig, too, the Jew's participation in history takes the form of an antagonism to its dominant narrative, a refusal of the Western state's 'coercion' of redemption.[46]

Cast in Levinas' retrospective light, this refusal need not be read, as it conventionally is,[47] as an unambiguous rejection of historical experience; Jewish experience according to Rosenzweig is rather a participation in history that resists history's totalizing terms of participation, just as Levinas' Jewish state enters history by rubbing against its grain.

Zionism, then, stages the necessary risk of justice, of the traffic between ethics and politics in the absence of 'any assured passage' (*AEL*, 20; 45) between the two. If, for Levinas, it is religion that might illuminate such a passage, it certainly cannot do so by transforming itself into political law. Far from 'rais[ing] the soul to a state of full self-possession', religion's role in the new State promises a diversion of the coercive and self-preserving logic of the state towards the 'difficult and erudite [*savante*] work of justice' (*DF*, 217; *DL*, 281) which is the very 'social law of Judaism' (*DF*, 218; *DL*, 282): 'Religion and religious parties do not necessarily coincide. Justice as the *raison d'être* of the State: that is religion' (*DF*, 219; *DL*, 283).

The truth of religion is always traduced by its accommodation to politics ('religious parties'). Politics keeps faith with religion only when it recognizes its absolute distance from it, when that distance awakens the political from its self-interested slumber to 'the difficult and erudite work of justice'. The promise of the State of Israel, in short, is that of politics become restless. What Levinas terms, in a 1971 essay, a 'monotheistic politics', would open the terrain of 'political invention' (*BV*, 187; *AV*, 220), of a State which does 'not contradict the absolute order, but is called by it' (*BV*, 180; *AV*, 213). This State would never come to rest in itself, never realize itself, but only perpetually invent itself, calling its institutions and legal structures towards the absolute of justice and peace which exceeds them. Such a peace, Derrida observes, 'interrupts itself or deconstructs itself so as to form a sort of enclave inside and outside of itself . . . the political interiorization of ethical or messianic transcendence' (*AEL*, 80; 146). Politics interiorizes, that is, what cannot be interiorized, what interrupts or deconstructs every interiorization – this would be the mutual 'eating into' of ethics and politics, Israel and State.

And yet this promised Israel – 'the Zionist *commitment*' – must be set apart from 'the Zionist *fact*', 'the actual situation of the State of Israel in its political visibility' (*AEL*, 79; 144). This distinction is what preserves Levinas' Zionism as a rich resource for ethico-political thought even for those of us who cannot share his political analyses of this 'actual situation'. If this situation – which (for all its undoubted achievements) includes institutionalized social and legal discrimination against the State's Arab citizens, the repressive military occupation and quasi-colonial settlement of the Palestinian territories, and the corrupt ransoming of the State by religious parties – has rarely seemed more distant from the 'Zionist commitment',[48] that is, from the promise of *another* politics, Levinas has nevertheless provided the terms for recognizing and thinking this distance.[49] The necessary friction between ethics and justice, between the demands of the Other and the third, is the ineluctable risk of the political. The State presents the ever-present temptation to forget the Other, and if Zionism's history tells repeatedly of the force of this temptation, its promise is the demand of a perpetual vigilance against it.[50]

If Judaism can have a role in the State, it is only as the prophetic inspiration that awakens politics to this demand. The Talmudic readings frequently hinge on the infinitesimal distance holding the good apart from evil, and as such harbour the resources for a potent if implicit critique of the temptations of politics, Israeli or otherwise.

POLITICS, RELIGION AND TEMPTATION

Levinas' 1964 reading, 'The Temptation of Temptation', a discussion of Tractate *Shabbat* 88a–b, draws out Judaism's contribution to the thinking of ethical subjectivity and its relation to evil. The extract from *Shabbat* is a dialogue on the guiding logic of Jewish practice as expressed by the Children of Israel in Exodus 24:7, shortly after Moses has read them the Book of the Covenant: 'All that God has spoken, *we will do, and hear*' (my emphasis).[51] The *gemarah* discussed by Levinas cites a *midrash*, in which the commitment to doing before hearing is accompanied by the visitation of 600,000 angels who adorn each Israelite with two crowns, 'one for the *doing*, the other for the *hearing*' (*NTR*, 42, Levinas' emphasis; *QLT*, 92). Yet this exaltation of each Israelite is attended, according to the statement of Rav Hama bar Hanina, by a surrender of these crowns. Levinas comments on this near simultaneous gift and withdrawal: 'The Jew at Horeb is to be adorned, and already he is stripped: We are simultaneously armed against all accommodation with the situation of someone who is tempted by evil and already falling [*succombant*]. The excellent choice that makes doing go before hearing does not prevent a fall. It arms not against temptation but against the temptation of temptation' (*NTR*, 43; *QLT*, 94).

What, then, is the 'temptation of temptation'? The doubling of the term refers to the rational mediation through which temptation comes to Western – or philosophical – consciousness. In the logical order of hearing prior to doing, the lure of evil can touch the soul without capturing it. The ego that seeks knowledge of evil is protected in this search by the autonomy of an intellect which can simultaneously participate in and exclude itself from what corrupts it. No longer excessive in the sense we have discussed above, evil in the order of hearing (or understanding) before doing is integrated into an economy of knowledge, an object which consciousness can conceptualize and so neutralize: 'What is tempting is to be simultaneously outside everything and participating in everything' (*NTR*, 34; *QLT*, 74).

Israel's temptation differs from that of the West, then, in its precarious lack of *mediation*.[52] The commitment to a doing before hearing – what the phenomenological texts call an immemorial obligatedness or responsibility – insinuates an absolute distance between good and evil which is simultaneously a radical proximity (a paradox expounded in our earlier discussion of 'Transcendence and Evil'). The immediacy of Israel's vulnerability to 'the fall' is inextricable from its always-prior responsibility. As hostage to the Good, Israel is always already immune to the temptation of temptation, to which only a consciousness assuming a choice between good and evil can fall prey. Assigned to the Good prior to any choice, Israel's sin 'does not question the certainty of good and evil. It remains unadorned sin, ignorant of the triumph attained by faults liberated from scruple and remorse. Thus a path back is available to the sinner' (*NTR*, 42; *QLT*, 94–5).

The simultaneity of gift and withdrawal of the crowns figures the insomniac condition into which this 'ignorance' plunges Israel. The crowns must be surrendered as soon as they are received because the Good is never an object to be worn – that is, never experienced as such – but rather an absolute always awaited: 'The experience of evil would thus also be our waiting for the good – the love of God' (*OGW*, 131; *DDQ*, 203). Israel's naked vulnerability to sin is what keeps intact the possibility of the Good, what opens a path back to the sinner. The temptation of temptation, in contrast, by interposing knowledge between consciousness and evil, relates evil to the good in an economy of opposition, in which both become objects of a choice. To hear before doing is to coerce into relation that which is without relation.

The two temptations delineated in Levinas' reading provide a point of entry into thinking critically of the gap between Zionist promise and Zionist fact. If the idea of the State of Israel promises the exposure of 'hearing before doing' – the logic of the State – to 'doing before hearing' – the commitment of Israel, its history is haunted by a forgetting of the latter, by the threat of its collapse without remainder into the former. The temptation of the political, Levinas' reading teaches, is unavoidable – for if the gift of the crowns is an immemorial ethics, its withdrawal is a necessary politics. But in the State, this temptation – the temptation of the 'unadorned sin' – is in danger of yielding to the temptation of temptation, where evil becomes the object of a rational political calculus, a means to the State's interested ends. Sabra and Shatilla can occur only where 'books are in jeopardy' (*TLR*, 296), that is, where Israel's sobriety is intoxicated by the State.

The task of thinking after Auschwitz might be defined as a tireless vigilance against such political intoxication. If the illusory horizon of the State is the attainment of the good, the possibility of ethics can only be a waiting for the good, a waiting that consigns us necessarily to being – to 'comparison, coexistence, contemporaneousness, assembly, order, thematization' (*OB*, 157; *AE*, 200). As Levinas insinuates from his earliest writings, evil can take hold only when this sovereignty of being becomes absolute. Concluding his 1935 essay, *De L'Evasion*, written in the shadow of Hitler's rise, he writes, '[e]very civilization that accepts being, the tragic despair it entails and the crimes it justifies, merits the name of barbarism'[53] (*DE*, 98). It is hard to avoid hearing in this diagnosis the anticipation of pervasive murder Levinas would describe in his Talmudic reading of forty years later: 'Everywhere war and murder lie concealed, assassination lurks in every corner, killings go on on the sly. There would be no radical difference between peace and Auschwitz' (*NTR*, 193; *DSS*, 174). The condition of possibility for Auschwitz is thus not the forgetting of Being, but of the immemorial beyond Being.[54] As in the vision of the simple goodwill gesture which leads the narrator of 'The Madness of the Day' to the chilly anonymity of a dark courtyard, the possibility of peace must endure the permanent shadow of war, of its own forgetting.

This is the predicament that responsibility shares with writing: both are destined to a desire for the Absolute which exceeds every desire, which ab-solves itself from every relation. Writing and responsibility converge at this moment of dispossession, where subjectivity is in contact with what tolerates only separation, remembers that which can only be forgotten. There is, moreover, no possible liberation from this insatiate desire, no redemption from the finitude which withholds the Good from me, for ethical and writerly desire seek only their own non-fulfilment, only that which draws desire perpetually towards 'one degree more'. The perpetual awakening to this one degree more is the measureless task of religion after Auschwitz.

CHAPTER 4

'To Preserve the Question':
Interrupting the Book, or Jabès

In the course of his 1982 speech to the Foundation for French Judaism, Edmond Jabès offers perhaps his most succinct and direct response to a question that haunts his entire corpus: what is Jewish writing?

> No, a Jewish theme is not enough to make a book Jewish. The Jewish tale [*récit*] is much less in the anecdote, the confession, the local color, than in the writing. You cannot tell [*raconte*] Auschwitz. Every word tells it to us. (*BM*, 173; *LM*, 182)

The argumentative sequence here is immediately disquieting; why does Jabès follow the dissociation of the Jewish tale from a particular narrative or descriptive content with the assertion that Auschwitz cannot be told? What is it that ties this proscription to the priority of 'writing' over 'theme'?

In insisting that it is writing itself rather than a given thematic or descriptive content that confers 'Jewishness' on a tale, Jabès undoes a key literary–critical distinction between form and content. Far from being one content among others to be appropriated and formed according to the author's will, Jewish experience announces instead the very exhaustion of both a communicable content and a bounded form, giving voice to the impossibility of its own 'telling'. This dissolution of the form–content distinction is what, for Jabès, gives Auschwitz to be thought through the twin terms of Judaism and writing. Where the anecdote would seek to disavow this crisis of telling, a 'Jewish' writing exposes it; and this difference points both to what prohibits the telling of Auschwitz and what demands its (Jewish) writing. If to tell Auschwitz is to contain it within a bounded form, to write it is first of all to acknowledge its inassimilability to any form. The 'horrible image' of 'six million burned bodies' (*BM*, 173; *LM*, 182) disperses the very language that would seek to comprehend it. Writing is the undergoing of this dispersion; in it, the power to tell is displaced from the subject to language itself, whose every word tells Auschwitz to us.

The dispossession of the subject's power of telling is illuminated by Giorgio Agamben's recent book, *Remnants of Auschwitz*. For Agamben, this dispossession characterizes precisely the predicament of the witness to the death camps: '*The authority of the witness consists in his capacity to speak solely in the name of an incapacity to speak . . .*' (RA, 158, Agamben's emphasis). The paradoxical imperative of the witness is to give voice to those who cannot speak, such that what is heard in that testimony is what dispossesses her as speaker; testimony begins where the subject's power of telling ends. Like Jabès, Agamben identifies the poet as the subject in which this 'desubjectified' condition finds its original expression.

The poet's significance lies in his status as the agency through which the unsayable lets itself be heard as such, as Agamben shows in his reading of Keats' letter of October 1818 to John Woodhouse. In this letter, Keats describes the ' "poetical Character" ' as without self or identity, a perpetual other to himself, and as such, '*the most unpoetical of all things*' (RA, 112, Agamben's emphasis). The poet's incapacity to coincide with himself makes his the exemplary experience of 'desubjectification', in which the impossibility of speaking in his own name comes to speech.

Agamben's description of poetic experience casts into relief the meaning of Jabès' claim that it is language itself, rather than the individual writer or text, that 'tells Auschwitz to us'. Exposed to mass death, the writer runs up against the abyssal absence of foundation which conditions his language; this experience is the means through which the silence of the dead comes to speech in its impossibility, the silence which is told to us by 'every word'. The demand of thinking after Auschwitz would be above all to expose and bear witness to this silence at the heart of language.

We have seen a demand of this kind staged in the previous chapters through the structures of art and religion, and their specific unfolding in poetry and Judaism. This chapter will seek to unfold the convergence of these twin itineraries in the sustained and singular project of writing pursued by Jabès from 1962 until his death in 1991. In this sense, the readings that follow, while ranging widely across the motifs and concepts that govern his texts, are intended as a kind of extended interpretation of one of his texts' most famous self-descriptions, written by Yukel, the spectral 'protagonist' of the third of *The Book of Questions*' seven volumes:

First I thought I was a writer. Then I realized I was a Jew. Then I no longer distinguished the writer in me from the Jew because one and the other are only torments of an ancient word [*parole*]. (BQ1, 361; LQ1, 398)

In a later text, Jabès revisits this pronouncement in the light of those who have read it as an assertion of the identity of Jew and writer; instead, he counters, it should be understood as 'suggesting their common relation to the text' (LP, 89).[1] The sameness of Judaism and writing, in other words, is not the cancellation of their differences. It points rather to the ways in which their irreducibly different languages and traditions articulate the same passion for the impossible, the same 'torments of an ancient word'. We have glimpsed intimations of this ancient word in previous chapters: in the Hölderlinian name which signifies the irredeemable promise of redemption for Adorno, in the pre-original saying which conditions the insomniac human relation in Levinas. In Jabès, these poetic and religious approaches to the Absolute converge in their differences. This chapter will therefore be concerned in large part with the ways in which he draws on and rewrites those moments in both poetic and Judaic tradition which expose this 'ancient' word and exacerbate its torments. Rather than seek its redemption, Jabès makes torment's irredeemability the organizing principle of his writing. And yet, in keeping with the paradox explored across this book, this irredeemability is not to be seen in opposition to redemption. The messianic horizon which haunts all of his texts takes the paradoxical form of its non-achievement; the affinity of Judaism and writing lies in their shared thinking of redemption as that which is maintained in its promise rather than its realization. It is for this reason that perhaps the most privileged term in Jabès' thought is the *question*, for the question is the form which maintains itself only in its irresolution, the originary mode of incompletion.

Jabès' approach to Auschwitz and the task of thinking that it imposes has raised the serious charge of mystification. Does the characterization of the Nazi genocide as the unsayable at the heart of every said not render it interchangeable with the void, language or God?[2] Jabès seems to speak directly to this charge when he describes his writing as 'starting from two limits. /Beyond [*Au-delà*] there is the void./ On this side [*En-deça*], the horror of Auschwitz' (*LP*, 95). Writing, on this account, is the point at which the limit of thought and the limit of history converge; Jabès is quite conscious that these limits occupy different spaces, and as such cannot be identified. And yet to run up against the limit of history is to be dispossessed of the resources for conceptualizing it, such that to start from the horror *en-deça* is already to be exposed to the void *au-delà*. Far from mystifying Auschwitz, Jabès' writing seeks to delineate with the utmost specificity and precision its meaning and implications for the future task of thought.

This precision is what confers on his texts their striking singularity of form. Generically unclassifiable, they shift incessantly between skeletally intimated narratives, imaginary rabbinic quotations, poetry, philosophical meditation, anonymous monologue and dialogue, all of whose mutual interpenetration and interruption is mimed through constant changes in typeface. If in Jabès philosophy has become writing, it is because it has been dispossessed by history of the capacity to express itself in the form of conventional discursive propositions. In the face of events which disperse rather than determine meaning, philosophical concepts undergo their own ruin; in Jabès, writing and Judaism are the modes through which this ruin unfolds itself.

INCOMPLETE WRITING

The meaning of writing, Judaism and their convergence in Jabès can be clarified by setting them against the Ideals which condition the judgement of art and religion in Hegel's system. Hegel's *Aesthetics* defines the Ideal of poetry as the unbroken unity of matter and spirit, content and form. The 'essential nature of works of art proper (i.e. of the Ideal)' involves 'both a subject-matter not inherently arbitrary and transient and also a mode of portrayal in correspondence with such a subject-matter'. Against the backdrop of this Ideal, Hegel questions whether romantic works of art are 'still to be called works of art' (*A* 1, 596; *VA* 2, 223); for the history of romantic art as he recounts it is the history of an ever-widening divide between the inner life and the external world, such that both in themselves and in relation to one another each becomes increasingly arbitrary, contingent and meaningless.

Hegel's critique of romantic art finds an uncannily precise correlation in his critique of Judaism. As the actualized unity of being and knowledge, religion attains its highest form in knowledge of God: 'The object of religion, like that of philosophy, is the eternal truth, God and nothing but God and the explication of God' (*LPR*, 152–3). As such, Judaism is repeatedly impugned across Hegel's authorship for falling short of the true religious object, for its sublime conception of God places an infinite and insuperable distance between human and divine. The *Aesthetics* takes pains to show how this distance makes itself felt in the sublime depths of Biblical Hebrew poetry. The Psalms exemplify the lyric restlessness which results from the irreconcilability of inner life and its divine object. Psalm 29, for example, bears witness to God's infinite greatness by way of a potentially endless attestation to the different modalities of his 'might and truth' (' "The voice of the Lord is powerful; the voice of the Lord is full of majesty. The voice of the Lord breaketh the cedars; yea, the Lord breaketh the cedars of Lebanon" '). In such 'lyrical sublimity', no 'peaceful beauty' can be achieved, for consciousness is always running anxiously behind its object:

> Caught in this vagueness, the subjective inner life cannot portray its unattainable object to itself in peaceful beauty or enjoy its self-expression in a work of art. Instead of a peaceful picture, imagination seizes on external phenomena and juxtaposes them fragmentarily and in disorder, and since in its inner life it does not achieve any firm articulation of its particular ideas, it avails itself in its external expression of only an arbitrary and irregular rhythm. (*A* 2, 1140; *VA* 3, 453)

The Psalms, then, reveal the restless inner life that is the irremediable failure of both lyric poetry and Judaism. Yet, as we have seen, it is precisely in this restlessness that Adornian art and Levinasian religion find their points of departure.

For the former, rather than recover its lost ideal, '[a]rt must turn against itself, in opposition to its own concept, and thus become uncertain of itself right into its innermost fiber' (*A T*, 2; *GS* 7, 10); poetry after Auschwitz becomes the perpetual revocation of its own reconciliatory ideal. Levinas, in turn, far from positing God as object of the highest knowledge, thinks religion as that which maintains God outside the reach of the concept, as the relation to an Absolute which 'ab-solves' itself from every relation. In Judaism the irremediable restlessness or 'desire' which characterizes this relation becomes the very substance of religious experience. Measured against the Hegelian religious Ideal of the reconciliation of finite and infinite, Levinasian religion too can be described as 'turning against itself'.

Cast in the light of these twin renunciations, Jabès' project reveals itself as the unfolding of writing and Judaism in the impossibility of their completion. Such a project is caught in a necessarily ambivalent relation to the poetic and religious traditions it must simultaneously invoke and interrupt. Jabès' peculiar continuity with both traditions consists in drawing out what in them is most resistant to comprehension or resolution, that which reveals the voiding rather than fulfilment of meaning. But where in the histories of writing and Judaism does Jabès find such resources?

THE SILENCE OF WORDS: MALLARMÉ AFTER CELAN

Literary tradition offers a range of possible genealogies in which to situate Jabès' project. Born into the francophone context of the Egyptian Jewish community, his early poetry of the 1930s and 1940s was written under the immediate influence of surrealism, and in particular of his earliest mentor Max Jacob. In the course of his instructive dialogues with Marcel Cohen, he further invokes Baudelaire, the symbolist poets, Kafka, Proust and Joyce as key texts in the formation of his writerly identity (*FDB*, 10; *DDL*, 27–8).[3] Undoubtedly, however, the writer whose lexicon resonates most directly through Jabès' corpus is Stéphane Mallarmé. From the idea of the Book – the term around which the mature Jabès' corpus orbits – to the interruptive fracture of the page's visual format, this resonance is felt at every level of Jabès' texts.

Philippe Lacoue-Labarthe's account, in his *Poetry As Experience*, of Celan's reading and rewriting of Hölderlin provides an apposite framework for theorizing Jabès' relationship to Mallarmé. Both poets write in a displaced relationship to their adoptive literary tradition, and each recasts his chosen predecessor in the shadow of Auschwitz. The predecessors in question, moreover, are chosen because they perhaps more than any other poets in their respective traditions expose the abyssal truth of language. For Lacoue-Labarthe, the poem as Celan conceives it is the interruption of art from within, an estrangement of art's eloquence by the abyssal silence which founds it:

> poetry, if it ever occurs, occurs as the brutal revelation of the abyss that contains art (language) and nevertheless constitutes it, as such, in its strangeness ... Poetry, by this account, can be called the abyss of art (language): it makes art [language] abysmal. [*La poésie, à ce compte, dite abîme de l'art (le langage): elle abîme l'art (le langage)*][4]

The central motif for this abyss is the Hölderlinian 'retreat of the divine', in which God is manifest only in his concealment; revelation, on this model, is not Hegel's 'perfect being-in-evidence' (Lacoue-Labarthe, 117, 162), but an exposure of the void which conditions being. In a reading of Celan's poem 'Tenebrae', Lacoue-Labarthe finds the profound affinity and immeasurable distance between the earlier and later poet in an image of God's revelation–withdrawal:

> Gegriffen schon, Herr,
> ineinander verkrallt, als wär
> der Leib eines jeden von uns
> dein Leib, Herr.

> [Handled already, Lord,
> clawed and clawing as though
> the body of each of us were
> your body, Lord.]

Lacoue-Labarthe's gloss of this passage takes pains to distance the resemblance it insinuates between the divine and the human body from any anthropomorphism. Celan is following Hölderlin in conceiving this resemblance in terms of an absence at the heart of both the human and the divine. Yet where in the earlier poet this absence is the means by which (in the words of 'In Lovely Blueness' ['*In Lieblicher Bläue*'], '"Man not unhappily can measure himself with the divine"' (cited by Lacoue-Labarthe, 114, 158), in Celan's poem this measure is reversed, 'in order to signify that God's image is man's blood shed: God present, which is to say withdrawn, not in "the figure of death", but in the face of the dead – the exterminated' (Lacoue-Labarthe, 119, 166). This is not to render God and the exterminated interchangeable, but to locate in the image of the dead the abyssal figure of divine concealment.

In *Le Memoire des Mots*, a tribute to Celan as both friend and poet, as well as an implicit description of his own poetic, Jabès places this abyssal or 'silent' language at the heart of his response:

At a given moment, . . . silence is so strong that words express nothing else.

This silence, capable of making language collapse [*basculer*], has it not its own language in that to which we can attribute neither origin nor name? . . . But the question still to be posed: would the language of silence be that of the refusal of language or, on the contrary, that of the memory of the first word? (*MDM*, 13–14)

The difference between 'the refusal of language' and 'the memory of the first word' is the difference between silence as the simple negation of speech, and as the unsayable condition of speech's possibility. To refuse language is to remain caught within its restricted economy, whereas to maintain the memory of the first, immemorial word is to recognize the silence internal to words, the silence which, in confronting language with its own perilous lack of foundation, causes it to fall in on itself. It is this internal silence in 'every word' which 'tells Auschwitz to us'.

The task that Jabès' writing assumes is above all to let this silence be heard without traducing or (to take advantage of the resonance of the French '*traduction*') *translating* it. This affinity of translation and betrayal is brought into focus by Hans-Jost Frey's reading of metaphor in Mallarmé in his *Studies in Poetic Discourse*.[5] Taking the example of the 1895 'A la nue accablante tue' sonnet, Frey reveals in its image of 'babbling foam' (*écume . . . baves*) nothing less than a metaphor for the play of language itself. However, where metaphor is conventionally understood as the indirect expression of an expressed content, Mallarmé's metaphor singularly fails to yield up any such content to its interpreter. Metaphor here is rather what enables the 'expressing of something' without its becoming 'something expressed' (Frey, 28, 28), that is, without translation. Foam thus figures the very noncorrespondence which ruins figuration, separating language from reference. The sonnet unfolds the impossibility of its own translation, expressing nothing but expression itself, severed from any content or message.

Frey's reading of Mallarmé brings into focus his centrality for the development of Jabès' poetic and philosophical lexicon, for Mallarmé's poetry, essays and correspondence attest to an unrelieved obsession with the possibility – and impossibility – of giving expression to the 'first word', or language itself. The untranslatable metaphor, as the taking place of a word without reference beyond itself, lets the unsayable be heard at the heart of speech. From this perspective, Jabès' statement of the impossibility of my telling Auschwitz points to the same untranslatability. For 'you' to tell Auschwitz would be to render it intelligible as an expressed content, that is, to translate it. If instead 'every word tells it to us', its untranslatability is maintained, for this telling by the word is not the communication but the erasure of content. Auschwitz can be told only via the paradoxical means of this erasure. In Blanchot's words, from his fragmentary meditation on 'writing the disaster',

This is the era destined to the intermittence of a language unburdened of words
and dispossessed ... writing which distinguishes itself by deleting from itself all
distinguishing marks, which is to say perhaps, ultimately by effacing itself .....
(*WD*, 34; *ED*, 58)

If Blanchot's description of the era's writerly destiny cannot but evoke Jabès'
project, it equally points backward to the logic of the Mallarméan poem. For as
Blanchot himself teaches in successive studies, Mallarmé's poetry is modern literature's most passionate and sustained articulation of the desire for a 'supreme
language', an 'immortal Word'[6] at the heart of ordinary words. In his writing, this
desire insinuates itself ruinously into the texture of everyday language: 'Essential
language shines suddenly in the heart of the skies, and its brilliance attacks, consumes, devours historical language, which is compromised but not replaced'.[7]
There is no 'replacing' historical language, because no way of realizing the desire
for the immortal Word, inasmuch as this Word is precisely what evades the
phenomenal world. Only in its silent consumption of 'historical language', that
is, of the semantic content of words – Blanchot's self-effacing writing – does
Mallarmé's essential language make itself present. His poetry is nothing but this
consumption, a perpetual witness to the impossible dream of the absolute Word:
'We dream of words brilliant at once in meaning and sound, or darkening in meaning and so in sound, luminously and elementally self-succeeding. But, let us
remember that if our dream were fulfilled, *verse would not exist* ...' ('CV', 38,
CC 364, Mallarmé's emphasis). The existence of verse, that is, expresses the
poet's simultaneous hope and the despair of the essential language. Poetry would
be annihilated by the fulfilment of the dream it expresses; for if the poem's dream is
the absolute coincidence of 'meaning and sound', its reality is their insuperable disjunction. The dream is in this sense inseparable from, indeed *is*, its own impossibility.

The term that most precisely compacts this dream in Mallarmé's thought is, of
course, the Book. The Book is the container of 'all earthly existence', 'an immacu-
late grouping of universal relationships come together for some miraculous and
glittering occasion' (*SP*, 24–5; *OC*, 378). Every historical book is born of the
desire for its own consummation in this ultimate Book, in which the dream of an
immortal Word would finally take on form. Yet, notwithstanding the Hegelian
resonances of these statements, the Book, far from being a figure for absolute
knowing, is the very sign of its undoing. If Mallarmé's poetry and thought has
become a central resource for recent continental philosophy's questioning of literature, it is because it persistently wrenches the word away from, as Derrida puts
it, 'any sure revelation of meaning',[8] and towards what he calls (invoking one of
Mallarmé's key motifs), a ceaseless and irreducible textual *folding*. The folding
of the text prevents all attempts at interpretative mastery by way of an infinite

suspension of referentiality: 'In folding back on itself, the text thus *parts* (with) reference, spreads it like a V, a gap that pivots on its point, a dancer, flower, or Idea' (Derrida, 239, 211, Derrida's emphasis).

Hegelian absolute knowing sees the final reconciliation of the concept's disparate elements: between its 'individuality' ('*Einzelheit*') and its 'universality', and between its 'abstract universality' and 'the Self'. The realization of the identity of these elements is 'Spirit that knows itself in the shape of Spirit', or the 'self-certainty' of Truth (*PS*, 485; *PG*, 581–2). The Book – ostensibly Mallarmé's correlative term to Absolute Knowledge – in fact effects the very ruin of such self-certainty; where Absolute Knowledge cancels the disparity between universal and particular, the Book exacerbates it, exposes its irreparability. For the instrument of the Book's realization – the sum of individual books – is also what will have always already prevented its realization. As expressions of the 'imperfect' multiplicity of languages, books and the words which comprise them have by virtue of their imperfection blocked the way to 'Truth Herself Incarnate' (*SP*, 38; *OC*, 364). The existence of verse, and especially Mallarmé's verse, signifies the necessary non-fulfilment of the very dream that engenders it.

As Frey painstakingly shows, the structuring principle of his poetry is an irresolvable contradiction between wish and fulfilment, for the one of necessity negates the other. The Faun of Mallarmé's great poem is exemplary here, for his desire to appropriate his desired nymphs in language effects their annihilation in reality, such that he remains perpetually caught between 'meaningless reality and unreal meaning' (Frey, 38, 34). To choose between the 'wish' of meaning and the 'fulfilment' of reality is thus to point up their essential irreconcilability: 'The Faun is trapped in language, because on the one hand he tries to go beyond language in order to achieve what he does not have in it and on the other hand must stay in language in order not to lose what he cannot find outside it' (Frey, 42, 38). The predicament of the Faun is that of writing (or the book) itself, whose movement towards its own transcendence (or the Book) is consigned to the very language which prevents it.

If we have taken pains to distinguish the self-destructive character of Mallarméan teleology from the self-certainty of Hegel's, it is in order to specify just how the former insinuates itself into Jabès' thought and writing. In an important interview with Paul Auster, Jabès acknowledges the centrality of his predecessor's terms, and most obviously the Book, for the development of his own thought, while measuring his distance from them. This distance consists in a different ambition for the book; where Mallarmé dreamed of putting all knowledge in a single Book, he says, '[t]he book that would have a chance to survive, I think, is the book that destroys itself, that destroys itself in favour of another book that will prolong it'.[9] The distinction appears to align Mallarmé with Hegel in order to establish the non-teleological status of his own Book. Yet from this perspective, Jabès would fall foul of Paul de Man's critique of a continuous literary history (exemplified for de Man by Jauss and his school) which conceives of literary modernity in terms of a progressive intensification of obscurity and fragmentation. On that model, Jabès develops and radicalizes the destabilized poetics only nascent in Mallarmé.

Yet de Man suggests a different way of thinking the relation between the poet and his predecessor which would cast Jabès' statement in a different light. Again, it is Celan and Hölderlin that provide the exemplar; in citing Hölderlin, Celan's 1963 poem 'Tübingen, Jänner' does not set the 'light' of the former's language against the 'darkness' of its own. Rather, 'Celan repeats quotations from Hölderlin that assert their own incomprehensibility'.[10] Poetic tradition tells the story not of a progressive advance in technique but of a perpetual repetition of the impossibility of advance, of the poet's destiny to repeat the incomprehensibility of his predecessor without redeeming it.[11]

Read from this perspective, Jabès' contrast between the Mallarméan Book and his own is less an attempt to set his own self-destructive poetic in opposition to his predecessor's 'teleological' poetic, than to draw out and expose that which in Mallarmé has already ruined his ostensibly teleological presuppositions. Mallarmé's projected book of the future, in which 'all earthly existence must ultimately be contained' (SP, 24; OC, 378), is revealed by Jabès' statement as the very same book which 'destroys itself in favour of another book that will prolong it'.

Jabès' relationship to tradition – both poetic and Judaic – is thus staked above all in those moments which interrupt tradition's continuity, exacerbating its inner tendency to prolong rather than complete itself. Tradition provides him with terms – the Book, the Law, God – which designate the Absolute as that which, far from founding and guaranteeing meaning, perpetually disperses it. The importance for Jabès of Mallarmé's inventory of poetic strategies – not only the motif of the Book, but the fascination for the blank page which founds writing, the paradoxical figuration of nothingness, and, in the famous instance of *Un Coup de Dés*, the derangement of the verse page's spatial organization – lies in their yoking of the Absolute to its own constitutive incompletion.[12]

If Derrida and Frey's penetrating readings have revealed this structure of incompletion and so pointed to the profound affinities between Mallarmé and Jabès' writings, it remains to show in just what the difference between them consists. What is the transformation that Mallarmé's lexicon – and particularly the motif of the Book – undergoes in its reinscription by Jabès?

THE EXILE OF THE BOOK

If Mallarmé's poetic telos is distinguished by its impossibility, there is nevertheless a tendency at work in his early poetry, essays and correspondence to characterize this impossibility as the consequence of a tragically insurmountable gap between the Real and the Ideal. The exemplary document of this tendency is a letter of June 1863 to his close friend Henri Cazalis, in which he insists, against Baudelaire's 'lament' that 'Action was not the sister of the Dream', on the Dream's necessary and absolute inviolability:

> Dear Lord, if it were otherwise, if the Dream were thus debased and deflowered, where would we retreat to, we unlucky ones whom the earth repels and for whom the Dream alone offers refuge? Henri, my friend, seek your sustenance from the Ideal.[13]

The Ideal as Mallarmé evokes it here is less impossible than *unattainable*; the rhetoric of lament which opposes its quasi-Platonic transcendence to the ignobility of 'earthly happiness' confers upon it a higher substantiality not unlike that of the God of negative theology. It is to this Mallarmé that Jabès could be said to be addressing himself when he responds thus to a silent and anonymous interlocutor:

> We have nothing in common and at the same time everything: an unshakable faith in the book. But for you, the book is a place of refuge, for me, a link with exile, with death, that is, a link with a word [*parole*] which for dying of its merits deprives us of our place, link with the sacrifice to a word to which we cannot come back and which is closed against our fervor. (*BQ2*, 301; *LQ2*, 415)

The faith that Jabès shares with his interlocutor is directed towards an object both the identical and absolutely different; the book which the Mallarmé of 1863 gestures towards as the only possible 'refuge' against the world has become in Jabès' text the point of contact with the impossible, with 'exile', 'death' and 'a word to which we cannot come back'. Jabès' texts unfold in the irremediable exhaustion of any refuge, in the shadow of the immemorial world which refuses our 'fervor'. In this sense, the 'nothing in common' they have with the Mallarmé of 1863 is shadowed by the 'everything' they have in common with the Mallarmé of 1894 and *Un Coup de Dés*.

The first word of the later poem's third folio – 'SOIT' – will invoke the Ideal with an allusion to the 'Let there be' of Genesis,[14] only to expose not divine light, but 'l'Abîme/blanchi/étale/furieux' ('the Abyss/blanched/spread/furious') (*CP*, 129; *OC*, 460). Between these two texts, then, the Ideal as 'refuge' has yielded to the Ideal as 'Abyss'. Far from providing the secure guarantee against the Real conjured by the letter to Cazalis, the thought of the Ideal in the later poem engenders only a fall into abyssal Nothingness (mimed by the vertiginous diagonal drop of single-word lines down the page).

What this necessarily compacted and schematic comparison points to is the simultaneity of continuity and rupture which characterizes Jabès' relationship to

Mallarmé. In distinguishing his from Mallarmé's Book, Jabès is both divesting the term of any residual 'architectural' (to use Cahen's term) connotations, and drawing out for his own project that dimension of his predecessor's thought which 'asserts its own incomprehensibility'. In this respect, *Un Coup de Dés* anticipates *The Book of Questions* in more than its radical typographical strategies; it augurs the later text's positing of the Absolute as that which undoes rather than guarantees meaning.

For Jabès, every attempt to approach the Absolute – writing's approach to the Book, man's approach to God – takes the doubled form of an infinite diversion.[15] Once again, Blanchot helps illuminate this paradoxical movement; in an essay entitled 'The Most Profound Question', he describes the posing of this question as the affirmation of 'the Entirely Other where there is no longer any return to the same' (*IC*, 19; *EI*, 25). But the Entirely Other (like the *Âbime* of Mallarmé's poem) dissolves the very language of the question that would comprehend it. The Other to which the profound question addresses itself can remain other only by being kept in reserve, by refusing to lend itself to any conceptual or dialectical resolution. It must derail the question which approaches it, such that the question becomes this very derailment, an approach in the mode of detour.

Jabès' thinking of the Book, then, consists not in setting himself against Mallarmé's project, but in revealing at its heart this detour which haunts and per-petually erases its Dream. It is to this detour which the following examination of the Jabèsian Book will now submit.

'*The ... of ... or the Absent Book*': this title of one of the most explicit of Jabès' many attempts to describe the condition of the book – a section from the first volume of *The Book of Resemblances* – signifies by its silent ellipses the impossible thought of the Book. In the course of this description, Jabès brings these ellipses to speech without thereby 'translating' them:

> Such a work, being boundless [*illimité*], cannot be. It accompanies our books. It inspires them. It would be their model if it existed. Because it does not exist, it is the obsession of the book and, in practice, its explosion [*éclatement*] of which we cannot state precisely where it happened or how far it was felt – mingled cries of mother and child? – but which is perhaps only a scream of letters, of words [*vocables*] torn from themselves, as the supposed author of this book was torn from his life to become its writing:
>
> the writing of his death. (*BR1*, 18; *LR*, 32)[16]

The Mallarméan 'obsession of the book' begins from the impossibility of attain-ing its object, which is not an object; non-existent in the Levinasian sense of being other to the phenomenal realm, the 'work' that accompanies and inspires all books is the ruin of every will to objectify. The 'supposed author' of this and every book is destined to this ruin, to dispossession by the very Book he would like to possess.

This dispossession is the death of the writer as subject, the exposure of what Blanchot calls the absurdity of wanting to write where '[w]riting is the decay of will, just as it is the loss of power' (*WD*, 11; *ED*, 24). Jabès' non-existent work can never be brought into being as such; it can only haunt the text in the (non)form of an 'explosion', a tearing of words from sense, of writer from life; the tearing of the book is the trace of the Book.

Jabès' description of the 'Absent Book' thus brings to speech the unsayable ellipses of *The ... of ...* without negating or redeeming their unsayability. Like the Mallarméan metaphor elaborated by Frey, the 'work' which accompanies and inspires every book is refractory to every attempt at translation, indeed, is untranslatability itself. It is this untranslatability which destines the book to 'remain unappeased desire for the book, longing for a refused word [*parole*].' (*BQ2*, 331; *LQ2*, 452).[17] Yet like Adornian *Sehnsucht* or Levinasian Desire, this longing seeks not its fulfilment but its maintenance. The 'refused word' it desires is the dissolution of the language that would contain it, the Absolute that ab-solves itself, keeping book and Book apart.

The Jabèsian book refuses every form which would sate this longing. It is in terms of this refusal that we must understand his polemic against 'the novel' in *Yaël*, the fourth volume of *The Book of Questions*. Comprising fragments from a letter to his friend, the critic Gabriel Bounoure, this polemic is staked above all in the distinction between book and narrative:

> I now believe (and I have come to see this as a truth on which the book's reality depends), I now believe that narrative in the usual sense is not the business of the book, that it is extraneous to the book.
>
> The writer who declares himself a novelist or a storyteller does not serve the book; he does not care about it for one moment and even considers it less than nothing.
>
> A novel is a writer's triumph over the book, and not the opposite, because the novelist makes a strong entrance with his characters and, with them as go-betweens, gives free rein to his innumerable voices. The book is trampled by them, its voice choked by theirs.
>
> [...]
>
> The day I shall write a novel I shall have left the book, have lost it. (*BQ2*, 35–6; *LQ2*, 54–5)

The novel is the forgetting of the book, the illusory mastery of writing's abyssal truth. To 'tell' a story, as Jabès intimated in his pronouncement on telling Auschwitz, is to appropriate the sovereignty that belongs to language itself. Where the novel is subject of language, the book is subject to it; where the writer of the novel claims possession over what dispossesses him, the writer of the book submits to this dispossession.

Jabès' image of the book choking under the novelist's grasp needs to be read in the broader context of *Yaël*, a text haunted by the intimated (rather than 'told') narrative of a writer who strangles to death his faithless lover. Jabès' writing of this tale plunges the lover (Yaël) into the same condition of ontological undecidability which characterized the nymphs in Mallarmé's 'L'Après-midi d'un Faune'. Frey's reading of the poem described the Faun's predicament as a desire split between the 'meaningless reality' of the nymphs outside language (the fulfilment and annihilation of his wish) and their 'unreal meaning' within it (the maintenance of his wish and suspension of its fulfilment). The decision of Yaël's lover to 'kill' her arises from his inability to bear the same predicament; murdering her is a vain attempt to put an end to her insuperable otherness, to place her finally in his grasp by way of the absolute consummation of his desire to possess her.

Yet it is precisely at this point of apparent possession that she eludes him. In the course of an erotic embrace, the writer feels himself transform under her gaze into her lover – '*the other*'. In the transitory delirium of gratitude that he experiences in finally taking the place of *the other*, he presses her to him until she 'collapsed without a sign of life' (*BQ*2, 69; *LQ*2, 98). Staring at her corpse, he realizes the illusory nature of his union with Yaël:

> I was no longer *the other*. He stood behind me. I realized that the immense distance Yaël had tried to put between us canceled the apparent distance between *the other* and me, so that I was the nightmare she fought by clutching her lover across my hands which did not let go of her neck. Her eyes told [*racontaient*] him her love, told him her repulsion for me. They told [*disaient*] him her faithfulness beyond death. (*BQ*2, 70; *LQ*2, 100, Jabès' emphasis)

In murdering Yaël, the lover seeks an absolute coincidence between himself and his other, such that the 'immense distance' she places between them would collapse.[18] Yet the transitory illusion of this coincidence in the act of love/murder gives way to a confrontation with its impossibility. The writer awakens from the dream to find himself still irreparably divided, 'no longer *the other*', still irreducibly distant from the object of his desire. Yaël's dead pupils – 'so cruelly, so stubbornly hard' (*BQ*2, 69; *LQ*2, 99) – taunt him with this unredeemed distance; even in the moment of extinction, they reach toward *the other*.[19]

If the ontological status of Yaël in the text is undecidable, it is because she is a figure for what escapes the will's attempt to impose itself on language. The text suspends her, like Mallarmé's nymphs, between the real and the figural, making of her both faithless lover and (untranslatable) metaphor for language itself. Jabès deliberately employs stock novelistic tropes – Yaël is caught writing surreptitiously to her lover and assures the writer, 'I was writing to my mother' (*BQ*2, 86; *LQ*2, 123). Yet the effect of the text is to undermine the referential stability of such tropes; the straying lover dissimulating her affair is simultaneously the 'writing' whose itinerary defies the writer's capacity to direct it, even as it seems to assure him otherwise.

Read in this context, Jabès' meta-narrative digression on the novel and the book comes into focus. The fragmentary tale of the writer and Yaël's doomed love mimes the novelist's ambition to take command of the book, and the book's stubborn indifference to this ambition. Even 'choked' in the grip of the novel, the book's voice, like Yaël's eyes, whispers its fidelity to another horizon, to the horizon of *the other*.

Yet the Yaël narrative also attests to the impossibility of hearing the book's voice other than through its 'choking'; the pure language of the book is perpetually consigned to the referential language of the novel and of everyday speech. As thought of absolute alterity – her name's two syllables are both Hebrew Names of God – Yaël can assume textual existence only by 'dying', that is, by a betrayal of her non-being and silence. Yaël, like Jabès' Book, 'does not exist' and 'cannot be', except through her trace in the book.

Jabès' writerly strategies and motifs form an intricate network of signs by which this silence is brought to speech without being translated, that is, as silence. In this sense, the insistent interruption of text by blank space is the exemplary Jabèsian gesture. Whiteness is here to be understood not as a making visible of the invisible, which would keep intact an economy of representation, but as an undoing of their very opposition. White space in Jabès' texts *makes nothing visible*, or is the making visible of no thing or content; what is signified instead is an impossibility of truth's presentation. It is what is named, in the essay on Celan, a 'language of silence' which, far from being 'the refusal of language' is 'the memory of the first word'.

In *Aely*, the sixth volume of *The Book of Questions* and perhaps the most explicitly self-descriptive, the white page is described as the 'preferred repository' of a truth which 'takes ruthless revenge' on 'those who claim to own [*détenir*] it' (*BQ*2, 284; *LQ*2, 392):

> Untransmissible truth, a sister of silence and the abyss. Is the white page perhaps its privileged repository [*détentrice*]? All whiteness is violence, like the wall's mute determination to block our road. All whiteness is God's color, which in the silence of an infinite truth pierces our eyes and crushes. Is the writer's struggle not this mad effort to sink his hands into the sand of the shore just once before the wave takes him back? (*BQ*2, 284; *LQ*2, 392)[20]

In what does the 'violence' of whiteness consist? It is a violence with no object because it is without subjectivity, is subjectivity's very dissolution. Whiteness, with the mute indifference of the wall, places an infinite distance between the hand and the object it would grasp, the distance which taunts the writer of *Yaël* at the very moment he believes himself to have mastered it. This is why the murderous writer's predicament is that of writing itself; adrift on the sea of language, the writer's attempt to anchor himself on shore is also an awakening to the vanity of his gesture, of his insuperable groundlessness. If the murderous writer and the novelist are figures for the intolerability of this groundlessness, and for the 'mad effort' to forget it, the intrusion of the white page is the tormenting insinuation of its memory.

'To speak of the book of the desert', writes Jabès at the end of the first volume of *The Book of Resemblances*,[21] 'is as absurd as to speak of the book of nothing. /And yet, on this nothing I have built my books' (*BR*1, 112; *LR*, 148). Any reading of Jabès' project must begin from its foundation in this nothing, this abyssal absence of foundation. Its will to its perpetual self-erasure cannot be thought apart from this nothingness, for erasure is the mark of the book's search for its own impossible ground. If '[m]aking a book, or, rather, helping it to come into being means above all blurring its utopian tracks, wiping out the trace' (*BQ*2, 30; *LQ*2, 47),[22] it is because its 'utopia' – its consummation as Book – is what presents itself only in the form of an erasure. In *Intimations The Desert (Le Soupçon Le Desert)*, the second volume of *The Book of Resemblances*, Jabès elaborates the inextricability of the book's impossible origin and its infinite prolongation in erasure:

> But the book is always the beginning of the incomplete book defined by its very incompleteness, the beginning of an interrupted rebeginning whose sense and key lie in the hands of death. Remains to be seen [*reste à savoir*] what the book is and what was the book of our very first childhood. An erased book, no doubt whose erasure is remembered by all books. (*BR* 2, 76; *LR*, 236)

The book as yet unknown, the book which precedes and conditions all books, is 'an erased book'; it comes to the memory of 'all books' by withdrawing from them, destining them to their condition of irredeemable incompleteness. The 'book of our very first childhood' is never revealed other than as what Blanchot calls, in his essay on Jabès, 'the unoriginal text of the origin' (*F*, 225; *A*, 254). The text of the origin is 'unoriginal' because it can never appear as such, but only in the guise of the texts which ceaselessly repeat or 'rebegin' it.[23]

It bears reiterating, however, that this condition of repetition is not to be opposed to the book's fulfilment. For Jabès, the book can be redeemed only in the paradoxical mode of its non-redemption, as he intimates in an aphorism from *The Little Book of Unsuspected Subversion (Petit Livre de Subversion hors de Soupçon)*: 'An endless book can find completion only in that of its unforeseeable prolongations' (*LBUS*, 78; *PLS*, 84). In prolongation, endlessness and completion enter into a zone of indistinction.[24]

But how can a text actualize the logic of prolongation? Above all, it is through the modality of the question that the end undergoes, in Blanchot's phrase, its own 'measurelessness'. Not merely one mode of thinking amongst others, the question is the site of a paradoxical ontology, as Jabès suggests in this passage from *Elya*:

> Being means questioning. Means interrogating yourself in the labyrinths of the Question put to the other [*autrui*] and to God, and which does not expect any answer. (*BQ2*, 153; *LQ2*, 218)

As questioning, being is divested of its substantiality, defined not by a determinate essence but by a process that cannot be contained by the finite logic of the answer. The question as thought by Jabès is not a dialectical step awaiting its negation and consummation; its meaning and ethical force derives rather from its perpetual maintenance *as question*. As Andrew Benjamin argues, 'the distancing of completion should not be understood as failure, as something still undone. It is not as though identity has yet to be achieved or finality to be attained' (*PH*, 149). Rather, the question has always already dissolved the attainment of finality.

Yet if questioning is the condition of writing, what authorizes Jabès to claim that it shares this condition with Judaism? What is it in Jewish tradition that suggests this affinity?

THE QUESTION OF THE FUTURE: JUDAISM

Judaism is conjugated in the future.

(BS, 22; LP, 32)

So that writing always means waiting for salvation by a word still to come, *the writer being unable to express himself except in the future.*

(BS, 36; LP, 52–3, emphasis Jabès')[25]

These two sentences from Jabès' 1987 text, *The Book of Shares* (*Le Livre du Partage*),[26] reveal the term that draws Judaism into a common space with writing. Eight years on, Jacques Derrida's book *Archive Fever* (*Mal d'Archive*) will similarly invoke futurity – *l'à-venir*, or the future/to come – as the point of convergence between 'being-Jewish' and the 'archive'. Like Derridean writing, the archive finds its identity in its own perpetual prolongation: 'the archivist produces more archive, and that is why the archive is never closed'. Jewishness '*beyond all Judaism*', that is, a Jewishness beyond and irreducible to any doctrinal or theological tenet of Judaism, is defined for Derrida by this archival principle, a 'messianic' openness to the future *as future*.[27] Developing some suggestive lines of thought in the work of Y. H. Yerushalmi, Derrida finds in the Judaic imperative to remember ('*Zachor*') a practice of memory distinguished by this openness, such that, '[t]he being-Jewish and the being-open-toward-the-the-future would be the same thing'.[28] The messianic future indissociable from being-Jewish is a future that '*remains to come*'; like Levinas' sober Messiah, its irreducible futurity could only be annulled by its realization: 'The condition on which the future remains to come is not only that it not be known, but that it not be *knowable as such*'.[29] The unknowability of the future that draws together being-Jewish, writing and the archive is not a temporary condition anticipating its redemption in knowledge, but a constitutive unknowability, an exteriority to the order of knowledge *as such*.

Derrida's text helps to specify just what is at stake philosophically and religiously in the affinity of writing and Judaism which Jabès ceaselessly elaborates. Both thinkers effect a disjunction between the messianic principle and its fulfilment (this is what Derrida terms the radical distinction of the '*messianic*' from 'all messianism').[30] In 'The Trial', the final section of *The Book of Resemblances*, the author of Jabès' texts is put on trial by the arbiters of normative Judaism for 'publishing, about fifteen years ago, a disturbing book, followed by others as embarrassing' (*BR1*, 104; *LR*, 139). Among the litany of charges levelled by the witnesses for the prosecution is the confounding of Judaism's key terms: God, the Book, the Messiah. Of the last, the second witness says: 'You called for the Messiah. But only the better to turn away from us, to open larger breaches onto the void, our abyss' (*BR*, 106; *LR*, 141).

The defendant responds by acceding to this as to all other charges; rather than denying their heretical character, he seeks paradoxically to find in this heresy an inner truth of Judaism itself. Thus, of his calling on the Messiah, he states: 'I said that the Messiah was the ultimate [*extrême*] opening of the book, being the vocable designated by this opening' (*BR1*, 107; *LR*, 143). The Jabèsian Messiah thus articulates the logic of Derrida's 'being-Jewish'; if its opening of the book is 'ultimate', it is because it is not one possible opening among others but opening *itself*, the impossibility of bringing the book to completion. Judaism and the book are animated by the same passion for what Blanchot terms this 'word of impossibility';[31] to experience the limits of poetry and religion, writing and Judaism, is to be exposed to this word.

In Judaism, as in writing, this exposure occurs with the event of the question. As spectral inheritors of the tradition of Talmudic commentary, the interventions and dialogues of Jabès' imaginary rabbis are premised on the intensification rather than resolution of the questions they raise (*F*, 223; *A*, 253). The exchange in *The Book of Questions* between Reb Mendel and his disciples provides an exemplary enactment of this strategy. Mendel's opening pronouncement that ' "Our hope is for knowledge" ' is questioned by his oldest disciple:

'We have first to agree on the sense you give to the word "knowledge" '

[...]

'Knowledge means questioning', replied Reb Mendel.

'What will we get out of these questions? What will we get out of all the answers which only lead to more questions, since questions are born of unsatisfactory answers?' asked the second disciple.

'The promise of a new question,' replied Reb Mendel.

'There will be a moment,' the oldest disciple continued, 'when we have to stop interrogating. Either because there will be no answer possible, or because we will not be able to formulate any further questions. So why should we begin?'

'You see,' said Reb Mendel: 'at the end of an argument, there is always a decisive question unsettled [*en suspens*].' (*BQ*1, 116; *LQ*1, 129–30)

In defining knowledge in terms of the question, Mendel from the outset opens the definition itself to questioning. It is tempting, and not altogether inaccurate, to read Mendel's responses to his disciples' objections dialectically, that is, as negations and higher syntheses of their various misrecognitions. Mendel's dialectic, however, is rigorously negative, placing perpetually *en suspens* the identity of question and answer with which Hegel's *Phenomenology* ends.[32] His disciples' objections are thus not errors awaiting correction, but the necessary subjection of the master's pronouncement to the very questioning it opens. Once commonly assented to, Mendel's formulation would contradict itself, restoring knowledge to the sovereignty of the answer. 'Knowledge means questioning' can only be rescued from its own abstraction as a foundational maxim by being itself put in question.

THE IMPOSSIBLE: GOD

If the Book is the term with which Jabès designates the yielding of writing to the question, it is with the word God that he signifies the homologous limit of Judaism. A passage in *Le Parcours* elaborates this limit character of God:

In every possible, there is an impossible which taunts it. Yet this impossible is not the impossible. It is only the failure [*l'échec*] of the possible.
[. . .]
This impossible is God. Do not insist, in your pride, in willing his transformation into a permanent possible. (*LP*, 38)

What is at stake in the contradictory claim that 'this impossible is not the impossible'? Jabès' sentence insinuates a self-division into the term which prevents its reader from substantializing it, from comprehending it as an object. The language of the impossible, precisely because it draws the impossible into language, always threatens this temptation. It is for this reason that Jabès must go on to insist that the impossible is not 'the unreachable point' (*'point l'inatteignable'*), not, that is, a transcendental signifier which, though outside the grasp of finite consciousness, guarantees the integrity and meaning of the possible. It is rather 'the opening onto the Nothing; the Nothing of the opening' (*LP*, 38); every aspiration to assimilate the impossible to knowledge, to make it equal to itself, can only run up against this ruinous Nothing.

In naming this experience of the impossible 'God', Jabès sets the term apart from every theology that would comprehend it, transform it 'a permanent possible'. God, on the contrary, is the term which disables every such transformation before it begins, the exposure of an irremediable disjunction between the possible and its other. When Jabès' texts invoke God, they invoke the immemorial memory of this disjunction, of language voided at its limit.

The experience of this disjunction, as André Neher has shown, is inscribed deep in the text of Jewish tradition. In a reading of Psalm 22, Neher discloses an experience of God which is simultaneously an experience of radical abandonment. The phrase around which this experience orbits is '*lo dumiyah*' or 'no respite', as in the Psalmist's plaintive, 'I cry by day – You answer not, and by night, but there is no respite for me'.[33] For Neher, no translation can be adequate to the doubled negativity of '*lo dumiyah*', a doubling he renders with the phrase 'nonsilence'.[34] Where the day's silence is other to speech, the night's *lo dumiyah* places silence and speech in a zone of indistinction, an indistinction that wrenches God terrifyingly from the stable economy of speech and silence. The night gives rise to 'a silence more silent than silence' (Neher, 68, 75–6), in which the divine speaks only in the obscurity of its desertion: 'Nonsilence confronts with a God whose Being may be grasped only from the fleeting roots of Nothingness' (Neher, 69, 76).

The *lo dumiyah* of the Psalmist is the torment of the Nothing's consitutive untranslatability, the refractoriness of Jabès' 'impossible' to the permanence of the possible. The ineluctability of the *échec* that turns the finite being away from the God it would approach assigns the Jew to a condition of unrelieved wandering:

> Nomadism!. *Le Nom*, 'the Name', justifies the nomad. The Jew inherited the Name and, at the same time, lost his place on earth. The nomad takes on himself the unstated [*informulé*] Name. (*BQ2*, 347; *LQ2*, 472)

The Jew's inheritance of the Name is profoundly intricated with his loss of place; because the Name names only its own 'unstatedness', its own otherness to the statement, it destines its inheritors to a perpetual displacement. Only allegiance to a determinate name – a State, a people, a god – can guarantee a place on earth; allegiance to the Name that ruins every such determination is for this reason the irretrievable loss of place, as Blanchot's description of '*être-Juif*' makes clear:

The exigency of uprooting: the affirmation of nomadic truth. In this Judaism stands in contrast to paganism (all paganism). To be pagan is to be fixed, to plant oneself in earth, as it were, to establish oneself in a pact with the permanence that authorizes sojourn and is certified by certainty in the land. Nomadism answers to a relation that possession cannot satisfy. (*IC*, 125; *EI*, 183)

Blanchot's words illuminate the Jabèsian (and indeed Blanchotian) affinity between Judaism and writing; the nomadism of the people pledged to the Name is always simultaneously that of the writer pledged to the Book. In this respect, the pagan is to Judaism what the novelist is to writing; each attains possession of their territory at the expense of forgetting the Nothing which conditions all possession. The drive to draw God and the Book into the present is the disavowal of their ineliminable futurity, and of the state of incompletion to which this futurity destines writing and Judaism.

THE IMAGE OF GOD: RESEMBLANCE

Writing and Judaism, then, share a passion to maintain, rather than redeem, this state of incompletion. In relentlessly exposing each of them to the demand of the other, Jabès prevents either from coming to resolution. Judaism is made to undergo the boundlessness of writing, such that its messianic horizon becomes the very opening of the book. But how, in turn, is writing exposed to Judaism's imperative?

Undoubtedly, writing confronts the peculiarly religious character of its predicament in Jabès' ongoing meditation on idolatry. Moreover, where his thinking of literary language placed him in a doubled relation of continuity and rupture to poetic tradition, his thinking of religious language positions him in a homologous relation to Jewish tradition. And where Mallarmé stood as the exemplary antecedent in the former tradition, it is in Maimonides – medieval philosopher, Biblical exegete and codifier of Jewish law – that the anticipatory resonance of a Jabèsian religion can be heard.

Judaism in Jabès is characterized above all by a radical and even transgressive fidelity to the second commandment, a divestment of any residual vestige of Platonism from the thought of God. His authorship presents itself as an unending enactment of the impossible struggle to keep faith with this commandment, to stave off through writing the ever-present temptation of idolatry which writing itself harbours. Perhaps the key text of Hebrew tradition at stake in this context is the description in Genesis 1 of man as created 'in the image of God, after his likeness' ('*b'tselem Adonai, ke-demuth*'), a text which insistently haunts Jabès' books.

In a pivotal philosophical and hermeneutic text of later Jewish tradition, the first chapter of his *Guide to the Perplexed*, Maimonides points forcefully to both the theological meaning and the religious dangers which this description entails. Both Hebrew terms denoting man's resemblance to God – *tselem*, or image and *demuth*, or likeness – are 'equivocal' or homonymous, insofar as their use in ordinary language might imply the corporeality of God, and hence His representability to human consciousness. By employing the traditional Jewish exegetical strategy of reading the terms in the context of their other usages throughout the Bible,[35] Maimonides concludes that, on the contrary, the 'image' and 'likeness' to which Genesis 1 alludes are in respect of a *notion* rather than a form. This notion is 'intellectual apprehension' or the rational soul, and can be likened to the divine only insofar as it signifies that within the human which eludes sensual apprehension.[36]

In their *Idolatry*, Moshe Halbertal and Avishai Margalit suggest a construal of Maimonides whereby God's unrepresentability implies, beyond the determination of His simple unity, 'the absolute otherness of God and the essential categorical difference that exists between him and all familiar objects'.[37] On this view, God's negative attributes point not to a special mode of existence, but to a confounding of the very predication of existence (and so equally of non-existence). Thus, inasmuch as language's sphere of reference is bounded by what exists, God is that term *in* language which marks the *limit* of language.

Jabès' reading, scattered across his texts, of the text from Genesis 1, makes of this limit the paradoxical basis of the human's resemblance to God. The rational soul which enables Maimonides to speak of a notional resemblance is now divested of any substance; from this perspective, the self-image in which God creates the human is only the image of this non-substance. The resemblance of man to God partakes of the same logic as the book's resemblance to the Book, for neither God nor the Book designate resembled objects. Both are names rather for the exhaustion of language and image, bearing witness, in Adorno's phrase, to 'an impossibility at their very core' (*NL2*, 139; *GS*11, 480). Reb Betesh's pronouncement in *The Book of Resemblances* articulates this impossible logic of resemblance: 'God is in All means outside All, He is nothing./Man is in God means he is only the portion this nothingness grants him' (*BR1*, 31; *LR*, 49). If God is in All – that is, in the idealist Universal which would comprehend and subsume everything other to itself – He is nevertheless not contained by it. The All cannot contain the nothingness which precedes and conditions it, as the famous opening sentence of *The Star of Redemption* reminds us: 'From death, from the fear of death, comes all cognition of the All' (*SR*, 3; *SE*, 3).[38] The sovereignty of the All is made possible by the death it cannot acknowledge without making vulnerable its claim to comprehension of the Absolute. To acknowledge the ineluctable negativity of death would be to put in question the All's originality and universality.

For Reb Betesh, this vulnerability to the question is precisely the effect of the All's exposure to the word God. And it is in terms of this exposure that the resemblance of the human to God ('Man is in God') must be understood. The human's

creation in God's image describes the abyssal foundation of the subject, the unsayable nothingness or death on which her existence depends. Under Jabès' gaze,
Judaism and writing are the twin forms which bring this nothingness to the surface
of language.

Indeed resemblance is arguably the term on which the itineraries of Judaism and
writing converge. The Judaic proscription of idolatry and the writerly movement
of self-erasure are both governed by the logic of resemblance. In an essay on Michel
Leiris, Blanchot draws out this logic with exemplary lucidity:

> Let us remember the bewitching power with which any passerby seems to be
> endowed if, for an instant, he becomes the bearer of some resemblance; how
> his face attracts us, haunts us, familiar and remote, yet also frightens us a little;
> we are in a hurry to identify it, that is, to erase it by redirecting it to the circle of
> things in which men are so bound up with themselves that they are without
> resemblance. ... Whom does the resembler resemble? Neither this one nor
> that one; he resembles no one or an ungraspable Some one . . . .[39]

Read next to Blanchot's description, Jabès' gloss on man's creation in the image
of God reveals this logic of resemblance in its pre-original form. The ungraspable
Someone registered in the uncanny experience of the passerby discloses imperceptibly the God — the 'no one' or void — in whose image the human is created,
a disclosure nearly simultaneous with its own forgetting, its redirection into 'the
circle of things'. Nor is this forgetting a choice; the experience of resemblance must
always also be that of its erasure, for what it reveals is only an impossibility of revelation; resemblance is this impossibility come to sight.

If writing is the privileged bearer of resemblance, it is because it is the memory
of this necessary erasure. In writing, God — the 'no one' that conditions and haunts
every someone — comes to presence only by way of a revocation of presence. The
final volume of *The Book of Questions* — • *El, or the Last Book* — is nothing other than
the obsessive enactment and reenactment of this revocation. Jabès begins the book
by citing a kabbalistic articulation of the paradoxical logic of divine revelation:
'When God, El, wanted to reveal Himself/He appeared as a point' (*BQ2*, 341;
LQ2, 465). The point refers to no object outside itself; it signifies rather only the
fact of signification itself, before and beyond any content. This fact can appear only
as the limit of appearance, as the erasure of all particular signifieds:

> 'God refused image and language in order to be Himself the point. He is image
> in the absence of image, language in the absence of language, point in the
> absence of point', he said. (*BQ2*, 353; *LQ2*, 477)

The anonymity of the speaker throughout the book follows inexorably from the
paradox in which he is caught; the expression *in* language of the absence of

language enacts that condition of 'desubjectification' which for Agamben is the essence of poetic experience. The 'Poetical Character' described by Keats in his letter to Woodhouse, we recall, offered exemplary testimony to this experience; to 'be' a poet is for Keats to expose the self to its own annihilation, to the impossibility of ' "speaking from myself" ' (*RA*, 113). The 'he' of Jabès' text marks the displacement of subjectivity that must result from this impossibility; God names the exhaustion of the author's descriptive resources, coming to language and image only as absence of language and image. This exhaustion is the transfer of writerly subjectivity from 'I' to 'he', from the determinate (represented) to the anonymous (resembling) speaker.

In Jabès' ongoing interpretation of the Genesis text, the creation of man in the image of God is the pre-original manifestation of resemblance, annulling the logic of representation. Nowhere is the meaning of this difference laid bare more explicitly than in a section from *The Book of Shares* entitled 'Adam, or the Birth of Anxiety', in which he draws out the consequences of Adam's creation out of Nothing. 'And God created Adam', Jabès writes, '... depriving him of memory ... without childhood, without past':

> Man come out of Nothing, unable even to claim a portion of Nothing.
> [...]
> Man chained to the Void, chained to the absence of all absence.
> The past reassures us. Man without such security, delivered to whom? to what?
> Man without light or shadow, without origin or road, without place, unless part of that place outside time, indifferent to man.
> [...]
> O emptiness! Nothing to lean against, nothing to rest on, is this anxiety?
> Time molds [*pétrit*] us. Without past there is no present, and the *I* cannot be imagined. (*BS*, 26; *LP*, 37–8)[40]

Adam's absence of past is the absence of any means of self-representation. The process described by Blanchot, whereby the bewitching power of resemblance is neutralized by its redirection into 'the circle of things', is not available to him, for he exists prior to any such circle. His precession of the representable world renders him the original bearer of resemblance, image of the absence of image. The difference between Adam and all who come after him, moreover, lies only in the illusory power of the latter to draw resemblance into representation (Blanchot's 'hurry to identify'). The narrative of Adam erodes this power of representation by exposing the Void which conditions it, recalling the absence which representation is destined to forget.

If man is 'unable to claim even a portion of this Nothing', it is because any such claim would be based in a fundamental misrecognition. To make a claim on Nothing would be to substantialize it, to make a ground of the groundless. Adam lacks the means to forge even the illusory security provided by the past; he can ally himself only to that which breaks all alliances, to 'that place outside time which is indifferent to man'. Born into a restless anxiety he has not chosen and cannot be released from, his predicament brings to light an original dispossession of the subject. Read from Agamben's perspective, Adam's is the primordial poetic experience, the model of desubjectification: 'Without past there is no present, and the *I* cannot be imagined.' In Adam, is disclosed the abyssal condition of the human, of the self prior to the I:

> Orphaned in the fullest sense of the term, of father and mother, but also of himself – are we not engendered in that moment of carnal and spiritual experience? – what could seeing and hearing be for him? What speaking or acting mean? What weight had a word, what reverberations in the future? (*BS*, 26; *LP*, 38, Jabès' emphasis)

Creation from Nothing is an originary orphaning, a loss which conditions the very ontology of selfhood and its acts. Without a past through which to define his present, he is author neither of his words nor his actions; in speaking he voids rather than expresses himself.

'SYLLABLES OF ASH': WRITING AFTER AUSCHWITZ

But what bearing does this disclosure of the abyssal ground of being and language have on the task of thinking after Auschwitz? In what sense does it answer to the urgent ethico-political demand 'to arrange thoughts and actions so that . . . nothing similar will happen'? Jabès' texts never cease responding to this question, not least by exposing the intrication of the Nazi war against the Jews with the logic of representation. If the Jew attests to the groundlessness of resemblance, Nazism is premised on the pathological drive to erase this testimony. *The Book of Resemblances* opens with the image of Sarah Schwall, the suicidal survivor of *The Book of Questions*, contemplating her naked body in the mirror 'thirty-two years later':

> If she takes time to examine it closely, it is because she knows it escapes her.
> Who could be absolute master of the body? We can make the soul speak or fall silent. We can take refuge in it entirely. But in our body?
> All around Sarah, women and men are arrested (*appréhendés*) for bodies labeled 'of Jewish race' in police files. No passport is needed for the soul.
> [. . .]

> 'O Sarah', Yukel had written, 'your body is beautiful, enchanting like the distant landscapes of childhood which outshine the most celebrated sights.' (*BR1*, 5–6; *LR*, 16)

The Vichy police are bound to destroy all traces of the vertiginous truth which Sarah – literally – embodies. If the soul provides a place of refuge, it is on account of its insuperable inaccessibility to sight; the invisible defies the discipline of classification. The body's vulnerability to the same discipline, however, indicates not simply its visibility but its displacing of the very boundary between the visible and the invisible. Its availability to sight fosters the illusion that it can be mastered in representation. The comprehension and objectification of the Jewish body – its subjection to a classifying gaze – is never far from its annihilation.

Adorno and Horkheimer, we recall, had articulated this insight in a different register in *Dialectic of Enlightenment*, in theorizing Nazi anti-Semitism as 'the morbid expression of repressed mimesis' (*DE*, 187; *GS3*, 211–2). The Jew's bodily comportment – the gestural language of the grimace, for example – in its expressive excess, disturbs the logic of identity which drives hatred of the racial other. This is not a matter simply of Jewish cultural difference, but of the unmasterable non-identity to which such difference attests. Mimetic expression confronts Nazism with an image of the groundlessness of identity it seeks to forget; the classifying logic of anti-Semitism is the violently delusory means through which it achieves that forgetting.

Read alongside Adorno, the meaning of the body that Sarah discovers before the mirror comes into focus. Close examination yields not its mastery, but the recognition of its inevitable escape from the discipline of the visible. The mirror shows her not only the visible representation of her form, but the 'resemblance to no one' which conditions and haunts that form. Yukel's description of her body's beauty accentuates its unmasterability, drawing it closer to 'the distant landscapes of childhood' than 'the most celebrated sights'. The visibility of the childhood landscapes is of a different order than that of the sights; where the latter are seen by yielding themselves to the gaze, the former are seen only through distance, through their indifference to the gaze. Revealed as resembling, the body is no longer visible without thereby having passed over to the invisible; it is rather the point at which the very distinction dissolves.

Sarah's insight is above all the insight of a survivor, as Yukel's figure for the camp inmates shows: ' "In the Nazi camps", Yukel had written, "we were starveling books whose titles you could no longer make out. The resemblance, between creatures barely alive, had reached – O noon of crime – its zenith" ' (*BR1*, 47; *LQ*, 69). The nothingness which resemblance discloses, merely intimated in everyday experience, insinuates itself in the camps into the very surface of the face. No longer able to claim title to his name ('The disaster', writes Blanchot, 'is the disappearance of the proper name' (*WD*, 40; *ED*, 68), the inmate makes manifest the 'orphaned' condition of the human. Adam, the original name for this condition, is orphaned 'of father and mother, but also of himself'. In Auschwitz, every prisoner becomes Adam, orphaned of self in the violating exposure of the Nothing from which he is born, and which he resembles.

As the passage cited at the outset of this chapter reminds us, this experience cannot be told, if telling is thought in terms of narration. To narrate Auschwitz would be to impose the logic of representation on the abyssal truth of resemblance, to render determinate that which escapes every determination. How, then, could Auschwitz be written without violating its untellability? The story of Sarah and Yukel as unfolded in the first three volumes of *The Book of Questions* constitutes Jabès' most explicit response to this question.

A passage from *A Foreigner Carrying in the Crook of His Arm a Tiny Book*, a late text written some seventeen years after the first of *The Book of Questions*, helps to establish the logic that governs Jabès' writing of Auschwitz:

> Because we can never say more than the beginning of the intolerable, the beginning – O tonic ingenuity – of a word that refuses itself, does not speak, in order to be captured silent.
>
> 'Auschwitz', he had noted, 'escapes this beginning, is always prior to it, wound of an unsayable name rather than name of an unhealable wound.'
> (*AFC*, 67; *EAS*, 95)[41]

The refusal of the intolerable to be spoken is at the same time its capture in silence. This is the only means by which Auschwitz, always prior to the opening of speech, can come to speech. Wound of the unsayable rather than name of the unhealable, Auschwitz maintains – indeed *is* – the impossibility of its own telling, an impossibility no name could render determinate.

The 'story' ('*roman*') of Sarah and Yukel is exposed to and ruined in advance by this impossibility of telling. It is, writes Jabès at the outset of *The Book of Questions*, 'the account [*récit*], through various dialogues and meditations attributed to imaginary rabbis, of a love destroyed by men and by words. It has the dimensions of the book and the bitter stubbornness of a wandering question' (*BQ1*, 26; *LQ1*, 30). Why does the *récit* of Sarah and Yukel come to writing only through the modality of imaginary rabbinic commentary? The 'dialogues and meditations' of Jabès' rabbis disperse rather than gather the elements of the story; rather than imposing a bounded form upon it, they release the boundlessness and irresolution it shares with the book and the question. In the commentaries of the rabbis, Auschwitz, to adapt Jabès' pronouncement, tells itself in language rather than being told by it:

Aside from challenging God, the center formed by the many extermination camps left the Jews – chosen people of the center – grappling with the interrogations of their race. Even those who could no longer think.

'It is in questions that the Alliance is renewed', wrote Reb Assim. 'Interpreting the Law is our daily task. Questioning, the pledge of our truth in God' (*BQ*1, 364; *LQ*1, 401)

The extermination camps confer a monstrous ambiguity on the 'center' to which the Jews are destined. Only through the agency of the question can this ambiguity be thought in its essential irreducibility. If questions renew the Jews' covenantal relation with God, it is because they alone can articulate the irredeemable doubt cast by the camps on that relation. The renewal proper to questioning, far from reconciling human and divine, only exacerbates their irreconcilability.

The writing of Sarah and Yukel's story subjects the order of telling to the disordering logic of questioning. The effect of this encounter is made evident in a passage from *The Book of Questions* relating the skeletal biography of Sarah's father, Solomon Schwall. A parenthetic interruption of the (already interruptive) text, Solomon's life comes to speech only in and as its unnarratability:

> (. . . The life of one or two generations of men may fill one sentence or two pages. The gross outline of four particular or ordinary lives: 'He was born in . . . He died in . . .' Yes, but between the scream of life and the scream of death? 'He was born in . . . He was insulted for no good reason . . . He was misunderstood . . . He died in . . .' Yes, but there must be more? [*Oui, mais encore?*] . . . 'He settled in the South of France with his wife . . . He was an antique dealer . . . He was called "the Jew" . . . His wife and son were called "the wife and son of the Jew" ' . . . Yes, but there must be more? . . . 'Sometimes, he spoke in public to brand (*flétrir*) racism, to affirm the rights of man . . .' Yes, yes, but there must be more? 'He died in a gas chamber outside France . . . and his wife died in a gas chamber outside France . . . and his daughter came back to France, out of her mind . . .') (*BQ*1, 166–7; *LQ*1, 187–8)

The aporia of telling is inextricable here from what struggles (and fails) to be told. Solomon's life is shaped by exclusion, displacement and violence, by forces which rebuff every attempt at assimilation to narrative. As 'Jew', as migrant and as anti-racist in Nazi-occupied France, he is set outside the boundaries of national identity and community, that is, outside those structures which found narrative and keep it intact. No form is available to give shape to his life; its writing is impelled rather by the very lack it persistently seeks to fill. In this sense it exemplifies the experience desribed by Hans-Jost Frey as 'mourning', whereby the survival of that which is lost is also the loss of hope for its completion:

The end is sad because it is only a half end and something else comes after it. What stops in such a way that one loses it while it comes to an end is not completed ... The hope of completion ends with the end. The end of hope survives as mourning. ... Mourning is a living on without future, in the monotony in which every place is like the next.[42]

Jabès' recounting of Solomon's story is inscribed by just this mourning for the impossibility of its own completion. Every fact the narrator offers draws attention to its own insufficiency, to an insistent supplement which the listener's '*oui, mais encore?*' tries to make heard. The attempt is in vain, however; nothing the narrator says could assuage the force of the *encore*, for the story is marked in advance by an excess to itself. The '*oui, mais encore?*', as the repeated remarking of this excess, both drives and ruins telling, drawing the narration forward whilst denying it the possibility of completion.

Sarah and Yukel's own words are similarly marked in advance by this denial. In the course of a discussion of wisdom and madness in *The Ineffaceable The Unperceived* (*L'Ineffaçable L'Inaperçu*), Reb Nidam says, ' "... there were two kinds of fruit: one claimed by the earth [*que la terre revendique*] and one, invisible, the pride of the sky [*que le ciel s'enorgueillit*]./"The first was the ruin of man [*a perdu l'homme*], the second, of God" ' (*BR3*, 23; *LR*, 311). If the first fruit is the knowledge which destines the human to eternal self-division and so to separation from the divine, what is the second? God is 'ruined' by the very medium through which he is known: language. In language, God's unsayability is said; that which is without relation enters into relation. Sarah's subsequent words must be read in the light of Reb Nidam's:

And Sarah said: 'It is not from the tree that we plucked the fruit, but from our lips.

'The tree was burned one night, and our lips, since, have formed [*remuent*] only syllables of ash.

'Inarticulable'. (*BR3*, 24; *LR*, 311)

It is through the lips that celestial speech – fruit of the sky – comes to earthly beings. In Sarah's experience, however, the passage from sky to earth has been insuperably blocked. The tree that assured this passage has been burned, leaving the lips to form only inarticulable 'syllables of ash'. It is difficult to avoid hearing in this phrase the echo of Derrida's reading of Celan, in which ash is the figure for the paradoxical singularity of the signature or 'date' which cannot be mastered. In Celan's invocation of dates, that which occurs just once must efface its own origin order to be made readable or 'iterable'. The poem, must expose its secret, risk losing it if it is to keep it. It must blur the border, crossing it and recrossing it, between readability and unreadability. The unreadable is readable as unreadable, unreadable insofar as readable; this is the madness or fire which consumes a date from within. Here is what renders it ash, here is what renders it ash from the first moment.[43]

Sarah's 'syllables of ash' partake of just this predicament. The 'secret' she would reveal consumes its own readability in the act of being spoken, rendering itself 'inarticulable' from the first. Only in the form of this fiery self-annulment can her experience enter the word. The poetic character of her speech is not an attempt to aestheticize that experience, but to expose to reading its unreadability, its essential ashenness.

This unreadability is insinuated into the fragments from Sarah's journal which punctuate *The Book of Yukel*. The first entry cited reads 'I will not write of [*sur*] what I have seen. I write at the foot of the moment I dodge [*l'instant que j'esquive*], in tow of a question which carries other questions./ ... /I will not write of men's brutality, of the profaned word [*parole*]' (*BQ*1, 236; *LQ*1, 268). Here, bearing witness takes the form of its own revocation. The relation of not writing to writing can no longer be framed in terms of opposition, for not writing is now the modality through which what is witnessed comes to writing; what she has seen incinerates from within the word which would attest to it. 'At the foot of the moment' – that is, at the cusp of writing's coincidence with experience – the writing 'I' reveals itself as that which slips away (*esquive*) from any such coincidence, yielding instead to the tow of the question. As carrier of other questions, prolonging and intensifying rather than completing itself, the question is the mode through which Sarah attests to the 'men's brutality' of which she declines to write.

It is important, then, that Sarah's not writing 'of' the brutality of the camps be read as more than the silenced voice of a traumatized consciousness. What she has seen refuses being written of, that is, as the representable object of a writing subject. Her writing enacts instead the dispossession of its subject, her experience's ruinous effect on the will to contain it in language or image. Yet if it registers the disintegration of the will, writing is also affirmation of the question's sovereignty and refusal of the logic which would silence it. Sarah's submission to this sovereignty is thus an act of defiance in the sense suggested by Reb Fina in *Intimations The Desert*: ' "They sewed a star on our hearts to appropriate the clarity of our nights; for though we were prey to their abusive power, deep down they knew that, transparent and vast like the sky, we could never be seized" ' (*BR*2, 61; *LR*, 219).[44] To write in tow of the question is to affirm this unseizability; the yellow star which captures the Jew in a fatal logic of representation fails to extinguish the transparency – 'resemblance to no one' – which gives the lie to that logic. Nazism labours in vain to close the question.

The privilege given by Jabès to Judaism and writing as carriers of the ethico-political task imposed by Auschwitz should be coming into focus. As the twin terrains of the question, Judaism and writing keep in reserve the Nothing which Nazism's representational regime would appropriate and destroy. The question undoes idolatry by exposing it to its own groundlessness, to the abyssal 'transparency' which conditions its delusory images. Nor is this undoing a question of opposing the idolatrous image with a refusal of the image; rather, as the anonymous speaker of *The Little Book of Unsuspected Subversion* has it,

'See how paradoxical, the whims [*volontés*] of God.

'On the one hand, He appeals to consciousness to develop in us the idea, the sentiment, of the divine; on the other hand, by prohibiting the image, He throws us back into the unconscious, where He reigns without us' . . . (*LBUS*, 17; *PLS*, 23)

The prohibition of the image is inextricable from its temptation. Just as, for Adorno, the unconditional can be thought only from the conditionality of experience, so for Jabès the unconscious reign of the divine is intimated only in and through consciousness. The difference of human consciousness and divine unconsciousness is, as Levinas puts it, 'a difference more different than opposition' (*OGW*, 134; *DDQ*, 204), for it is through conceptual language that the human is enjoined by God to 'develop . . . the idea . . . of the divine'. Yet this solicitation by God is simultaneously a prohibition which turns us away from Him, ruining the very language through which we would comprehend him. In the approach to the divine, consciousness thus comes to know itself, in its essential incompleteness, as a question.

THE SHARE OF NOTHING

Jabès' mobilization of the question against the temptations of idolatry is neither a hermetically literary nor a narrowly religious enterprise. The interpenetration of writing and Judaism in his texts cannot be thought apart from its implications for the future of ethico-political solidarity and responsibility. If the question interrupts every logic of foundation, it must interrupt the founding of community on the basis of a determinate origin or identity. The Jabèsian community of imaginary rabbis is exemplary in this respect; their coexistence is underwritten not by the promise of final resolution or consensus, but by the perpetual dissolution of this promise. Theirs is a community with 'nothing to rest on' (*BS*, 26; *LP*, 38), freed of the illusion of its substantiality and knowing in advance its 'orphaned' condition. The God they name ' "our truth" is, in Reb Mendel's words, "a question . . . which leads us to Him who is Light through and for us, who are nothing" ' (*BQ*1, 117; *LQ*1, 130). The Light God shines through the rabbis discloses only the nothing-ness of their origin; the path to the Absolute it illuminates leads not to the finality of an answer but to the prolongation of a question.

To speak of the God that founds the being of community as a question is to set in motion a radical rethinking of the ethico-political task, one that has as its horizon not its fulfilment but its maintenance *as a task*. The life of a community founded in the question would no longer sustain itself by way of a shared principle of identity, but by the sharing of the impossibility of such a principle, as expressed in the decep-tively simple question posed by Jabès at the end of *The Book of Shares*: '*Could sharing be impossible because of our differences?*' (*BS*, 94; *LP*, 135, Jabès' emphasis).[45] Differ-ence here must be understood as, to invoke Andrew Benjamin's term, 'anoriginal' (*PH*, 150), both before and beyond the sameness that would comprehend it. In a community forged in the question, what is shared is precisely this difference which renders sharing impossible:

'How can we divide the name of God with its four unvoiced consonants?' he asked.

[…]

'And if we shared only the vital desire to share, our only means to escape our solitude, the void?' (*BS*, 98; *LP*, 140)

God's name – the name of the question – cannot serve community as its shared principle of belonging, for it is the name of what tolerates no belonging, of what '*remains forever beyond sharing* (hors du partage)' (*BS*, 98; *LP*, 140, Jabès' emphasis). The promise opened up by this ruin of communal identity, however, is a sharing without identity, a sharing of '*the vital desire to share*', prior to any content. Once determined by content, sharing must exclude what is other to that content; only sharing *itself* can open community without simultaneously enclosing it.

Writing and Judaism, forged in the indivisible and unpronounceable name of God, are the ciphers of such a sharing. In them is voiced insistently the imperative animating the task of thinking after Auschwitz. Concluding *The Book of Questions*, Jabès gives voice to this imperative, and in so doing prevents its conclusion:

The essential: in the throes of our crisis, to preserve the question. (*BQ*2, 442; *LQ*2, 581)

Conclusion: Sharing the Imperative

A counter-question might be put to Jabès' community of the question: is 'the vital desire to share' alone a sufficient condition for community? Does the actual experience of sharing not presuppose a content – a language, an identity, a tradition – shared? That such presuppositions everywhere structure the experience of community today is beyond doubt. No citizen of the liberal West can be unaware, after the events of 11 September, of how intimately their inclusion in its boundaries is tied to the exclusion of others from them. Phenomena as apparently diverse as the revocation by Western states of essential civic rights and freedoms in the name of security, the emergence of a global media debate as to when torture might be justified and the ominous rise of anti-immigration parties in Continental Europe, are intricated symptoms of the lines of division – visible and invisible – being ever more sharply drawn between 'our' community and its others.[1]

Jabès' imagined community provokes the question as to whether this economy of exclusion and exclusion, belonging and non-belonging, must always structure the political. No question could make Adorno's 'new categorical imperative' resound more urgently. To think and act in such a way that Auschwitz will not recur, it has been argued here, is to imagine a political – and so ethical – space liberated from the grasp of identity. This conclusion will locate the cipher of such a space not in a vision of the future but in the testimony of the past, specifically the testimony of the survivor.

To discover the truth of community here may appear the most painful of paradoxes; the Nazi concentration camps remain, after all, the site of the most radical experiment in exclusion yet known to history. In them is concentrated not just the visible image of genocidal terror, but the negative image of a purged nation, the enraged attempt to restore the lost wholeness and integrity of (Aryan) community by the creation of, in Edith Wyschogrod's words, a 'death-world' which functions 'by consigning to itself all that seems worthy of death'.[2]

The poem that gives its title to the most famed of survivor testimonies, Primo Levi's 'Shema', speaks out of the ruined landscape of this death-world, out of the assaulted humanity of its inhabitants:

> Consider if this is a man
> Who works in the mud
> Who does not know peace
> Who fights for a scrap of bread
> Who dies because of a yes or a no.
> Consider if this is a woman,
> Without hair and without name
> With no more strength to remember,
> Her eyes empty and her womb cold
> Like a frog in winter.[3]

These lines, like the testimony that follows them, are haunted by the possibility that the answer to this question is 'no'; that to be dispossessed of all that gives form to life – rest, sustenance, the right to life, a distinct identity and memory – is to be robbed of humanity itself.

And yet what if it is this very experience of being expelled from the established community of the human that enables the victim to refuse the 'no' that Levi's anguished questions imply? No survivor testimony – not even Levi's – shows more profoundly than Robert Antelme's *The Human Race* how the Nazi conviction in the divisibility of humanity brings to light its ineliminable and absolute *unity*. In Antelme's startling formulation, the horrors of the camp – 'darkness, absolute lack of any kind of landmark, solitude, unending oppression, slow annihilation'[4] – confer on those who undergo them 'an ultimate sense of belonging to the human race' (*'un sentiment ultime d'appertance à l'espèce'*) (*HR*, 5; *EH*, 11).

How is it that this 'ultimate sense of belonging' is forged in and by the 'slow annihilation' of selfhood, in the deprivation of the very power to say 'I'? This paradox can be understood only once this sense of belonging and the annihilation which attends it are thought outside of a relationship of opposition. It is worth recalling here Levinas' insistence in 'Transcendence and Evil' that the movement towards the Good consists not in a progression away from evil, but in 'a difference more different than opposition' (*OGW*, 134; *DDQ*, 204). Good's distance from evil takes the form, for Levinas, not of opposition but of *proximity*, a 'contact-in-separation' whereby the encounter with evil is always already an awakening to its other.

Antelme's expression of 'an ultimate sense of belonging to the human race' is structured by just this proximity. Antelme is awakened to this imperative truth not by ways of some subjective act of defiance against evil, but through his radical proximity to it. *The Human Race* is nothing less than a record of this proximity, of an intimacy with suffering that exposes the very limit of the human – a doubled limit of power (the SS) and affliction (the deportee). The end at which the SS remorselessly aim is the destruction, by way of hunger, cold, exhaustion, disease and the pervasive rule of gratuitous violence, of his victim's very selfhood, of his capacity to speak and act in his own name.

And, undoubtedly, as Antelme shows unsparingly, the SS attain this end, interposing through terror an irrecoverable distance between the inmate and his own singularity. Faced with his own image in a shard of mirror, each inmate is both compelled and repelled by this intimation of distinctiveness lost to the person facing it: 'the face of the guy who when his term came to look at himself in it remained reduced to the state determined by the SS. Only the one in the mirror was distinct' (HR, 52; EH, 58). For the inmate inhabiting the body 'determined by the SS', his mirror image recalls the singularity that is both undeniable and – as 'what one could – really could – become again tomorrow … impossibility itself' (HR, 53; EH, 58). At the limits of abjection, he is separated from his own image, dispossessed of all that would distinguish him:

> We are being transformed. Our faces and bodies are going downhill, there's no more telling the handsome from the ugly. In three months' time we'll be more different still, we'll be even less distinguishable from one another. (HR, 87; EH, 92)

Yet this descent into the mute anonymity of suffering, in attesting to human destruction, discloses simultaneously the *indestructibility* of the human. Blanchot's essay on Antelme formulates this paradox thus: 'man is the indestructible. And this means there is no limit to the destruction of man' (IC, 135; EI, 200). Blanchot captures in these apparently contradictory sentences the essential aporia of Nazi violence as characterized by Antelme; the limitless cruelty of the SS is engendered not by the putative infinity of their power but by their enraged experience of its *limit*. For the moment at which the singularity of each man appears destroyed is the very same moment at which it resurfaces, invisibly yet unmistakably:

> The SS who view us all as one and the same cannot induce us to see ourselves that way. They cannot prevent us from choosing. On the contrary: here the need to choose is constant and immeasurably greater. The more transformed we become, the farther we retreat from back home, the more the SS believe us reduced to the indistinctness and to the irresponsibility whereof we do certainly present the appearance – the more distinctions our community does in fact contain, and the stricter those distinctions are. The inhabitant of the camps is not the abolition of these differences; on the contrary, he is their effective realization. (HR, 88; EH, 93)

The appearance of indistinctness, visible index of the limitlessness of his destruction, is equally the invisible marker of his indestructibility. It is neither, Antelme continues, the 'liberation' nor the 'resurrection' of his body that will defy destruction. Not in the impossible recovery of the body's singularity does the humanity of the victim come to light; rather, as Antelme's apostrophe to an imagined SS[5] proclaims:

> For it to be shown that we are in the right we no more count on our bodies' liberation than on our resurrection. It's now, alive and wasted as we are, that our righteousness triumphs. True, this can't be seen; but the less it is visible, the greater our righteousness is; the less are the chances of seeing anything at all, the more in the right we are. Not only are right and reason on our side, but we are the very righteousness that you have vanished to a clandestine existence. And so less than ever can we bow before seeming triumphs. Let this be well understood: owing to what you have done, right-thinking transforms itself into consciousness. You have restored the unity of man; you have made conscience irreducible. No longer can you ever hope that we be at once in your place and in our own skin, condemning ourselves. Never will anyone here become to himself his own SS. (*HR*, 89; *EH*, 94–5)

The SS's destructive power over the apparent is indissociable from his impotence before the clandestine, just as the inmates' righteousness cannot be thought apart from its invisibility. The destroyed man attests to the very 'unity of man' his destruction was intended to deny. As long as he continues to inhabit his afflicted body, his self-perception can only interrupt the perception of the SS. In Blanchot's words, '[t]he Powerful One is the master of the possible, but he is not master of this relation that does not derive from mastery and that power cannot measure: the relation without relation wherein the "other" is revealed as "*autrui*" ' (*IC*, 132; *EI*, 194).

By bearing witness to the SS's infinite and brutal mastery of the possible, Antelme discloses the ineliminable excess to the possible that constitutes both the human and the 'ultimate sense of belonging to the human race'. All powerful over the victim's visible body, the blows of the SS flail impotently – and unwittingly – against his sense of belonging.

Each of the thinkers discussed above have brought to light – through the agency of the poem, of Judaism, and of their difficult sameness – an otherness to power that must always refuse its reach, a refusal concentrated in the words of Jabès' Reb Fina: ' "They sewed a star on our hearts to appropriate the clarity of our nights; for though we were prey to their abusive power, deep down they knew that, transparent and vast like the sky, we could never be seized" ' (*BR2*, 61; *LR*, 219). Antelme reveals just how intimately the demand of the new categorical imperative is tied to preserving this inappropriable alterity for thought and action. It is a difficult demand, for it defies thought's naturalized mechanisms of conceptualization, representation and identification. It is also an essential one, because it exposes the indelible unity that conditions every attempt to divide the human into the opposed terms of included and excluded, powerful and powerless. Auschwitz is a possibility wherever this unity is forgotten or erased, a possibility named by racism above all. But as Antelme shows, the vain struggle to erase the unity of the human ultimately causes it to appear 'with absolute clarity':

> We have come to resemble whatever fights simply to eat, and dies from not eating; come to where we exist on the level of some other species, which will never be ours and towards which we are tending ... Yet there is no ambiguity: we're still men, and we shall not end otherwise than as men. The distance separating us from other species is still intact. It is not historical. It's an SS fantasy to believe that we have an historical mission to change species ... No, this extraordinary sickness is nothing other than a culminating moment in man's history. And that means two things. First, that the solidity and stability of the species is being put to the test. Next, that the variety of relationships between men, their colour, their customs, the classes they are formed into mask a truth that here, at the boundary of nature, at the point where we approach our limits, appears with absolute clarity: namely, that there are not several human races, there is only one human race ... everything happens ... as though there were a number of human species, or rather, as though belonging to a single human species wasn't certain, as though you could join the species or leave it, could be halfway in it or belong to it fully, or never belong to it, try though you might for generations, division into races or classes being the canon of the species and sustaining the axiom we're always prepared to use, the ultimate line of defense: 'They aren't people like us.' (*HR*, 218–9; *EH*, 228–9)

Here, in this irrefutable demonstration of the indivisibility of the human, is ciphered the ethico-political task of the future. Nor is this task, in spite of the simplicity of Antelme's affirmation – 'there are not several human races, there is only one human race' – reducible to the fulfilment of an easy universalism. The essential unity of the human race, far from authorizing the subordination of singularity to collective identity, demands the maintenance of singularity – and so alterity – as its first and last imperative. The true ethical counteraction to the destruction of the human is not the restoration of the destroyed 'Self-Subject' to its rightful power over the other. Rather, the 'Self-Subject' that emerges from blinding exposure to Antelme's testimony – and the imperative it carries – will function, writes Blanchot, 'no longer as a dominating and oppressing power drawn up against the "other" that is *autrui*, but as what can receive the unknown and the foreign, receive them in the justice of a true *speech*' (*IC*, 134; *EI*, 196).

The true unity of the human will be disclosed only through such a self and such a speech, only in 'receiving' rather than refusing or dominating 'the unknown and the foreign'. Only those who have undergone the near total abjection experienced by Antelme can know the unity of the human with the 'absolute clarity' he describes. For those of us consigned – gratefully – to the 'real world' of a humanity divided by 'colours', 'customs' and 'classes', this unity can never appear as such; but its trace is concealed in the just receptivity to the Other of which Blanchot speaks.

This receptivity cannot rest in what Levinas would call 'the concupiscence of the two' – that is, in my singular relation to the Other – if justice is to be possible. And only justice – responsibility to the many others beyond the Other – can carry the demand of the new categorical imperative. This necessary collective dimension of the imperative is confirmed by Sarah Kofman's reflections on Antelme and Blanchot in her philosophical memoir *Smothered Words* (*Paroles Suffoquées*). Kofman points to the inextricability of Nazi exterminism from its vision of community:

> An idyllic community which erases all trace of discord, of difference, of death, which pretends to rest on a perfect harmony, a fusion conferring immediate unity, can only be a fictional community, a beautiful (psychotic?) story.[6]

To this 'perfect harmony' of fusion, Kofman counterposes a community founded in 'the foreignness of that which can never be held in common' (Kofman, 30). The community that refuses Auschwitz and its recurrence is one that ceaselessly resists the 'psychotic' temptation of fusion, the subordination of alterity to the law of identity. If, as Jean-Luc Nancy memorably writes, 'the fulfillment of community is its suppression'[7] – if, that is, community is realized at the expense of the very difference that renders it possible, then the new categorical imperative demands the perpetual *interruption* of this fulfilment.

In art and religion, it has been argued, the promise and the interruption of fulfilment are at one. This simultaneity of promise and interruption speaks in the name of neither the beautiful nor the sacred, but of the one name adequate to the task of thought: the human race.

Notes

Preface

1. The phrase is, of course, Emil Fackenheim's, whose work is discussed in Chapter 1.
2. Of course, this proximity is frequently contested by Levinas himself; the relationship of Levinasian ethics to Blanchotian writing is discussed at some length in Chapter 3.

Chapter 1: The Interrupted Absolute

1. Standard histories of the Nazi genocide repeatedly confirm this paradox. In the patient and unfailingly sober factual accounts of Raul Hilberg and Lucy Dawidowicz, for example, sober documentation is attended by repeated avowals of the genocide's inassimilability to any previous historical logic. As Dawidowicz puts it, 'The Final Solution transcended the bounds of modern historical experience ... History has, to be sure, recorded terrible massacres and destruction that one people perpetrated against another, but all – however cruel and unjustifiable – were intended to achieve instrumental ends, being means to ends, not ends in themselves'. See *The War Against the Jews 1933–45* (London: Pelican, 1977), pp. 18–19. The insistence on the pathological irrationality of the genocide has attracted criticism for its implicit portrayal of the Jews as passive objects rather than actors in an undoubtedly unequal conflict of social and ideological interests. As early as 1948, Hannah Arendt criticized the liberal 'scapegoat theory' of anti-Semitism for reducing the dense complex of social and historical forces in which racial hatred is intricated to the expression of an inexplicably baseless malice. More recently, Richard Rubinstein has directed the same criticism explicitly at Hilberg, Dawidowicz and Nora Levin, charging that in each of them '[a]nti-Semitism is depicted as something that happens to Jews rather than an expression of a conflict between Jews and their enemies'. See Hannah Arendt, *The Origins of Totalitarianism* (New York, NY: Harcourt Brace, 1979), pp. 5–9; Richard Rubinstein, *After Auschwitz: History, Theology and Contemporary Judaism*, second edition (Baltimore, MD: Johns Hopkins University Press, 1992), pp. 88–92. Following the Arendtian critique of the mystification of anti-Semitism, the present chapter will argue that the renewal of thought after Auschwitz is indissociable from the task of a thorough philosophical and ethico-political anatomy of Nazism's racialized metaphysics. This anatomy, however, is intended not to bring the death camps into conformity with some determinate historical logic, but to show precisely the conditions under which any such logic is ruined. This position is elegantly set out by Giorgio Agamben: 'The aporia of Auschwitz is, indeed, the very aporia of

historical knowledge: a non-coincidence between facts and truth, between verification and comprehension. Some want to understand too much and too quickly; they have explanations for everything. Others refuse to understand; they offer only cheap mystifications. The only way forward lies in investigating the space between these two options'. See *Remnants of Auschwitz: The Witness and the Archive* (trans. D. Heller-Roazen, New York, NY: Zone Books, 1999), pp. 12–13.

2. The ongoing debate on terminology, and the requisite justificatory footnotes it has engendered, is of course a related symptom of conceptual crisis. I have chosen 'Auschwitz' as the term of reference for the Nazi genocide precisely because it renders this crisis explicit. As many have pointed out, the Greek term 'Holocaust' translates the Bibilical Hebrew word 'olah', or sacrificial offering, and so confers an explicit theological determination on the death camps. While the Hebrew term *Shoah*, or 'destruction' avoids this redemptive connotation, its use is motivated by the desire to maximize the adequation of name to event. The explicitly synecdochic character of 'Auschwitz', on the other hand, makes evident the necessary inadequacy of any name to the event named. For the most sustained critique of the term 'Holocaust', see Agamben, *Remnants of Auschwitz*, pp. 28–31; for a more historically grounded justification of 'Auschwitz', see Enzo Traverso, *Understanding the Nazi Genocide: Marxism After Auschwitz* (trans. P. Drucker, London: Pluto Press, 1999), pp. 8–9.

3. Zygmunt Bauman, *Modernity and the Holocaust* (Cambridge: Polity, 1989).

4. In addition to drawing the Other into the economy of the visible, this sentence misses the crucial doubleness of the face's signification in Levinas: precisely because the face announces the *ethical* impossibility of the Other's murder, it is a permanent temptation to such a murder: 'I can wish to kill only an existent absolutely independent, which exceeds my powers infinitely, and therefore does not oppose them but paralyses the very power of power. The Other is the soul being I can wish to kill' (*TaI*, 198; *TeI*, 224).

5. Maurice Blanchot, *Friendship* (trans. E. Rottenberg, Stanford, CA: Stanford University Press, 1997), p. 92; *L'Amitié* (Paris: Gallimard, 1971), pp. 107–8.

6. As Howard Caygill perceptively observes, the theological category of evil is absent from the 1934 essay; its introduction into the 1990 note thus points to the religious entailments of the essay's analysis of Nazism. See *Levinas and the Political* (London: Routledge, 2002), p. 31.

7. See Chapter 3 below for an elaboration of Levinas' monotheistic critique of myth.

8. The prefatory note of 1990 clearly implicates the Heideggerean ontology 'of a being concerned with being' ('RPH', 63) in the 'elemental Evil' against which Christendom is insufficiently insured. This charge cannot be thought of apart from the undoubted debt Levinas' analysis of the West's doctrine of the Spirit owes to Heidegger. As I will come to argue in my reading of Levinas' essays on evil, his ultimately decisive distance from Heidegger is indissociable from an extreme proximity.

9. This is the term Levinas will use in his compelling phenomenological description of the impotent desire to escape being in *De L'Evasion* his essay of the following year.

10. It is here, of course, that we must locate the decisive and fateful difference between Christian and Nazi anti-Semitism. It is not a crime of belief but of being that defines the Jewish offence for the latter.

11. I focus here on Agamben among other contemporary philosophical interpreters of Nazism because of the explicit continuity between Levinas' and his own analysis. It is worth pausing to note, however, the affinities between Agamben and a number of other recent philosophical texts on this question. Edith Wyschogrod, for example, interprets the 'death-world' of Auschwitz as the result of a demonic struggle to recover the mythic integrity of social life from its fracture and alienation by technological modernity: 'The death-world makes its appearance upon . . . demythologized ground as an effort to sacralize a world of impoverished symbolic meanings by creating a totalizing structure to express what is irreducible even in technological society: the binary opposition of life

and death'. See *Spirit in Ashes: Hegel, Heidegger and Man-Made Mass Death* (New Haven, CT: Yale University Press, 1985), p. 28. In their powerful analysis of the rhetoric of Nazism, Philippe Lacoue-Labarthe and Jean-Luc Nancy excavate an Aryan 'type' in which the power of a *mythic* Absolute is incarnated. This power is the power to dream and shape the world in conformity with itself: 'The Aryan world will have to be much more than a world ruled and exploited by the Aryans: it will have to be a world that has become Aryan (thus it will be necessary to eliminate from it the nonbeing or nontype par excellence, the Jew, as well as the nonbeing or lesser being of several other inferior or degenerate types, gypsies, for example)'. See 'The Nazi Myth' (trans. B. Holmes), in *Critical Inquiry* 16, Winter 1990, p. 311. The authors have elaborated their thesis further in their as yet untranslated *Le Mythe Nazi* (La Tour d'Aigues: Editions l'Aube, 1991). I offer readings of both Adorno and Jabès' interpretations of Nazism in Chapters 2 and 4 below.

12. The separation of the analytic of Dasein from biology is set out as an explicit task in ¶10 of *Being and Time*: 'In the order which any possible comprehension and interpretation must follow, biology as a "science of life" is founded upon the ontology of Dasein, even if not entirely. Life, in its own right, is a kind of Being; but essentially *it is accessible only in Dasein*' (Heidegger, 75/50, my emphasis).

13. This refusal is at the heart of the ethics of testimony elaborated in Agamben's sequel to *Homo Sacer, Remnants of Auschwitz*.

14. The best study in this field is Zachary Braiterman's *(God) After Auschwitz* (Princeton, NJ: Princeton University Press, 1998). For discussions covering a broader range of thinkers, however, see Stephen Katz, *Post-Holocaust Dialogues: Critical Studies in Modern Jewish Thought* (New York, NY: New York University Press, 1983), and most recently Michael Morgan, *Beyond Auschwitz: Post-Holocaust Jewish Thought in America* (Oxford: Oxford University Press, 2001).

15. See, however, Rubinstein's serious caution towards the Christological connotations of this term in his essay 'Death-of-God Theology and Judaism' (in *After Auschwitz*). Rubinstein insists on the distinction between the death of God as a *theological* and as a *cultural* event, and couches his own diagnosis strictly in terms of the latter.

16. All three of these thinkers, even the neo-Orthodox Berkowitz, would likely contest this characterization of their positions. My claim in what follows, however, is that this premise structures their thought even when (perhaps especially when) it is most emphatically denied.

17. Rubinstein's book was first published in 1966 with the subtitle 'Radical Theology and Contemporary Judaism', and reissued in substantially revised form in 1992 ('nine of the fifteen chapters have been eliminated from the second edition, which has sixteen chapters, ten of them new to *After Auschwitz*') with the subtitle 'History, Theology and Contemporary Judaism'. For a statement of the differences between the two versions of the book, see the Preface to the 1992 edition. Because my concern in this study is not with the history of theological responses to Auschwitz but rather with the task of thought it imposes on the present, I have confined my reading of Rubinstein to commentary on the 1992 edition.

18. This sentence is Rubinstein's own citation from the 1966 edition. While his gloss on this self-citation initially suggests a softening of this either/or position on the viability of covenantal theology, the alternative theological interpretations of Auschwitz he goes on to acknowledge – Jewish Messianism and Christian eschatology – are hardly credible from his perspective. The essential argument with regard to the collapse of the providential view of History thus remains unchanged.

19. See Braiterman, *(God) After Auschwitz*, pp. 92–3. Among many examples of such texts, we can invoke the discussion in the first chapter of the Talmudic tractate *Berachot* of '*yissurin shel ahava*' or 'chastisements of love' (5a–b). The concept of chastisements of love emerges from the rabbis' attempts to account for sufferings that seem to defy all logic of

reward and punishment – for example the man who 'busies himself in the study of Torah and in acts of charity and nonetheless buries his children'. Once all traditional theodicical and legal explanations have been explored and rejected, they suggest that certain categories of suffering can be understood as 'chastisements of love' – sufferings visited by God upon human beings in this world in order to enhance their reward in the next. Far from resolving the problem of 'useless suffering' (to use Levinas' term), however, the discussion only points up its irresolvability. The issue as to just what constitutes a chastisement of love remains inconclusive, rendering futile any attempt to render determinate the relation of human suffering to divine intention. See *The Soncino Talmud, Zeraim I: Berakoth* (ed. and trans. I. Epstein, London: The Soncino Press, 1948), pp. 20–2.

20. My discussion below of Marc-Alain Ouaknin's reading of the Talmud, and more substantially of Levinas' rabbinic hermeneutics in Chapter 3, is intended as a philosophical elaboration of this principle.

21. This confident prediction of a neo-paganist revival in Israel is offered in the 1963 essay 'The Rebirth of Israel in Contemporary Jewish Theology', one of the essays from the first edition retained in the second. It should be noted that Rubinstein acknowledges the hastiness of this prediction in more recent essays, and suggests that such a revival has ironically been confined to the Gush Emunim ('Block of the Faithful'), the militant West Bank settlers whose messianic zeal for the Land is for Rubinstein an unconscious response to the awesome potency of the earth.

22. Again, this deployment of Heidegger is starkly at odds with Agamben's, for whom the ontological difference – Being's original consignment to entities – renders impossible any meaningful distinction between authentic and inauthentic existence: '*Authentic existence has no content other than inauthentic existence; the proper is nothing other than the apprehension of the improper*'. See 'The Passion of Facticity' in *Potentialities: Collected Essays in Philosophy* (trans. D. Heller-Roazen, Stanford CA: Stanford University Press, 2000), p. 197.

23. The prefix 'neo' is intended to indicate Berkowits' distance from the theodicy prevalent among ultra-Orthodox interpreters for whom Auschwitz is an expression of God's punishment '*mipnei chateinu*' – 'for our sins'. While remaining very much within normative Judaic boundaries, Berkowits creatively mobilizes the text of tradition against such an interpretation.

24. This is of course the subtitle to Fackenheim's major work of 1982, *To Mend the World*.

25. I cite here from the preface to the second edition of 1994.

26. Chapter 2 will attempt to develop the ethico-political entailments of such a position.

27. Perhaps the most telling index of the persistence of Hegelianism in Fackenheim's interpretation of Auschwitz is to be found in a footnote to the second edition of 1994, which responds to a review of the first edition by Susan E. Shapiro. In response to Shapiro's criticism that *To Mend the World*'s privileging of physical and spiritual resistance in the death camps implicitly denigrates 'the mute testimony of the *Muselmänner*', Fackenheim writes: 'Her error in the cited criticism is due to her failure to recognize that post-Hegelian thought like Hegel's own, *moves*. Hence the *Muselmänner* are not left behind as this thought reaches the resistance that mends its own ontological foundations: it can reach, come to possess and continue to possess these foundations only as it, ever again, *moves through* the mute testimony of the *Muselmänner* by which it is paralyzed. Not accidentally does the present essay end with the statement that while a mending of the wound of Spirit is possible, a healing is not' (*MW*, 336). As will be argued presently, the distinction between Hegelian and post-Hegelian, or between healing and mending, is vulnerable to Hegelian critique precisely because it remains within Hegel's terms. The 'movement through' the *Muselmän*'s testimony to the ontological ultimacy of resistance leaves the Hegelian Absolute intact while slackening the rigour of its metaphysical determination. From Hegel's perspective, 'mending' is merely healing in a state of misrecognition; and, as long as Fackenheim insists on the dialectical sublation of the *Muselmän*, there is no arguing with Hegel's perspective.

28. This is the title of Fackenheim's 1978 collection of essays (New York: Schocken, 1978).
29. Nor is this a Heideggerean ontology of finitude; it is rather a sacral ontology, invested inexplicably by a divine authority, as indicated by the name Fackenheim famously gives to this task of self-affirmation: 'the 614th commandment'. See 'The 614th Commandment' in *The Jewish Return Into History*, pp. 19–24.
30. Chapter 3 will argue that Levinas' treatment of the relation between the people and the State of Israel turns – not accidentally – on the very same tension.
31. For a more concentrated elaboration of this relation, see the essay 'The Holocaust and the State of Israel: Their Relation' in *The Jewish Return Into History*, pp. 273–86.
32. For a more recent attempt to appropriate the fragmentary logic of Jena Romanticism for contemporary philosophy, see Simon Critchley, *Very Little . . . Almost Nothing: Death, Philosophy, Literature* (London: Routledge, 1997) pp. 85–117.
33. Philippe Lacoue-Labarthe and Jean-Luc Nancy, *The Literary Absolute: The Theory of Literature in German Romanticism* (trans. P. Bernard and C. Lester, Albany, NY: SUNY Press, 1988, p. 83; *L'Absolu Littéraire: Théorie de la Littérature du Romantisme Allemande* (Paris: Seuil, 1978), p. 266.
34. F. W. Schlegel, *Philosophical Fragments* (trans. P. Firchow, Minneapolis, MN: Minnesota University Press, 1991), p. 32; 'Fragmente' in *Athenaeum: Eine Zeitschrift von A. W. Schlegel und F. Schlegel*, Vol. 1 (ed. C. Grutzmaster, Munich: Rowolt Verlag, 1969), pp. 29–30.
35. Mark-Alain Ouaknin, *The Burnt Book: Reading the Talmud* (trans. L. Brown, Princeton, NJ: Princeton University Press, 1995); *Le Livre Brûlé: Lire le Talmud* (Paris: Lieu Commun, 1986). See also, however, Susan Handelman, *The Slayers of Moses: The Emergence of Rabbinic Interpretation in Modern Literary Theory* (Albany, NY: SUNY Press, 1982) and most recently Robert Gibbs, *Why Ethics: Signs of Responsibilities* (Princeton, NJ: Princeton University Press, 2000), especially pp. 210–24.

Chapter 2: 'The Ever-Broken Promise of Happiness'

1. Adorno himself quickly warns us against understanding his imperative too quickly – 'this imperative', he continues, 'is as refractory as the given one of Kant was once upon a time. Dealing discursively with it would be an outrage . . .' (*ND*, 365; *GS* 6, 358). By pursuing the question of what it might mean to keep faith with the categorical imperative, we perhaps risk this 'outrage'; this is why we must avoid attempting to specify formal criteria for its fulfilment, and recognize the *absence* of any such criteria as constitutive.
2. Jephcott's translation thus misses the allusion to and provocation against Hegel in Adorno's title: '*Zum* Ende' – '*Towards* an End' – indicates a break in the closed circle of Absolute Knowledge. Invoking terminology from Philippe Lacoue-Labarthe and Jean-Luc Nancy, we might say that Adorno's text 'incompletes' itself at its very completion. See Philippe Lacoue-Labarthe and Jean-Luc Nancy, *The Literary Absolute* (trans. C. Lester and P. Barnard, Albany, NY: SUNY Press, 1988).
3. The subtitle of *Minima Moralia* is, of course, *Reflections from Damaged Life* (*Reflexionen aus dem beschädigten Leben*).
4. In spite of the wide range and massive volume of his writings on other art-forms – most obviously and importantly music – I have chosen to confine my discussion of the particular instantiations of the Adornian aesthetic to his writings on poetry. This choice is dictated by reasons both pragmatic and substantive; pragmatic insofar as a reading of the musical writings in the terms set out here would render the scope of this chapter unmanageably large; substantive insofar as the essays on poetry give particularly potent voice to a tension at the heart of both this chapter and this book, between what Adorno would call the conceptual and the expressive. That is, because poetry's medium

is language –and as such irreducibly conceptual – it enacts in its very texture the negative dialectical play of the concept and its inassimilable other – in other terms, the non-
identity of identity and non-identity.

5. Probably the most rigorous rebuttal of the 'negative theological' reading of Adorno is
to be found in Jay Bernstein's *The Fate of Art: Aesthetic Alienation from Kant to Derrida*
(Oxford: Blackwell, 1992). Bernstein protests Albrecht Wellmer's reading of the art–
philosophy relation in Adorno as 'secularized negative theology'. 'Unlike the negations
of negative theology', he writes, 'Adorno's negations are determinate and not abstract.
Because these negations are determinate, the result is finite' (260). Bernstein is right to
reject the characterization of Adorno's aesthetic as 'secularized negative theology'. As I
hope to show, art is not theology by another, secular name, but the place where theology
is preserved *in its impossibility*. However, to oppose determinate to abstract negation and
place Adorno on the side of the former is to miss the crucially *doubled* character of the
negative dialectic: both abstract, because it creates a space for the unnamable beyond any
determination, and determinate because unnamability is itself the condition of an
ineluctable finitude.

6. The following remark from Section 99 ('Gold assay') of *Minima Moralia* is instructive at
this point: 'He who holds fast the self and does away with theological concepts helps to
justify the diabolical positive, naked interest' (*MM*, 154; *GS* 4, 176).

7. Max Horkheimer, *Die Sehnsucht nach dem ganz Anderen, Ein Interview mit Kommentar von
Helmut Gumnior* (Hamburg: Furche-Verlag, 1970). All translations from this text are
my own.

8. For a reading of Adorno on religion heavily informed by the interview with Horkheimer (to the point of paraphrasing large, mostly unacknowledged, passages), see Rudolf
J. Siebert, 'Adorno's Theory of Religion' in *Telos* 58 (winter 1983–4).

9. The phrase, of course, is Walter Benjamin's, from the first of the 'theses' from 'On the
Concept of History' ('Über den Begriff der Geschichte'). See *Illuminations* (trans.
H. Zohn, London: Fontana, 1992), p. 245; *Gesammelte Schriften 1.2* (eds R. Tiedemann
and H. Schweppenhäuser , Frankfurt: Suhrkamp, 1974), p. 693.

10. See for example Susan Buck-Morss, *The Origin of Negative Dialectics* (New York, NY:
Free Press, 1977); Martin Jay, *Adorno* (Cambridge, MA: Havard University Press,
1984); and more concentratedly, Wayne Whitson Floyd, Jr., 'Transcendence in the
Light of Redemption: Adorno and the Legacy of Rosenzweig and Benjamin', *Journal
of the American Academy of Religion*, LXI/3.

11. Indeed, Adorno's displaced recognition of this affinity is suggested in one of his rare
allusions to Rosenzweig, where he suggests that Benjamin shares with him (and
others) a certain 'conception to the concrete', which despite its opposition to idealism,
'has a theological colouring even where thought has reservations about theology'
(*NL* 2, 320; *GS* 11, 688).

12. For a fascinating attempt to bring together these two thinkers by way of this terminological affinity, see Alexander Garcia Düttmann, *The Gift of Language: Memory and Promise
in Adorno, Benjamin, Heidegger and Rosenzweig* (trans. A. Lyons, London: Athlone, 2000),
especially the opening chapter, 'Constellations'.

13. The elements Creation – Revelation – Redemption are the 'conversion' of the previously isolated elements, respectively God – Man – World. The isolation of each element is negated by its counterpart: God negates this isolation in Creation, Man in
Revelation, the World in Redemption.

14. Rosenzweig's distinction between State and Jewish law finds unmistakable echoes in
Walter Benjamin's 'Critique of Violence' ('*Zur Kritik der Gewalt*') and its analogous distinction between the 'mythic violence' of the State and the 'divine violence' of God.
Both thinkers oppose the religious submission to commandment to the citizen's subjection to law; the former sustains life, the latter curtails it. See *Selected Writings*, Volume 1

(ed. M. Bullock and M. Jennings, Cambridge, MA: Harvard University Press, 1996); *Gessamelte Schriften*, Volume 2.i. (ed. R. Tiédemann and H. Schweppenhäuser, Frankfurt am Main: Suhrkamp Verlag, 1977).

15. For further biographical information on Adorno's Jewish origins see Susan Buck-Morss, *The Origin of Negative Dialectics* (New York: Free Press, 1977) and Martin Jay, *The Dialectical Imagination* (Berkeley, CA: University of California Press, 1996 (revised edn)).

16. Simon Jarvis, *Adorno: A Critical Introduction* (Cambridge: Polity, 1998), p. 11.

17. We will return to this perennial Adornian theme, the struggle for a non-Hegelian critique of the Kantian 'block', in more detail.

18. From the end of Bloch's short text: 'Everything that was ever made in this way, out of love and necessity, leads a life of its own, leads ito a strange new territory, and returns with us formed as we could not be in life, adorned with a certain, however weak sign, the seal of our self'. See *The Spirit of Utopia* (trans. A. A. Nassar, Stanford, CA: Stanford University Press, 2000), p. 9.

19. Adorno's defence of the 'imagelessness' of utopia against Bloch's 'positivistic cataloguing' of redemptive images is treated with great clarity and precision by Rolf Tiedemann in his essay 'Concept, Image, Name: On Adorno's Utopia of Knowledge', in T. Huhn and L. Zuidevaart (eds), *The Semblance of Subjectivity: Adorno's Aesthetic Theory* (Cambridge, MA: MIT Press, 1997).

20. It is Benjamin that first employs the term 'constellation' ('*Sternbilder*') in the 'Epistemo-Critical Prologue' to *The Origin of German Tragic Drama* to describe a method aimed at redeeming phenomena. See *The Origin of German Tragic Drama* (trans. J. Osborne, London: Verso, 1985), p. 34, *Gesammelte Schriften* 1.1, p. 214.

21. Düttmann offers a sustained (and very demanding) exploration of the relationship between name and promise in both Benjamin and Adorno in *The Gift of Language*. See especially Chapter 4, 'Apparitions': 'The appearance of a name is never without a certain promise, even if we are hearing the name for the first time' (p. 79).

22. See *Selected Writings*, Volume 1, p. 65; *Gesammelte Schriften* 2.1, p. 144 (Benjamin's emphasis).

23. Walter Benjamin, *One-Way Street and Other Writings*, p. 155 (London: Verso, 1995); *Gesammelte Schriften*, 2.1, p. 204.

24. We will expound Adorno's complex understanding of mimesis more fully below.

25. References to the English translation are to the pagination of the Norman Kemp Smith translation; references to the German are to the pagination of the first (or 'A') and, where appropriate, second (or 'B') editions.

26. Of course the second Critique, *Critique of Practical Reason*, accedes the possibility of such knowledge (which nevertheless cannot be derived theoretically) in the form of the moral Law.

27. Interestingly, despite the philosophical gap between them, the two thinkers are linked by their each having laid claim to Adorno as a key force behind their own thinking. Equally tellingly, their readings of Adorno seem to have moved in opposite directions. In an early critique, 'Adorno as the Devil' (*Telos* 19, spring 1974, hereafter 'AD'), Lyotard charges him with remaining in thrall to a dialectical theology. Rose's first book, *The Melancholy Science: An Introduction to the Thought of T. W. Adorno* (London: Macmillan, 1978) is an exceptionally perspicacious (though not uncritical) reading of Adorno's Marxism as 'the search for a style'. Where Lyotard's work (especially *The Differend* and *Heidegger and 'the Jews'*) becomes increasingly respectful of Adorno's 'micrology', Rose becomes increasingly impatient with what she sees as a regression from the power of the speculative proposition to the 'spellbound aporetics' of the negative dialectic ('From Speculative to Dialectical Thinking: Hegel and Adorno' in *Judaism and Modernity* (Oxford: Blackwell, 1993).

28. The relevant section in Kant is the 'Analytic of the Sublime' in *Critique of Judgment* (trans. W. S. Pluhar, Indianapolis, IN: Hackett, 1987), pp. 97–140; *Kritik der Urteilskraft* (Cologne: Parkland Verlag, 1999), pp. 349–98.

29. Jean-François Lyotard, *Heidegger and 'the Jews'* (trans. A. Michel and M. Roberts, Minneapolis: Minnesota University Press, 1990), p. 43, hereafter *Hj*; *Heidegger et 'le juifs'* (Paris: Galilée, 1988), p. 61.

30. Jean-François Lyotard, *The Differend* (trans G. Van Den Abeele, Minneapolis: Minnesota University Press, 1988), p. 56, hereafter *D*; *Le Différend* (Paris: Edition de Minuit, 1983), p. 91.

31. 'Our metaphysical faculty is paralyzed because actual events have shattered the basis on which speculative metaphysical thought could be reconciled with experience' (*ND*, 362; *GS* 6, 354).

32. See Jean-François Lyotard, *Discourse, Figure* (trans. G. Van Den Abeele, Manchester: Manchester University Press, 1986). *Discours, Figure* (Paris: Editions Klincksieck, 1971).

33. Samuel Weber, 'Afterword' to Lyotard's *Just Gaming* (Minneapolis: Minnesota University Press, 1985), p. 105. A different but not unrelated criticism of Lyotard's anti-representational politics and aesthetics is offered by Philippe Lacoue-Labarthe in his essay 'The Scene Is Primal'. Lacoue-Labarthe takes up Lyotard's critique of a Freudian 'theatre' in which the free play of desire is consigned to the '*disreal*' spaces of dramatic representation. Lacoue-Labarthe comments that Lyotard is right only if 'one posit (or imagine) that there is a reality "outside of representation" – that the real, far from being the impossible as it was for Lacan and Bataille, is what can actually present itself as such, and that consequently there is, in general, such a thing as presentation, a full, whole, virginal, inviolate, and inviolable presence'. See *The Subject of Philosophy* (trans. K. McPherson, Minneapolis, MN: Minnesota University Press, 1993), p. 101. See also Lacoue-Labarthe's critique of the Lyotardian sublime in *Poetry As Experience* (trans. A., Stanford, CA: Stanford University Press, 19), pp. 87–91; *La Poésie Comme Experience* (Paris: Christian Bourgois Éditeur, 1986), pp. 123–9.

34. These symptoms are tellingly compacted in Lyotard's famous injunction to 'wage war on totality'. See *The Postmodern Condition* (trans. G. Bennington and R. Bowlby, Minnesota, MN: University of Minnesota Press, 1990), p. 106.

35. Gillian Rose, *Mourning Becomes the Law: Philosophy and Representation* (Cambridge: Cambridge University Press, 1996), p. 21.

36. A question Rose argues should inform the visitor's experience of all memorial and museological representation of the Holocaust. See 'The Future of Auschwitz' in *Judaism and Modernity: Philosophical Essays* (Oxford: Blackwell, 1993).

37. Hannah Arendt, *Eichmann in Jerusalem: A Report on the Banality of Evil* (New York: Viking Press, 1964), p. 267.

38. Translation modified.

39. I quote from the chapter on Hegel's aesthetic in Gillian Rose's masterful *Hegel: Contra Sociology* (London: Athlone, 1981), p. 140.

40. Implied here of course is a wholesale rethinking of 'spirit' itself, for in this context it is 'no longer to be presupposed as substance' (*AT*, 91; *GS* 7, 140). Spirit is rather 'the mimetic impulse fixated [*festbegannte*] as totality' (*AT*, 90; *GS* 7, 139). Spirit cannot be presupposed as substance because it is rent by an irremediable internal division between the sedimented rationality of the concept ('totality') and the otherness ('mimetic impulse') which totality can never fully subsume.

41. For a very useful account of the complex interplay of the spiritual and mimetic in Adorno's aesthetic, see Peter Osborne, 'Adorno and the Metaphysics of Modernism: The Problem of a "Postmodern Art"' in A. Benjamin and P. Osborne (eds), *The Problems of Modernity*: Adorno and Benjamin (London: Routledge, 1989).

42. See *Friendship* (trans. E. Rottenberg, Stanford, CA: Stanford University Press, 1997), p. 92; *L'Amitié* (Paris: Gallimard, 1971), pp. 107–8.

43. In 'Music and Language: A Fragment', Adorno writes: 'The language of music is quite different from all signifying language. It contains a theological dimension. What it says remains concealed in its very utterance, while at the same time being precise and determinate: the message is both clear and veiled. The idea of this utterance is represented by the figure of the divine Name' (*Quasi Una Fantasia* [trans. R. Livingstone, London: Verso, 1992], pp. 2–3).

44. Jay Bernstein, *The Fate of Art: Aesthetic Alienation from Kant to Derrida* (Cambridge: Polity, 1993), p. 1.

45. Shierry Weber Nicholsen, *Exact Imagination, Late Work: On Adorno's Aesthetics* (Cambridge, MA: MIT Press, 1998), p. 93.

46. Benjamin writes, at the beginning of his essay: 'No poem is intended for the reader, no picture for the beholder, no symphony for the audience . . . For what does a literary work "say"? What does it communicate? It "tells" very little to those who understand it. Its essential quality is not communication or the imparting of information'. See *Selected Writings*, Vol. 1, p. 253; *Gesammelte Schriften* 4.1, p. 9.

47. Both also use the term 'language itself', Benjamin of course in 'On Language As Such and On Human Language', Adorno in his essay on Eichendorff.

48. The rethinking of mimesis has been central to the deconstructive turn in contemporary French philosophy. In 'The Double Session', the second of the three essays in *Dissemination* (trans. Barbara Johnson; Chicago, IL: Chicago University Press, 1988), Jacques Derrida brings the motif of the 'fold' into play as that which marks the text's parting of/with reference, with any 'mimetological' or 'Platonico-Hegelian' conception of mimesis: 'The syntax of the fold makes it impossible for us to arrest its play or indecision' (231). Mallarméan mimesis, that is, is 'mimicry imitating nothing . . . a double that doubles no simple' (206). Perhaps the most sustained exploration of the mimetic question, however, is to be found in Lacoue-Labarthe's essay 'Typography' (in *Typography: Mimesis, Philosophy, Politics*, trans. C. Fynsk, Stanford, CA: Stanford University Press, 1989). Martin Jay has attempted to show the affinities and disparities between Lacoue-Labarthe and Adorno, arguing that the latter's 'endlessly oscillating mimesis' breaks with Adorno's 'utopian impulse'. See 'Mimesis and Mimetology: Adorno and Lacoue-Labarthe' in T. Huhn and L. Zuidevaart (eds), *The Semblance of Subjectivity*, p. 44.

49. *One-Way Street and Other Writings*, p. 155; *Gesammelte Schriften*, 2.1, p. 204.

50. Translation modified.

51. Hullot-Kentor's translation exacerbates this separation by rendering 'mit der Paradoxie' as 'qualified by the paradox' (understandably from the perspective of clarity), as if the block were a second-order contingency of divine language as opposed to constitutive of it.

52. Translation modified.

53. Lacoue-Labarthe, *Poetry as Experience*, p. 88; *La Poésie Comme Experience*, p. 124. It is worth noting additionally in this regard Sarah Kofman's characterization of Adorno's 'new categorical imperative' as a Kantianism rid 'of its abstract and ideal generality'. See *Smothered Words* (trans. M. Dobie, Evanston, IL: Northwestern University Press, 19), p. 7.

54. While I have depended on Michael Hamburger's translation, I have revised it in a number of important respects. In particular, I have returned third-person verbs translated into the second person to their original form.

55. I am indebted here to Krysztof Ziarek's excellent discussion of the Celanian *Gegenwort*. See *Inflected Language: Toward A Hermeneutics of Nearness – Heidegger, Levinas, Stevens, Celan* (Albany, NY: SUNY, 1994), pp. 168–70.

56. Paul Celan, *Collected Prose* (trans. R. Waldrop, Manchester: Carcanet, 1986), p. 40; Paul Celan, *Der Meridian: Rede anlaßlich der Verleitung des Georg-Büchner-Preises 1960* (Frankfurt-am-Main: S. Fischer Verlag, 1961), p. 8.

57. Peter Szondi, 'Reading "Engführung": An essay on the poetry of Paul Celan' in *boundary 2*, Vol. XI 5 (spring 1983).

58. Again, I have modified Hamburger's translation, rendering the poem more 'literally'.

Chapter 3: 'Absolute Insomnia'

1. Translation slightly modified.

2. The most obvious example of which is the single sentence that follows the 'disparate' autobiographical 'inventory' which opens his short essay 'Signature': 'It is dominated by the presentiment and the memory of the Nazi horror' (*DF*, 291; *DL*, 374).

   Two of Levinas' most important philosophical contemporaries and commentators have placed the same question at the heart of his work. Maurice Blanchot demands, at the end of his 'Our Clandestine Companion', '[h]ow can one philosophize, how can one write within the memory of Auschwitz . . . It is this thought that traverses, that bears, the whole of Levinas' philosophy and that he proposes to us without saying it, beyond and before all obligation' (*FEL*, 50). Similarly, in his address at Levinas' funeral ('Adieu') Jacques Derrida remarks that 'the terrifying memory of our time . . . dictates each of these sentences, whether from nearby or afar . . .' (*AEL*, 5; 16).

3. Jacques Derrida, 'Violence and Metaphysics' in *Writing and Difference* (trans. A. Bass, London: Routledge, 1978), p. 111; 'Violence et métaphysique' in *L'écriture et le différence* (Paris: Seuil, 1967), p. 164.

4. Derrida offers fascinating anecdotal testimony to the priority of religion for Levinas: 'during one of those conversations I hold so dear . . . he said to me, "You know, one often speaks of ethics to describe what I do, but what really interests me in the end is not ethics, not ethics alone, but the holy, the holiness of the holy" ' (*AEL*, 4, 15).

5. Translated by Alphonso Lingis under the title *Existence and Existents*.

6. Levinas discusses the impact of Levy-Bruhl on French philosophy in 'Levy-Bruhl and Philosophy' in *Entre-Nous*, pp. 39–52, 49–63.

7. Friedrich Nietzsche, *The Birth of Tragedy and The Genealogy of Morals* (trans. F. Golffing, New York: Anchor Books, 1956), p. 46; *Die Geburt der Tragödie* (Leipzig: Reclam, 1937), p. 49.

8. The uncanny affinity between the early description of art and the later account of ethical substitution is at the heart of Thomas Carl Wall's reading of Levinas in his remarkable *Radical Passivity: Levinas, Blanchot, and Agamben* (Albany, NY: SUNY Press, 1999). Wall observes that the rhythmic participation subtending the known world in Levinas' description, 'realizes the paradox of immediacy – the paradox of an immediacy that drives out all mediation and, essentially empty, drives out itself and is thus outside memory' (16). The same paradox will characterize exactly that exposure to the Other which defines Levinasian ethics.

9. Levinas attributes these terms to his teacher Jean Wahl.

10. Jill Robbins, *Altered Reading: Levinas and Literature* (Chicago, IL: University of Chicago Press, 2000), p. 90.

11. This is not the place for a full elaboration of the difference between the Heideggerean and the Blanchotian poetic. However, some light may be cast on this question by the following gloss on Hölderlin from Heidegger's 'What Are Poets For?': 'Poets are the mortals who, singing earnestly of the wine god, sense the trace of the fugitive gods, stay on the gods' tracks, and so trace for their kindred mortals the way toward the turning' (in *Poetry, Language, Truth*, trans. A. Hofstadter, New York: Harper & Row, 1971, p. 95). To be sure, 'the turning' to which he alludes is decisively not a redemptive horizon at which all that has been concealed will be revealed; concealment and revelation are for Heidegger not opposed terms but indissociable modalities of one another. Nevertheless, Heidegger's language seems unmistakably to draw the poet closer to the fugitive truth of the divine than 'their kindred mortals'. For Blanchot, in contrast, poetry, far from bringing the poet closer to this truth, only sends him away from it. For an excellent discussion of this relationship, see Paul Davies' 'A Linear Narrative? Blanchot with Heidegger in the Work of Levinas' in D. Wood (ed.), *Philosopher's Poets* (London: Routledge, 1990).

12. The first version of the second text was published in *Le Nouveau Commerce*, No. 30–1 (spring 1975), under the title 'Discours sur la patience'.
13. Maurice Blanchot, 'The Madness of the Day' in *The Station Hill Blanchot Reader* (trans. L. Davis, Barrytown, NY: Station Hill Press, 1999), p. 195; *La Folie du Jour* (Montpellier: Fata Morgana, 1973), p. 20.
14. This is the same temporal experience that Levinas describes as 'indolence' in *From Existence to Existents*, a text near contemporary with 'The Madness of the Day', written when interned in a Nazi POW camp. Indolence is 'an impossibility of beginning' (*EE*, 26; *DEE*, 34), 'a refusal to undertake, to progress, to take charge . . . a holding back from the future' (*EE*, 29; *DEE*, 39).
15. Maurice Blanchot, 'The Madness of the Day', p. 194; *La Folie du Jour*, p. 18.
16. Paul Davies, 'A Linear Narrative?', p. 43.
17. Translation modified – Ann Smock omits from her translation the phrase 'responsabilité sans mesure'.
18. Maurice Blanchot, 'Literature and the Right to Death' in *The Work of Fire* (trans. L. Davis, Stanford, CA: Stanford University Press, 1995); 'La Littérature et le droit à la mort' in *Le Part du Feu* (Paris: Gallimard, 1949).
19. I use the feminine pronoun in spite of the ascription to the feminine, in *Totality and Infinity*, of a different alterity than that of the transparency of droiture – a silent, concealed and nocturnal alterity 'beyond the face'. See especially IV. B, 'The Phenomenology of Eros', pp. 256–66; 233–44 . While an explicit engagement with the question of the feminine in Levinas is beyond the scope of this chapter, its argument about the difficulty of distinguishing different modes of alterity may provide some suggestions as to the itinerary of such an engagement.
20. See *Being and Time* (trans. John McQuarrie and Edward Robinson, Oxford: Blackwell, 1962), Division Two, Chapter 1, pp. 279–311; *Sein und Zeit* (Tübingen; Max Niemayer Verlag, 1960), pp. 235–67.
21. The dispossession of the *Jemeinigkeit* of Heideggerean death is a motif present in Levinas from the earliest of his texts. In his lecture course of 1946–7, *Time and the Other*, he contests Heidegger's understanding of anxiety as 'the experience of nothingness. Is it not, on the contrary, – if by death one means nothingness – the fact that is impossible to die?' (*TO*, 57; *TA*, 29).
22. Dennis Keenan, *Death and Responsibility: The 'Work' of Levinas* (Albany, NY: SUNY Press, 1999), p. 8.
23. Levinas' phenomenology of fecundity, which we do not have the space to address here, finds in the relation between father and son the same unbridgeable distance experienced positively. Fecundity opens a future not my own, a time 'beyond the possible' which is 'mine' only in the form of a non-possession, in which a being becomes 'capable of another fate than its own' (*TaI*, 282; *TeI*, 258). See the entirety of Section IV, 'Beyond the Face', but especially Part C, 'Fecundity', pp. 267–70; 244–7.
24. The second of Derrida's three sustained engagements with Levinas, 'At This Very Moment In The Work Here I Am' is a painstaking interrogation of the necessary 'risk' of the Saying's detour through the Said (in S. Critchley and R. Bernasconi, eds *Re-Reading Levinas*, London: Athlone, 1991; 'En ce moment même dans cet ouvrage, me voici' in *Psyche: Inventions de l'autre*, Paris: Galilée, 1987). As the title indicates, this risk is conditioned above all by the aporetic temporality which renders the said perpetually 'out of phase' (in Levinas' phrase) with the Saying. *Otherwise Than Being* performs this temporality, suggests Derrida, when it draws attention to its own time, as in the phrase 'at this moment'. Derrida's essay hinges on the recurrence of this phrase in two successive paragraphs of *Otherwise Than Being*. Levinas questions, in the first one, whether ' "the act of talking and thinking about" ' the Soul's relation to the Absolute ' "*at this very moment*" ' (23; 34, Derrida's emphasis) does not demonstrate the sovereignty of thematization over that Relation. In the next paragraph, he responds that 'the language of thematization, which *at this*

moment we are using, has perhaps been made possible by means of that Relation' (23; 34, Derrida's emphasis). Derrida's 'reading' of this recurrence insinuates a decisive difference into this repetition of the same, a difference which points up precisely the intrication of the enigma of language with that of time, for the second 'moment' is revealed to be the condition of the first, such that 'the *same moment*, written and read in its difference, in its double difference, one belonging to dialectic and the other different from and differing from (*différant*) the first, infinitely and in advance overflowing it. The second moment has an infinite advance on the first. And yet it is the same' (24, Derrida's emphasis; 35).

25. Levinas' usage of this term both strictly conforms to and thoroughly alienates its Husserlian sense: strictly conforms in that it too denotes a radical suspension or *epokhē* of all that is secondary to the thing itself (the Saying); thoroughly alienates it in that this 'itself' cannot be made to appear to consciousness *apart* from that secondariness (the Said).

26. See, for example, the following lines from the 'Conclusions' to *Totality and Infinity*: 'When with Freud, sexuality is approached on the human plane, it is reduced to the level of the search for pleasure, without the ontological signification of voluptuosity and the irreducible categories it brings into play every being even suspected ... What remains unrecognized is ... that in sexuality the subject enters into relation with what is absolutely other, with an alterity of a type unforeseeable in formal logic, with what remains other in the relation and is never converted into "mine" ...' (*TaI*, 276; *TeI*, 253–4).

27. Sigmund Freud, 'Beyond The Pleasure Principle' in *The Penguin Freud Library, Volume 11: On Metapsychology* (London: Penguin, 1999), p. 301.

28. Levinas had elaborated the intimate bond between rest and consciousness as early as *From Existence to the Existent*: 'In lying down, in curling up in a corner to sleep, we abandon ourselves to a place; qua base it becomes our refuge. Then all our work of being consists in resting' (*EE*, 70; *DEE*, 119).

29. The argument I am developing here as to the relation between Auschwitz and the language of persecution differs from Robert Bernasconi's, who argues (though not without some caution) for a reading of this language in particularist terms (persecution as a historically specific experience rather than a general structure of subjectivity), on the grounds that a strictly universalist reading, in rendering everyone persecuted, divests persecution of its singularity. Yet Bernasconi is too careful a reader of Levinas not to recognize the difficulties involved in the attempt to determine that which tolerates no determination. The way out of this bind, I suggest, is to recognize a distinction between the universality of persecution and the election which is *awakening* to persecution. All are persecuted in the sense of being obligated prior to any contract or assumption – but persecution, being 'older' than consciousness, enables its own forgetting (indeed, like Heidegger's Being, it is *destined* to its own forgetting). For Levinas, to be Jewish is above all, and before any racial or religious identifcation, *not to forget* this immemorial persecution; such 'Jewishness' is anyone's possibility – hence a particularism which can extend itself infinitely without compromising its particularity. See R. Bernasconi, ' "Only the Persecuted": Language of the Oppressor, Language of the Oppressed' in A. Perpazak (ed.), *Ethics as First Philosophy* (London: Routledge, 1995).

30. Levinas' 1934 on Hitlerism, discussed in the first chapter, had implicitly identified a teleology of suffering at the heart of Nazism. The essay, we recall, reads Nazism as a demonic inversion of Christendom's decorporealization of the soul; where the latter prises body and soul apart, Nazism renders them equivalent; enchained to the body, the self's humanity becomes its racial destiny. The purgative discourse of Hitler's anti-Semitism, in which Jewishness is equated with a disease to be eradicated from the collective Aryan body is thus the ultimate logic of a restorative logic of suffering. See *Critical Inquiry* 17, autumn 1990 (first published in *Esprit* in 1934).

31. John Llewyellyn concludes his book on Levinas by suggesting that to remember the dead of Auschwitz is to perform 'the auto-accusation in suffering that is the turning of

the ego into a self'. See *Emmanuel Levinas: The Genealogy of Ethics* (London: Routledge, 1995), p. 213.

32. See also, however, a number of references to the Jewish experience of Nazism in *Difficult Freedom*. For example, from 'A Religion for Adults': 'They [the Jewish victims] experienced a condition inferior to that of things, an experience of total passivity, an experience of Passion' (*DF*, 12; *DL*, 26); and in 'Poetry and the Impossible': '... under Hitler, the Jews endured an ordeal that is without name, and that cannot be placed within any sociological category' (*DF*, 129; *DL*, 173).

33. For Dennis Keenan, 'The fact that the demonic is a modality of infinite goodness is what makes (true) responsibility possible'. See *Death and Responsiblity*, p. 82.

34. The qualifier 'metaphysical' is necessary, for Levinasian atheism is to be distinguished from all forms – logical, scientistic, existentialist – of rationalist atheism. For Levinas, to deny God is merely to invert positive religion's appropriative mode of knowing. Metaphysical atheism, in contrast, designates not the denial of God, but God's sovereign denial of Himself to human knowledge or representation.

35. I have restored the quotation marks which Lingis has removed from Levinas' original text.

36. Of Rosenzweig's *Star of Redemption*, Levinas famously writes at the outset of *Totality and Infinity*: 'We were impressed by the opposition to the idea of totality in Franz Rosenzweig's *Stern der Erlösung*, a work too often present in this work to be cited' (*TaI*, 28; *TeI*, xvi). Levinas went on to publish three essays on Rosenzweig: 'Between Two Worlds', a paper given in 1959 to the second colloquium of Franco-Jewish intellectuals and published in *Difficult Freedom*, his 1964 essay 'Franz Rosenzweig: A Modern Jewish Thinker', published in *Outside the Subject*, and 'The Philosophy of Franz Rosenzweig', a preface to Stéphane Mosès' 1982 study, *Système et Révélation*, reprinted in *In the Time of the Nations*.

37. The three-fold form of the term is elaborated in Hent de Vries' 'Adieu, A-Dieu, à-Dieu' in A. Perperzak (ed.), *Ethics as First Philosophy*. See also de Vries' more recent *Philosophy and the Turn to Religion* (Baltimore, MD: Johns Hopkins University Press, 1999), pp. 269–71, where the term is read from a more explicitly Derridean perspective.

38. See pp. 45–51 above for a discussion of Adorno's critique of positive religion.

39. Translation modified – Hand collapses the penultimate and last clauses of the sentence, losing the interesting ambiguity whereby the Messiah himself awaits the 'coming of Messiah'.

40. For a very useful account of the relationship between ethics and hermeneutics in Levinas' Jewish thought, see Tamra Wright, *The Twilight of Jewish Philosophy: Emmanuel Levinas' Ethical Hermeneutics* (Amsterdam: Harwood Academic, 1999), especially Chapter 5. In his recent *Why Ethics?: Signs of Responsibility* (Princeton, NJ: Princeton University Press, 2001), Robert Gibbs renders the Talmudic hermeneutic the performative as well as the conceptual basis of an ethics of responsibility, composing the text as a fluid and interpenetrative series of commentaries on 'pre-texts' or citations from a range of philosophical and Judaic sources which mimes the structure of the Talmudic page. Gibbs' book is thus a sustained enactment of the argument set forth here, namely that hermeneutics is responsibility – reading, questioning, disputing – impelled towards a state of infinition: 'I read and write commentary here to hold open for others, to call for other books to read. This text is a reading text, reading in the ethical exigency to call to other readers' (p. 113).

41. See Marc-Alain Ouaknin, *Médiations Erotiques* (Paris: Payot, 1992). For a fuller account of Ouaknin's Talmudic hermeneutics see his *The Burnt Book: Reading the Talmud* (trans. L. Brown, Princeton, NJ: Princeton University Press, 1995).

42. Deuteronomy 10:17 reads: 'For the LORD your God is God supreme and Lord supreme, the great, the mighty and the awesome God, who shows no favor and takes

no bribe'. Numbers 6:25 reads: 'The Lord deal kindly and graciously with you'. I quote from the Jewish Publication Society translation of the *Tanakh* (1985).

43. I have restored Levinas' emphasis of the word 'visibility' which Lingis removes from his translation.

44. The reverse, of course, is also the case: there is no justice worthy of the name that has not been immemorially conditioned by the ethical. For an excellent account of this conditioning, see Fabio Ciaramelli, 'The Riddle of the Pre-Original' in A. Perperzak (ed.), *Ethics as First Philosophy*.

45. See, for example, 'The Holocaust and the State of Israel: Their Relation' in Emil Fackenhcim, *The Jewish Return Into History* (New York: Schocken, 1978), p. 274.

46. For a fuller explication of this politics, see the previous chapter's section on Rosenzweig.

47. See, for example, Gillian Rose's trenchant critique of Rosenzweig along these lines in her essay 'Franz Rosenzweig: From Hegel to Yom Kippur', in *Judaism and Modernity: Philosophical Essays* (Oxford: Blackwell, 1993).

48. Following Derrida, I am referring here to the 'Zionist commitment' as Levinas envisions it, rather than to the historical project of pre-State Zionism. Needless to say, there can be no collapsing the two, not least because the Zionist commitment has a complex and internally variegated history which encompasses many different political and religious tendencies, from Marxism to ultra-nationalism, from secular humanism to religious Orthodoxy. Levinas' relationship to the different strains of Zionist thought, with its provocative disregard for entrenched religious and political boundaries, deserves a sustained study of its own which we cannot attempt here.

49. In a concluding footnote to his essay 'Being-Jewish', Blanchot addresses the same question of Judaism's relationship to the State, and in so doing illuminates the distance between the promise and 'actual situation' of Zionism. If, suggests Blanchot, Nazism has rendered the State of Israel an existential and political necessity, it is all the more urgent to keep the question of the State apart from that of 'being-Jewish': 'Yet if this task ['the reconstruction of a "place of sojourn"'] itself, which passes by way of the edification of a dwelling place and, finally, of a state, partially responds to the question of safeguarding the Jews, it cannot constitute a response to the question that being-Jewish poses, which is a universal question ... I would be tempted to conclude by saying that in the society that is being tried in Palestine – it is philosophy itself that is being dangerously measured against power inasmuch as this society, like the others, will have to determine the meaning and the future of "nomadic truth" in the face of the state' (*IC*, 447–8; *EI*, 190).

50. Levinas' radio dialogue with Alain Finkielkraut in the aftermath of the 1982 Sabra and Shatilla massacres, in spite of his unwillingness to attribute any direct culpability to the Israeli military command (in contrast to Finkielkraut), attests to his awareness of this temptation, and to Judaism's potential role as a counterforce against it: '... not enough has been said about the shock that the human possibility of events at Sabra and Shatilla – whoever is behind them – signifies in our entire history as Jews and as human beings. It's not only our thought that we must defend and protect, it's our souls, and that which upholds our souls: our books! Yes, for Jews this is an enormous question, and the supreme threat: that our books should be in jeopardy!'. See 'Ethics and Politics' in *The Levinas Reader* (ed. S. Hand, Oxford: Blackwell, 1989), p. 296.

51. *Nishmah* – the Hebrew word translated here as 'we will hear' translates also as 'we will understand' and 'we will obey' – an ambiguity which will feed into Levinas' reading.

52. It is worth invoking at this point Blanchot's enigmatic pronouncement in *The Writing of the Disaster* that 'Judaism is the sole thought that does not mediate' (*WD*, 63; *ED*, 104).

53. Emmanuel Levinas, *De L'Evasion* (Paris: Fata Morgana, 1982). Translation mine.

54. This forgetting of the immemorial is Lyotard's charge against Heidegger in the second essay ('Heidegger'), of his *Heidegger and 'the Jews'* (trans. A. Michel and M. Roberts, Minneapolis, MN: Minnesota University Press, 1990). In particular, Heidegger's silence on

the Holocaust is the necessary consequence of 'the "forgetting" that thought is without beginning and unfounded, that it does not that to "give place" to Being, but is owed to a nameless Law' (p. 94).

Chapter 4: 'To Preserve the Question'

1. All translations of texts by Jabès as yet untranslated are my own.
2. A charge of this sort is made and elaborated against Jabès by Berel Lang: '... only distortion can result when a writer "enlarges" on the Nazi genocide, by generalization, in making it a symbol for others. But this is in the end what Jabès does ... Thus Jabès is right: the history of the Jew and the life of language are closely linked. But to see the one or the other as symbolized in the Nazi genocide is not only to connect but to replace history with art – an exchange in which both lose'. See *Act and Idea in the Nazi Genocide* (Chicago, IL: University of Chicago Press, 1990), p. 116.
3. For further insight into the Jabès' place within both the French modernist context and the Egyptian literary community see the exhaustive research of Steven Jaron, including his PhD dissertation 'French Modernism and the Emergence of Jewish Consciousness in the Writings of Edmond Jabès' (Columbia University, 1997), along with his articles 'Repiquage poétique chez Edmond Jabès', in *Plein Marge* (No. 24, November 1996) and 'Edmond Jabès ou le fonctionnement du palimpseste' in *Entre Nil et Sable: Écrivains d'Égypte d'expression française* (1920–60) (ed. M. Kober, I. Fenoglio and D. Lançon, Paris: Centre Nationale de Documentation Pédagogique, 1999).
4. Philippe Lacoue-Labarthe, *Poetry As Experience* (trans. A. Tarnowski, Stanford, CA: Stanford University Press, 1999), p. 54; *La Poésie Comme Experience* (Paris: Christian Bourgois Editeur, 1986), p. 82.
5. Hans-Jost Frey, *Studies in Poetic Discourse: Baudelaire, Mallarmé, Rimbaud, Hölderlin* (trans. W. Whobrey, Stanford, CA: Stanford University Press, 1996); *Studien über das Reden der Dichter* (Munich: Wilhelm Fink Verlag, 1986).
6. Stéphane Mallarmé, 'Crisis of Verse' in *Selected Prose, Poems, Essays and Letters* (ed. and trans. B. Cook, Baltimore, MD: Johns Hopkins University Press, 1956), p. 38, hereafter *SP*; 'Crise de Vers' in *Œuvres Complètes* (ed. H. Mondor and G. Jean-Aubry, Paris: Gallimard, 1945), p. 364. Hereafter *OC*.
7. Maurice Blanchot, *Faux-Pas* (trans. E. Rottenberg, Stanford, CA: Stanford University Press, 2001), p. 168; *Faux-Pas* (Paris: Gallimard, 1943), p. 192.
8. Jacques Derrida, 'The Double Session' in *Dissemination* (trans. B. Johnson, Chicago, IL: University of Chicago Press, 1988), p. 293; 'La Double Séance' in *Dissémination* (Paris: Seuil, 1972), p. 261. Derrida is thinking explicitly here of Jean-Pierre Richard's influential Hegelian reading in *L'Univers Imaginaire de Mallarmé* (Paris: Editions du Seuil, 1961).
9. Paul Auster, 'The Book of the Dead: An Interview with Edmond Jabès' in E. Gould (ed.), *The Sin of the Book* (Lincoln, NE: University of Nebraska Press, 1985), p. 22. Didier Cahen's study of Jabès conceives his relationship to the earlier writer in a similar way: 'To the Mallarmean desire "to-describe-the book-which-contains-the book-of-the-world", Jabès opposes the expansion of the whole project of the book.' See *Edmond Jabès* (Paris: Belfond, 1991), p. 24 (translation mine). This way of distinguishing the two writers, I will presently suggest, is vulnerable to de Man's critique of progressivist literary history.
10. Paul de Man, *Blindness and Insight: Essays in the Rhetoric of Contemporary Criticism* (Minneapolis, MN: Minnesota University Press, 1983), p. 186.
11. Far from signifying the iteration of the Same, repetition here is precisely what allows for difference. As Andrew Benjamin suggests, 'literary' or 'poetic' repetition signifies not the determination of an infinite number of particulars by a grounding universal, but

rather exposes the ineliminable *inadequation* of a particular poem to a universal genre of poetry. Invoking Kant's notion in the 'Critique of Aesthetic Judgement' of the 'indeterminate concept' as the ground of particulars, Benjamin writes: 'Once it is acknowledged ... that what is recalled is the ground of universality, then it can be argued that what any poem recalls is its relationship to poetry. As such the particular instance always announces that relationship even though what is recalled does not have a determining role in regard to the content of the particular. What follows from this is that there cannot be a form adequate to the genre'. See *Philosophy's Literature* (Manchester: Clinamen Press, 2001), p. 21.

12. Once again, this paradoxical thinking of the absolute cannot but evoke Jena Romanticism, especially as read by Philippe Lacoue-Labarthe and Jean-Luc Nancy in *The Literary Absolute: The Theory of Literature in German Romanticism* (trans. P. Barnard and C. Lester, Albany, NY: SUNY Press, 1988). The Schlegelian model of literature, according to Lacoue-Labarthe and Nancy, is condemned 'to an inability to produce the concept it promises ... the "auto" movement, so to speak – auto-formation, auto-organization, auto-dissolution, and so on – is perpetually in excess in relation to itself' (p. 92).

13. Stéphane Mallarmé, *Selected Letters* (trans. and ed. R. Lloyd, Chicago, IL: University of Chicago Press, 1988), p. 22; *Œuvres Complètes* I (ed. B. Marchal, Paris: Gallimard, 1998), p. 647.

14. I am grateful for this insight to Henry Weinfeld's substantial and excellent commentary on his own translation of Mallarmé's *Collected Poems*.

15. This movement has of course been encountered above, notably in the form of Levinas' *À-Dieu*.

16. Translation slightly modified. It is further worth noting that while I have retained Waldrop's translation of '*vocable*' as 'word', it is important to be attentive to the term's difference from '*mot*'. The *vocable* is for Jabès a unit of language prior to or on the threshold of sense, 'voiced' prior to its integration into a network of meaning.

17. Translation slightly modified.

18. One of the epigraphs to the text, from Michel Leiris' *L'Âge d'Homme*, intimates a further meaning of Yaël and her murder – the impossible dream of suicide: 'Without trying to seem more than a coincidence I could not help noticing how exactly this meeting of symbols corresponds to what I think is the deep sense of suicide: to become at the same time *oneself* and *the other*, male and female, subject and object, the killer and the killed – our only chance of communion with ourselves' (*BQ2*, 3; *LQ2*, 11).

19. For a similar reading, see Rosmarie Waldrop's essay 'Mirrors and Paradoxes' (in E. Gould, ed., *The Sin of the Book*) for this insight.

20. Translation modified.

21. For ease of reference, this first will be referred to hereafter as *The Book of Resemblances*, while the trilogy's second and third volume will be referred to by their respective titles.

22. Translation modified.

23. In an essay on the question of the book, one of whose many points of entry is Derrida's essay on Jabès, Jean-Luc Nancy describes the condition of perpetual repetition in which the book as conceived by the West is perpetually 'knotted': 'Since the West – what Heidegger made us think of as the West – decided, as far back as human memory goes, to consigning to books the knowledge of a truth deciphered in a Book (of the World, of God, indeed of the Id) that was nevertheless impossible to read or write, the West is knotted up with writer's cramp ... According to a law that all these texts [Nancy is thinking of 'Mallarmé, Proust, Joyce, Kafka, Bataille, Borges, Blanchot, Laporte, Derrida] contain and articulate, and whose rigor needs no demonstration, this history stricken with writer's cramp can end only by repeating itself'. See 'Exscription' in *The Birth to Presence* (trans. K. Lydon, Stanford, CA: Stanford University Press, 1993), pp. 321–2.

24. Frey's 1989 book *Interruptions* (trans. G. Albert, Albany, NY: SUNY Press, 1996) reads as an extended meditation on this intrication of endlessness and completion. In a section that might be describing Jabès' texts, he names this condition 'Mourning': 'What stops without having been completed can no longer become what it would have liked to, could have or should have become. The hope of completion ends with the end. The end of hope survives uncompleted' (p. 75). *Unterbrechungen* (Zurich: Edition Howeg, 1989).

25. Translation modified.

26. The English translation of 'partage' cannot convey its doubled sense, so decisive for the text, as both 'share' and 'divide'.

27. It should be added that, at least in this text, Derrida is frustratingly reticent as to what Jewishness '*beyond all Judaism*' might consist in, or where it may be located. The danger of this reticence is that it conjures up the spectre of an essential Jewishness which exists beyond its particular forms. It is therefore important to insist that it is only in and through these forms that this Derridean Jewishness could be experienced; and, in addition, that precisely because this Jewishness does not function as a determining universal, its forms are necessarily plural: 'Levinas' and 'Jabès', indeed, are just two of their possible names.

28. Jacques Derrida, *Archive Fever: A Freudian Impression* (trans. E. Prenowitz, Chicago, IL: University of Chicago Press, 1996), p. 74; *Mal d'Archive: Une Impression Freudienne* (Paris: Galilée, 1995), p. 118.

29. Jacques Derrida, *Archive Fever*, p. 72, Derrida's emphasis; *Mal d'Archive*, p. 114.

30. Jacques Derrida, *Archive Fever*, p. 72; *Mal d'Archive*, p. 115.

31. This strategy of intensification is elaborated by Marc-Alain Ouaknin in his *The Burnt Book: Reading the Talmud* (trans. L. Brown, Princeton, NJ: Princeton University Press, 1995). By way of a series of readings in Talmud and the kabbalistic teachings of the eighteenth-century Hassidic mystic Rabbi Nachman of Bratslav, Ouaknin draws out a Jewish textual dynamic wherein the word's impoverishment, its inability to make present its object, is the very source of its plenitude, its availability to ceaseless interpretation and reinterpretation. The central texts of Judaism are holy precisely because they do not grasp the infinite in language; for the moment meaning freezes in interpretation, it must be 'burnt' by counter-interpretation.

32. In his impressive reading of Derrida's 1964 essay on Jabès, Joseph G. Kronick draws out the significance for Derrida of the counter-Hegelian motifs in *The Book of Questions*. The Jabèsian writer as read by Derrida is Hegel's Unhappy Consciousness; however, where in Hegel the Unhappy Consciousness is one of the shapes through which consciousness must pass in order to recognize and realize his identity with the Universal, the Jabèsian writer remains eternally behind this realization, and so terminally unhappy. It is Auschwitz above all that engenders the terminal deferral of the question's coincidence with its answer: as 'the excess that denies representation', Auschwitz, 'is the negative that inhabits the Hegelian system and marks its limitations from within; it is, in other words, that which escapes the merger of *Aufheben* [sublation] and *Errinerung* [memory] ... If Hegel is blind to what he lay bare, then our reading of Hegel must make the blind spot visible. As sacrifice, a sacrifice without supersession, this blind spot is a kind of writing – "Jewish" writing – that lies in the margins of the phenomenology of the Spirit – that is, it makes necessary and impossible the representation of that which the name "sacrifice" is blind to, annihilation'. See *Derrida and the Future of Literature* (Albany, NY: SUNY Press, 1999), pp. 83–4.

33. I have slightly modified the Jewish Publication Society's translation in *Tanakh: The Holy Scriptures* (Philadelphia, PA: Jewish Publication Society, 1985), p. 1129.

34. André Neher, *The Exile of the Word: From the Silence of the Bible to the Silence of Auschwitz* (trans. D. Maisel, Philadelphia, PA: Jewish Publication Society, 1981), p. 65; *L'Exil de la Parole: Du Silence Biblique au Silence d'Auschwitz* (Paris: Seuil, 1970), p. 72.

35. This strategy is known in rabbinic tradition as *Gezerah shavah*, and is the second of Rabbi Ishamel's thirteen rules of Talmudic exegesis. For a useful elaboration of these terms and a brief account of their history, see Ouaknin *The Burnt Book: Reading the Talmud,* pp. 70–2.

36. Maimonides is not alone in wishing to divest the verse of all anthropomorphic connotations; the same impulse animates the interpretations of all the major figures in the medieval Jewish exegetical tradition so central to the development of Rabbinic Judaism. Rashi, the eleventh-century French commentator, and perhaps the single most important figure in this tradition, reads 'after our likeness' (*ki-demuthenu*) as referring to 'our power to understand and discern' (*le-havin u'l'haskil*), while the Spanish twelfth-century commentator Ibn Ezra explains the terms 'image' and 'likeness' as alluding to 'the qualities of man's soul wherein it is similar to the God, viz. That it is immortal and fills man's body entirely, just as God fills the universe'. Finally, Nachmanides, the thirteenth-century Northern Spanish exegete, 'comments that man has a similarity to both his origins, viz. Bodily he is like the earth whence he was taken, and his spirit is immortal like God Who breathed it into him'. For Rashi, see *The Pentateuch and Rashi's Commentary* (trans. Rabbis Abraham Ben Isaiah and Benjamin Sharfman, New York, NY: S. S. and R. Publishing Company, 1949), p. 14. For a useful distillation of the other commentators, see *The Soncino Chumash* (ed. Rev Dr A. Cohen, London: Soncino Press, 1947), p. 6. Maimonides' reading, however, is undoubtedly the reading most rigorously and uncompromisingly insistent on God's otherness to language and image.

37. Moshe Halbertal and Avishai Margalit, *Idolatry* (trans. N. Goldblum, Cambridge, MA: Harvard University Press, 1992), p. 59. This is, it should be noted, the stronger of two possible readings of Maimonides suggested by Halbertal and Margalit (neither of which they explicitly endorse). A second more 'political' and less 'metaphysical' view would argue not that God is imageless, but that His image is inaccessible to human consciousness.

38. Translation modified.

39. Blanchot, *Friendship*, p. 145; *L'Amitié*, p. 167.

40. Translation slightly modified.

41. Translation modified.

42. Hans-Jost Frey, *Interruptions*, p. 75.

43. Jacques Derrida, 'Shibboleth for Paul Celan' in *Word Traces: Readings of Paul Celan* (trans. J. Wilner, ed. A. Fioretos, Baltimore, MD: Johns Hopkins University Press, 19), p. 43; *Schibboleth pour Paul Celan* (Paris: Galilée, 1986), p. 72.

44. Translation modified.

45. Translation modified.

Conclusion

1. Far from posing a challenge to these divisions, the 'others' invoked by the current rhetoric of the 'war on terror' – Islamist terrorism, despotic pan-Arab regimes, rogue Communist states – only confirm them (much like the Soviet empire which preceded them), as Jacques Derrida suggests in the course of his essay 'Faith and Knowledge'. Just as the 'rationality' of 'tele-techno-capitalistico-scientific' modernity is conditioned by an unacknowledged and irreducible 'faith' without which 'neither convention, nor institution, nor constitution, nor sovereign state, nor law . . .' would be possible, so its 'fundamentalist' antagonists are 'residues, surface effects' of 'the dislocation, expropriation, delocalization, deracination, disidiomization, and dispossession . . . that the tele-techo-scientific machine does not fail to produce'. Neither pole of this deadly geopolitical opposition, in other words, is uncontaminated by the other against which it defines itself: '. . . in principle, today, there is no incompatibility . . . between the "fundamentalisms", the "integrisms" or their

"politics" and, on the other hand, rationality, that is to say, the tele-techno-capitalistico-scientific fiduciary, in all of its mediatic and globalizing dimensions'. See 'Faith and Knowledge: the Two Sources of "Religion" at the Limits of Reason Alone', in *Religion* (eds J. Derrida and G. Vattimo, trans. S. Weber, Cambridge: Polity Press, 1998), pp. 44–5.

2. Edith Wyschogrod, *Spirit in Ashes: Hegel, Heidegger and Man-Made Mass Death* (New Haven, CT: Yale University Press, 1985), p. 28.

3. Primo Levi, *If This Is A Man/The Truce* (trans. S. Woolf, London: Vintage, 1979), p. 17.

4. '*Slow* annihilation' because Gandersheim, where Antelme was interned, was not an extermination camp ('there was no gas chamber, no crematorium' [5]) – nor was he, as a non-Jewish French political prisoner, destined for one. Unlike Levi, Antelme's daily suffering was not played out in the menacing shadow of the 'selections'; it is perhaps this consignment to the unrelieved monotony of his destruction which reveals to him both his limitless vulnerability and his ultimate indestructibility as a human being. To conclude with a meditation on Antelme – that is, on Gandersheim rather than Auschwitz – is to make explicit the synecdochic status of 'Auschwitz' throughout this book. Though less explicitly racialized or exterminist than Auschwitz, Gandersheim is infected by the same Nazi 'sorting myth' (to invoke Edith Wyschogrod's terminology once more) that separates unworthy from worthy life. 'Auschwitz' is a name both for this logic and for the place which most fully realized it.

5. As Sara Guyer points out, it is the very impossibility of such an address – 'is there such an SS? Is this a speech that could be heard and who would hear it?' – that confers on it its ethical force. The address brings the fictive SS face to face with the indestructible – that is, with the limit of his power; to the actual SS, whose can see in his victim only an object for destruction, this limit is as invisible as the address is inaudible. But to give voice to the indestructible from the depths of destruction is to return the inmate to the human from which the SS sought to expel him, just as it defies the SS's implicit claim to exist above and beyond the human. As Guyer puts it, 'to see Jacques, to allow Jacques to be seen by the SS . . . and to see him in the moment of positing the SS as an addressee is to present the human in destruction. Confusion becomes interruption. Here to speak is *not* to see, but to issue and address to another, out of this deprivation, is to already compel one to begin to see – to see the body in decay, to see the resistance that is somehow endless, and to break down every identity'. See Sara Guyer, 'Being-Destroyed: Anthropomorphizing *L'Espèce Humaine*' in D. Stone (ed.), *Theoretical Interpretations of the Holocaust* (Amsterdam: Rodopi, 2001), p. 121.

6. Sarah Kofman, *Smothered Words* (trans. M. Dobie, Evanston, IL: Northwestern University Press, 1998), p. 30.

7. Jean-Luc Nancy, *The Inoperative Community* (trans. P. Connor, Minneapolis, MN: Minnesota University Press, 1991), p. 60.

Index